Care Proceedings

Care Proceedings

Third edition

Linda Feldman, LLB

Solicitor

Longman

© Longman Group UK Ltd 1988

Published by
Longman Group UK Ltd
21/27 Lambs Conduit Street
London WC1N 3NJ

Associated offices
Australia, Hong Kong, Malaysia, Singapore and USA

First published 1978
Third edition 1988

A CIP catalogue record for this book
is available from the British Library.

ISBN 0 85121 309 X

All rights reserved. No part of this publication may be
reproduced, stored in a retrieval system, or transmitted,
in any form or by any means, electronic, mechanical,
photocopying, recording or otherwise, without the prior
written permission of the publishers.

Printed in Great Britain by
Biddles Ltd, Guildford, Surrey

Contents

Preface	xi
Table of Cases	xiii
Table of Statutes	xviii
Table of Statutory Instruments	xxiii
Abbreviations	xxv
Stop Press	xxvi

1 Introduction	1
1 What are care proceedings?	1
2 Can care orders be made in other proceedings?	3
3 When will a lawyer be involved?	7

Part I: The Children and Young Persons Acts 1933–1969

2 Detention in a Place of Safety	11
1 Place of safety order	11
2 Place of safety warrant	13
3 Detention by a police officer	15
4 Removal of a foster child	16
5 Removal of a protected child	17
6 Detention after arrest	17
7 Medical examination	17
3 Care Proceedings	19
1 Who may bring proceedings?	19
2 Jurisdiction of court	20
3 Grounds	20
4 Ill-treatment or neglect	21
5 Potential risk	26
6 Exposure to moral danger	27

7 Beyond control	28
8 The education ground	29
9 The offence condition	30
10 Care or control test	32

4 Procedure — 34
1 Commencing proceedings — 34
2 Which court? — 35
3 Who must attend? — 36
4 Parties — 37
5 Conflict of interest — 38
6 Appointment of a guardian ad litem — 38
7 Legal representation — 38
8 The role of the guardian ad litem — 40
9 The juvenile court — 42
10 The hearing — 43
11 The welfare principle — 43
12 Order of evidence and speeches — 44
13 Exclusion of the child or parent — 47
14 Exclusion of witnesses — 47
15 Adjournment — 47
16 Proving the offence condition — 48
17 The report stage — 49
18 Withdrawal of application — 51

5 Evidence — 52
1 The nature of evidence — 52
2 Relevance — 53
3 Expert opinion — 53
4 Hearsay evidence — 54
5 Privilege — 55
6 Oral testimony — 56
7 Documentary evidence — 57
8 Real evidence — 58
9 Tape and video recordings — 59
10 Witness summons — 60
11 Advance disclosure of evidence — 61

6 Orders — 62
1 Care order — 62
2 Interim care order — 63
3 Supervision order — 68
4 Hospital and guardianship orders — 71

CONTENTS

5 Recognisance by parent	72
6 Recognisance by child	72
7 Compensation order	73

7 Variation and Discharge of Care and Supervision Orders — 74
   1 Grounds for variation or discharge — 74
   2 Procedure — 76

8 Appeals — 86
   1 Crown Court — 86
   2 Divisional Court — 89
   3 Court of Appeal — 91
   4 House of Lords — 91
   5 Bail pending appeal — 92
   6 Application for judicial review — 93
   7 Appeal by the local authority — 94

9 Legal Aid and Costs — 96
   1 Legal advice and assistance — 96
   2 Legal aid in the juvenile court and the Crown Court — 97
   3 Legal aid in the High Court — 99
   4 Legal aid for parents — 100
   5 Costs — 100

10 Unauthorised Removal from Care — 102
   1 Absence without leave — 102
   2 Intervention of third party — 102
   3 Absence from a place of safety — 103
   4 Abduction abroad — 103

Part II: The Child Care Act 1980

11 Voluntary Reception into Care — 107
   1 Grounds for admission — 107
   2 Duty of a local authority — 108
   3 Leaving care — 110

12 Assumption of Parental Rights — 113
   1 Grounds for resolution — 113
   2 Joint exercise of parental rights — 116
   3 Termination of a resolution — 117
   4 Procedure — 118
   5 Complaint to the juvenile court — 118
   6 The hearing — 119

13 Application to Discharge a s 3 Resolution	125
1 Who may apply?	125
2 Grounds for discharge	125
3 Procedure	126
4 The hearing	126
14 Appeals	127
1 High Court	127
2 Court of Appeal and House of Lords	130
3 Application for judicial review	130
15 Legal Aid and Costs	131
1 Legal aid	131
2 Costs	133
16 Unauthorised Removal from Care	134
1 Assisting, harbouring or concealing a runaway child	134
2 Refusal to return a child	135
3 Recovery of a missing child	135
4 Abduction abroad	136

Part III: Children in the Care of Voluntary Organisations

17 Statutory Controls	139
1 The welfare principle	139
2 Parental rights and duties	140
3 Removal from care	142
4 Supervision of accommodation	142

Part IV: What Care Means

18 Powers, Rights and Duties of the Local Authority	147
1 To safeguard and promote the child's welfare	147
2 To review cases	148
3 To use available facilities	148
4 Accommodation	148
5 Maintenance	156
6 Access to information	160
19 General Matters of Care and Upbringing	162
1 Religion	162
2 Education	163
3 Medical treatment	164

4 Discipline	167
5 Access	168
6 Maintaining contact	174
7 Adoption	175
8 Custodianship	176
9 Emigration	177
10 Travel abroad	178
11 Legal proceedings	179
12 Consent to marriage	182
13 Welfare benefits	182
14 After-care	184
15 Death of a child in care	185
20 Resolution of Disputes	186
1 Local Government Ombudsman	186
2 Wardship	187
3 Judicial review	188
4 Action for breach of duty	189
5 European Court of Human Rights	190

Part V: Future Developments

21 Proposed Reform of Child Care Law	195
1 Investigation of child abuse	195
2 Emergency protection orders	195
3 Care proceedings	196
4 Interim care orders	197
5 Supervision orders	197
6 Custody orders	198
7 Discharge of care orders	198
8 Appeals	198
9 Duties of local authority	198
10 Unauthorised removal from care	199
11 Voluntary care	199
Appendix 1: Forms	201
Appendix 2: Draft letters	221
Appendix 3: Children and Young Persons Act 1933—First Schedule	223
Appendix 4: Useful addresses	224
Appendix 5: Sexual abuse: some recent medical publications	225
Index	227

Preface

When the second edition of this book was published in 1984 several important reforms of child care law had recently been implemented and it was too soon to judge how these changes would operate in practice. Important rulings in the higher courts have clarified matters and there is now a substantial body of new case law relating to both the substance and procedural requirements of the present law. In addition, Parliament has enacted the Children and Young Persons (Amendment) Act 1986 and the Family Law Reform Act 1987, both of which alter the existing law but have yet to be fully implemented.

It is essential for lawyers and others involved in child care cases to be aware of these developments and to be fully conversant with the law and practice in this field. The purpose of this book is to provide a practical guide to the law and procedure which is both concise and comprehensive. The writer has drawn upon her experience as a solicitor in local government, as a member of the Law Society's Child Care Panel working in private practice and as an adviser within the legal department of a large children's charity. The book is therefore written from a wide perspective and it is hoped that social workers, lay advisers and students will find it useful as a straightforward guide to a difficult area of law.

The basic framework of the book remains unaltered. It covers the various methods by which children can be admitted into care, the respective rights of child, parent and local authority while the child remains in care and the different routes out of care. Changes in law and procedure have been incorporated into this format and the law is as stated at 5 April 1988.

Child care law is in a state of flux. The shortcomings of the present legislation are widely acknowledged. The Government published its proposals for reform in a White Paper in January 1987 and is committed to early implementation. It is unlikely, however, that any new legislation will be drafted until there has been an opportunity to consider the recommendations of the Cleveland Inquiry due to report in July 1988. Whilst it is certain therefore that this will be the last edition of this book to cover the law in its present form, it is equally certain that the present law will be with us for some time to come.

May 1988   LINDA FELDMAN

Table of Cases

A v B and Hereford and Worcester CC [1986] 1 FLR 289 187
A v Liverpool City Council [1982] AC 363; [1981] 2 WLR 948; [1981] 2 All ER 385, HL 44, 187
Alhaji Mohamed v Knott [1968] QB 1; [1968] 2 WLR 1446, DC 27
AR v Avon County Council [1985] 3 WLR 311; [1985] 2 All ER 981; 129 SJ 541 87
Associated Provincial Picture Houses Ltd v Wednesbury Corporation [1948] 1 KB 223; [1948] LJR 190; [1947] 2 All ER 680, CA 109, 114, 191
Attorney-General *ex rel* Tilley v London Borough of Wandsworth [1981] 1 WLR 854; [1981] 1 All ER 1162; 125 SJ 148, CA 108
B and Another v Gloucestershire County Council [1980] 2 All ER 746; 78 LGR 468, DC 87
Barker v Westmorland County Council (1958) 56 LGR 267, DC 115
B (A Minor) (Wardship: Child in Care), *Re* [1975] Fam 36; [1975] 2 WLR 302 188
B (A Minor) (Wardship: Sterilisation), *In Re* [1987] 2 WLR 1213; [1987] 2 All ER 206, HL(E) 165
B (A Minor), *Re* (1978) *The Times*, 26 October, DC 128
Berkhamsted Rural District Council v Duerdin-Dutton [1964] Crim LR 307; 108 SJ 157, DC 52, 161
B v B (1976) 6 Fam Law 79, CA 112
C v Berkshire County Council [1987] 1 FLR 210 .... 83–4, 173
C (A Minor) (Justices' Decision: Review), *Re* [1981] 2 FLR 62 44
CB (A Minor) (Wardship: Local Authority), *Re* [1981] 1 WLR 379; [1981] 1 All ER 16; 125 SJ 219 188
C (Minors) v Martin and Another [1982] 2 All ER 636 87
Council of Civil Service Unions and Others v Minister for Civil Service [1985] AC 374; [1985] 1 WLR 1174; [1984] 3 All ER 935, CA 189
Coventry County Council v J [1986] 2 FLR 301 173
Croydon London Borough Council v N and Others [1987] 2 FLR 61 44
D, *Re* [1970] 1 WLR 1109 .... 50, 122
D v NSPCC [1978] AC 171; [1977] 2 WLR 201; [1977] 1 All ER 589, HL . 56
D (A Minor) (Justices' Decision: Review), *Re see* D (A Minor), *Re*
D (A Minor), *Re* (Wardship: Sterilisation) [1976] Fam 185; [1976] 2 WLR 279; [1976] 1 All ER 326 166
D (A Minor), *Re* [1977] Fam 158; 121 SJ 355; *sub nom* D (A Minor) (Justices' Decision: Review) [1977] 2 WLR 1006 43
D (A Minor), *Re* (1978) 76 LGR 653 114

TABLE OF CASES

D (A Minor), *Re* [1987] 1 FLR 422 22
Devon County Council *v* C [1985] 2 FLR 1159; 129 SJ 483; 149 JP 521, CA
.... 129, 171
Devon County Council *v* C (1986) 16 Fam Law 20 173
DJMS (A Minor), *Re* [1977] 3 All ER 582 .... 30, 90
DM (A Minor) (Wardship: Jurisdiction), *Re* [1986] 2 FLR 122 187
E (A Minor) (Child Abuse: Evidence), *Re* [1987] 1 FLR 269 .... 24, 59
E (A Minor) (Wardship: Court's Duty), *Re* [1984] FLR 457 187
Essex County Council *v* ILR and KBR (minors) (1979) 9 Fam Law 15, DC 12, 21
F (Minors), *In Re* (1987) *The Times*, 28 December 24
F *v* Suffolk County Council (1981) 125 SJ 307; 79 LGR 554 23
G *v* G (Minors: Custody Appeal) [1985] 2 FLR 894, HL 129
G *v* G (1962) 106 SJ 858 3
Gaskin *v* Liverpool City Council [1980] 1 WLR 1549; 124 SJ 498, CA ... 160, 190
G (A Minor), *Re* (1987) *The Times*, 30 July 52
Gillick *v* West Norfolk and Wisbech Area Health Authority and Another
  [1986] AC 112; [1986] 1 FLR 224, CA and HL(E) 165
G (Infants), *Re* [1963] 1 WLR 1169, [1963] 3 All ER 370; 107 SJ 682 112
Guevera *v* London Borough of Hounslow (1987) JSWL 374 190
H *v* Sheffield City Council (1982) JSWL 303 .... 12, 22
H (A Minor) (Wardship: Jurisdiction), *Re* [1978] Fam 65; [1978] 2 WLR 608;
  [1978] 2 All ER 903, CA 44
Hereford and Worcester CC *v* JAH [1986] 1 FLR 29 .... 171, 173
Hereford and Worcester County Council *v* EH [1985] 2 FLR 975; (1985) 15
  Fam Law 229 .... 128, 130
H (Minors) (Wardship: Cultural Background), *Re* [1987] 2 FLR 12 23
Home Office *v* Dorset Yacht Co Ltd [1970] AC 1004; [1970] 2 WLR 1140;
  [1970] 2 All ER 294 181
Humberside County Council *v* DPR (An Infant) *see* Humberside County
  Council *v* R
Humberside County Council *v* R [1977] 1 WLR 1251; 76 LGR 121, DC; *sub
  nom* Humberside County Council *v* DPR (An Infant) (1977) 121 SJ 693 . 55
Jarvis, *Re* [1984] FLR 350n 67
J Barber & Sons *v* Lloyd's Underwriter and Others [1986] 3 WLR 515; [1986]
  2 All ER 845; LSG 3253 59
K *v* Devon County Council (1987) 17 Fam Law 348 125
K (A Minor), *Re* [1978] 122 SJ 626 112
KD (A Minor), *Re* (1988) *The Times*, 19 February 172
Krishnan *v* London Borough of Sutton [1970] Ch 181; [1969] 3 WLR 683;
  [1969] 3 All ER 1367, CA 111
Laird (Inspector of Factories) *v* Simms (Gomersal) Ltd (1988) *The Times*,
  7 March 89
L (Child in Care: Access), *Re* [1985] FLR 95 169
Leeds City Council *v* West Yorkshire Metropolitan Police and Others [1982] 2
  WLR 186; [1982] 1 All ER 274; 126 SJ 79, HL 180
LH (A Minor) (Wardship: Jurisdiction), *Re* [1986] 2 FLR 306; 84 LGR 791 173
London Borough of Lewisham *v* Lewisham Juvenile Court Justices and
  Another [1979] AC 273; [1979] 2 WLR 513; [1979] 2 All ER 297, HL ... 110
M *v* Berkshire County Council [1985] Fam 60; [1985] 2 WLR 811; [1985]
  1 FLR 257, CA 39
M *v* M (Child: Access) [1973] 2 All ER 81, DC 168
M *v* Westminster City Council [1985] FLR 325 .... 22, 44-5, 82

TABLE OF CASES

M and Another *v* Wigan Metropolitan Borough Council [1979] Fam 36; [1979] 3 WLR 244; [1979] 2 All ER 958, DC 110
M and H (Minors) (Local Authority: Parental Rights), *In Re* [1987] 3 WLR 759, CA 170
M (A Minor) (Child Abuse: Evidence), *Re* [1986] 1 FLR 293 .... 24, 60
M (A Minor) (Wardship: Jurisdiction), *Re* [1985] Fam 60; [1985] 2 WLR 811; [1985] 1 All ER 745, CA 170
M (An Infant), *Re* [1961] Ch 328; [1961] 2 WLR 350; [1961] 1 All ER 788, CA 187
M (Minors), *Re* (1986) 16 Fam Law 336 56
Northamptonshire CC *v* H (1987) *The Times*, 7 November 37, 65
Nottinghamshire County Council *v* Q [1982] Fam 94; [1982] 2 WLR 954; [1982] 2 All ER 641 13
O'D *v* South Glamorgan County Council (Obligation of Parent) (1980) 78 LGR 522 115
O, H, W, B and R *v* UK (1987) *The Times*, 9 July 191
P (A Minor), *Re* (1982) 12 Fam Law; (1982) 80 LGR 301 ..... 165, 167, 188, 190
P (Infants), *Re* [1962] 1 WLR 1296 115
P (Minors: Access) P *v* P (Gateshead Metropolitan BC intervening), *Re* (1988) *The Times*, 19 February 170
Practice Direction [1988] 1 WLR 475 12
Practice Direction (Divisional Court: Appeal) [1977] 1 WLR 609 127
Practice Direction (Minor: Independent Reporter) [1983] 1 WLR 416; 4 FLR 800 54
Practice Note (Court of Appeal: New Procedure) [1982] 1 WLR 1312; [1982] 3 All ER 376, CA 91
P, *Re* (1979) JSWL 361 99
R *v* Aberdare Justices, *ex parte* Jones [1973] Crim LR 45, DC 50
R *v* Avon County Council, *ex parte* K and Others [1986] 1 FLR 443 147–8
R *v* Bedfordshire County Council, *ex parte* B [1987] 1 FLR 239 189
R *v* Bedfordshire County Council, *ex parte* C [1987] 1 FLR 239; 85 LGR 218 189
R *v* Birmingham City Juvenile Court, *ex parte* Birmingham City Council, CA (1987) *The Times*, 3 September 65
R *v* Birmingham Juvenile Court, *ex parte* G, R *v* Birmingham Juvenile Court, *ex parte* R (1988) *The Times*, 25 May 51
R *v* Birmingham Juvenile Court, *ex parte* N (An Infant) [1984] Fam 93; [1984] 3 WLR 387; [1984] 2 All ER 688 27
R *v* Birmingham Juvenile Court, *ex parte* P and S [1984] 1 WLR 610; [1984] 1 All ER 393; [1984] FLR 343 .... 43, 63, 65–7
R *v* Bolton Metropolitan Borough Council, *ex parte* B [1985] 1 FLR 343 .. 169
R *v* Bristol Justices, *ex parte* Broome [1986] 1 WLR 352 16
R *v* Cardiff Justices, *ex parte* Salter [1986] 1 FLR 162 93
R *v* Chertsey Justices, *ex parte* E [1987] 2 FLR 415 .... 45, 82–3
R *v* Corby Juvenile Court, *ex parte* M [1987] 1 WLR 55; [1987] 1 All ER 992; [1987] 1 FLR 490 169
R *v* Croydon Justices, *ex parte* N [1987] 1 FLR 252 64
R *v* Epsom Juvenile Court, *ex parte* G [1988] 1 WLR 145; [1988] 1 All ER 329 50, 64
R *v* Essex County Council, *ex parte* W [1987] 1 FLR 148 157
R *v* Exeter Juvenile Court, *ex parte* H (1988) *The Times*, 19 February 25, 43
R *v* Gravesham Juvenile Court, *ex parte* B [1982] 4 FLR 312; (1982) 12 Fam Law 207 .... 40, 44
R *v* Greenwich Juvenile Court, *ex parte* Greenwich London Borough Council (1977) 7 Fam Law 171; 74 LGR 99 .... 56, 122
R *v* Hendon Justices, *ex parte* D (1974) 118 SJ 756, DC 20

TABLE OF CASES

R v Inner London Juvenile Court, *ex parte* G (1988) 152 JP 239 .... 25, 44
R v Justice for Lincoln (Kesteven), *ex parte* M (a minor); R v Lincoln (Kesteven) Juvenile Court, *ex parte* Lincolnshire County Court. *See* R v Lincoln (Kesteven) County Justice, *ex parte* M (a minor); R v Lincoln (Kesteven) Juvenile Court, *ex parte* Lincolnshire County Council
R v K [1978] 1 WLR 139; [1978] 1 All ER 180; 121 SJ 728 92
R v Lincoln (Kesteven) County Justice, *ex parte* M (a minor); R v Lincoln (Kesteven) Juvenile Court, *ex parte* Lincolnshire County Council [1976] QB 957; [1976] 2 WLR 143; *sub nom* R v Justice for Lincoln (Kesteven), *ex parte* M (a minor); R v Lincoln (Kesteven), Juvenile Court *ex parte* Lincolnshire County Council [1976] 1 All ER 490; [1976] LGR 285, DC 13, 53
R v Manchester Justices, *ex parte* Salford City Council *sub nom* R v Manchester City Justices, *ex parte* Bannister [1983] 4 FLR 77; 147 JP 516; 81 LGR 755 .... 31, 62
R v Manchester Justices, *ex parte* Bannister *see* R v Manchester Justices, *ex parte* Salford City Council
R v Milton Keynes Justices, *ex parte* R [1979] 1 WLR 1062; 123 SJ 321, DC   44
R v Newham London Borough Council, *ex parte* McL (1987) *The Times*, 25 July 187, 189
R v Northampton Juvenile Court, *ex parte* London Borough of Hammersmith and Fulham [1985] FLR 193; (1985) Fam Law 125 153
R v Nottingham Justices, *ex parte* Davies [1980] QB 38; [1980] 3 WLR 15; [1980] 2 All ER 775, DC 65
R v Poole Juvenile Court, *ex parte* P [1988] 1 FLR 8 81
R v Plymouth Juvenile Court, *ex parte* F & F [1987] 1 FLR 169 ..... 38, 79, 81, 87
R v P (1979) 144 JP 39 92
R v Salisbury and Tisbury and Mere Combined JC, *ex parte* Ball [1986] 1 FLR 1 100
R v Slough Justices, *ex parte* B [1985] 1 FLR 384 .... 128, 172
R v Southwark Juvenile Court, *ex parte* C [1988] 1 FLR 8 81
R v Sunderland Juvenile Court, *ex parte* G (1987) *The Times*, 15 December 44, 50, 54, 123
R v Tower Hamlets Juvenile Court, *ex parte* London Borough of Tower Hamlets [1984] FLR 907; (1984) 14 Fam Law 307 .... 83, 93
R v Waltham Forest Juvenile Court, *ex parte* B (1988) *The Times*, 19 February 25
R v Wandsworth Juvenile Court, *ex parte* S [1984] FLR 713 81
R v West Malling Juvenile Court, *ex parte* Kendall [1986] 2 FLR 405 .... 51, 61, 85, 123
R v Wood Green Crown Court *ex parte* P [1982] 4 FLR 206 .... 54, 88
R v Worthing Justices, *ex parte* Stevenson [1976] 2 All ER 194; 120 SJ 333, DC 100
RM and LM (Minors) (Wardship Jurisdiction), *Re* [1986] 2 FLR 205 187
S v Walsall Metropolitan Borough Council [1985] 1 WLR 1150; [1985] 3 All ER 294; 129 SJ 685 181
S (A Minor) (Care Proceedings: Wardship Summons), *Re* [1987] 1 FLR 479 .... 34, 48, 117, 119, 187
S (Care Proceedings: Evidence), *Re* [1980] 1 FLR 301 25
S (Minors) (Wardship: Police Investigations), *In Re* [1987] Fam 199; [1987] 3 WLR 847 56
Simms v Moore [1970] 2 QB 327 44

TABLE OF CASES

Southwark London BC *v* H [1985] 1 WLR 861; [1985] 2 All ER 657; 129 SJ 397	171
Southwark London Borough Council *v* C (a minor) and Another; C (minors) *v* Martin and Another [1982] 1 WLR 826; [1982] 2 All ER 636	87
Surrey CC *v* S [1974] QB 124; [1973] 3 WLR 579; [1973] 3 All ER 1074	26
SW (A Minor) (Wardship: Jurisdiction), *Re* [1986] 1 FLR 24	5
T (An Infant), *Re* (1974) 118 SJ 78	47
Thompson *v* Thompson [1986] 1 FLR 212	124
Vicar of Writtle and Another *v* Essex County Council (1979) 77 LGR 656	181
W *v* Hertfordshire County Council [1985] 2 All ER 301; *sub nom* W (A Minor) (Wardship Jurisdiction), *Re* [1985] AC 791; [1985] 2 WLR 892, HL	189
W *v* Heywood [1985] FLR 1064; (1985) 15 Fam Law 282, DC	180
W *v* Nottinghamshire County Council [1981] 3 WLR 959; [1982] 1 All ER 1; 125 SJ 761, CA	121
W *v* Shropshire County Council [1986] 2 FLR 359	187
W *v* Sunderland Borough Council [1980] 2 All ER 514, DC	115
W (A Minor) (Wardship: Jurisdiction), *Re see* W *v* Hertfordshire County Council	
W and W (Minors), *Re* [1984] FLR 947	129–30
Wheelhouse *v* Woodward (formerly Wheelhouse) (1982) 12 Fam Law 180	87
Wooley *v* John and Patricia Haines (1975), unreported	21
Y *v* Kirklees Borough Council [1985] FLR 927	170

Table of Statutes

Adoption Act 1976—
s 16(2) 177
s 18 .... 63, 103, 116–17, 142–3, 177
s 26 6
s 34 14
    (3) 107
s 37(1) 14
s 55 .... 63, 116–17, 142–3
Affiliation Proceedings Act 1957 .. 160
Child Abduction Act 1984 137
s 1(1) 103, 137
Sched, para 1 103
        para 2 137
        para 3 103–4
Child Benefit Act 1975—
Sched 1, para 1 184–5
Child Care Act 1980 ... 114, 119, 141, 186
Pt 1A 170–1, 179–80, 193
s 1 .... 108, 180
s 2 .. 1–4, 11, 12, 14, 16, 32, 107–12,
    118, 134–5, 139, 147, 154, 164–5,
    169, 174, 176, 178–9, 182,
    184–5, 188
    (1) 2
    (2) 109
    (3) 109–10
    (4), (5) 108
    (10) 116, 140
s 3 . 1–3, 12, 21, 106–7, 110–11, 114,
    116–18, 121–2, 124–5, 127, 129,
    131–5, 141, 147, 157, 164, 169,
    175–6, 179, 181–2, 188
    (6) 121, 124, 127, 141, 171
    (7) 141
    (8) 114
s 4(3) 116, 162

Child Care Act 1980—*contd*
s 5 130–2
    (1) 117
    (2)(*a*)–(*c*) 117
    (3) 118
    (4) 2, 125–6, 127, 141, 171
    (*a*), (*b*) 125
s 6 .... 126, 131
s 7 .... 106, 122
    (1) 126
    (3) 123
s 8(2) 109, 116
    (3), (4) 116
s 9 174
s 10(2) 62
    (3) 164
s 11 .... 63, 174–5
s 12 174
s 12B 169–70
s 12C 2, 170
s 13 134
    (1) 135, 142
    (2) 110, 115
s 14 135
s 15(2), (3) 136
s 16(1)–(4) 102
Pt III 4, 5, 63, 110,
                    116, 135, 147
s 18 .... 114, 149
    (1) 147, 163–4
    (2) 148
    (3) 149
s 19 147
s 20 148
s 21 148–9
    (2) 115, 135, 149, 180
s 21A 2, 87, 94, 151, 153–4

TABLE OF STATUTES

Child Care Act 1980—*contd*
- s 23 185
- s 24 .... 4, 5
  - (1), (3) 177
- s 25 185
- s 26 .... 174, 185
- s 27 .... 182, 184
- s 28 .... 4, 5, 184
- s 29 185
- Pt IV 149
- s 31 .... 149, 154
- s 45(1), (1A) 156
  - (3) 157
- s 46 157
  - (4) 157
- s 47 157
  - (3), (4) 157
  - (5) 159
- s 48(1) 158
- ss 49, 50 158
- s 51 158
  - (4) 158
- s 52(1)(*a*), (*b*) 159
- s 53 159
- Pt VI 150
- s 57 142
- s 60(2) 142
- s 62(1) 140
- s 63(1) 142
- s 64 .... 140–2, 169
  - (3) 140
  - (7) 141
- s 64A 139
- s 65 141
  - (1), (2) 141
- s 67(2) 141
- s 68 142
  - (1), (2), (5) 150
- s 69 .... 139, 184
- s 72 .... 154, 184
- s 73(1) 11
  - (2) 12
- s 75(3) 14
- s 80 151
- s 84 134–5
- s 87(1) 109, 116, 139, 177
  - (2) 110
- s 90(3) 148
- Sched 4, para 3 185

Children Act 1948—
- s 2 171

Children Act 1975–
- s 33 5
  - (3) 176

Children Act 1975—*contd*
- s 36 5
- s 65 100
- s 85(1) 140
  - (3) 117
- s 88 139
- s 90 124
- Sched 3, para 67 26
  - para 75 4

Children and Young Persons Act 1933 44
- s 1 .... 164, 167
- s 25 12
- s 34 .... 37, 78
- s 39(2) 43
- s 40 13
- s 44 .... 66, 83
- ss 47, 49 42
- s 50 31
- s 53 154
- s 55 180
- s 86 66
- s 107 8
  - (1) 28, 37
- Sched 1 .... 10, 21
- Sched 2, Pt II 42

Children and Young Persons Act 1963—
- s 3 .... 28, 100–1
  - (1) 37
  - (3) 29
- s 23 .... 14, 17
  - (1), (3) 14
  - (5) 14, 64
- s 26 .... 57, 69, 121
- s 29 .... 6, 20
- s 57(4) 42

Children and Young Persons Act 1969 ... 1, 3, 6, 20, 28, 44, 100, 147, 182, 185
- s 1 .. 1, 2, 7, 11–13, 16–7, 23, 29–30, 66, 81–2, 84, 97, 109, 111, 123, 180, 188
  - (2) 2, 15, 20, 66, 83
  - (*a*) . 2, 11, 14, 15, 19–23, 26–7, 32, 43, 53, 62
  - (*b*) . 2, 11, 14, 15, 19, 20, 26–7, 32, 43
  - (*bb*) 14, 26
  - (*c*) 2, 11, 14, 19, 20, 27, 32, 43, 53
  - (*d*) 2, 11, 15, 19, 20, 28, 32, 43
  - (*e*) 2, 18–20, 29, 30, 32, 43

Children and Young Persons Act 1969—contd

- s 1(2)(f) ... 2, 7, 20, 31–2, 36, 43–4, 48, 92, 98
  - (3) 19, 20, 32, 62, 80, 86
- s 2(4) 17, 35
  - (5) 17, 35, 103
  - (6) 60
  - (7) 26, 31
  - (9) 36
  - (10) 49, 63–4, 71
  - (11) 35–6, 48
  - (12) 86
  - (14) 20
- s 3(1), (3) 31
  - (5) 36
  - (6) 32, 73, 87
  - (6A) 32
  - (7) 72
  - (8) 32, 86
- s 7 6
  - (7) 6
- s 7A 6
- s 9 85
  - (1), (2) 49
- s 12(1) 68
  - (2) 69, 70
  - (4) 69
- s 14 68
  - (A) 14
- s 15 .... 2, 204–6
  - (1) 68, 70, 74–5, 80
  - (5) 76
- s 16(2) 78
  - (3) 17, 78, 103
  - (4) 78, 83
  - (5) 78
  - (6) 75
    - (c) 75
  - (7) 75
  - (8) 86–7
- s 18(2) 4
  - (b) 68–9
  - (3) 70
- s 19 69
- s 20(1) 63
  - (b) 64
  - (2)(a) 62
  - (b) 66
  - (2A) 62, 180
  - (3) 63
- s 20A 63, 149, 180
  - (7) 182

Children and Young Persons Act 1969—contd

- s 21 2
  - (1) 74, 86
  - (2) 10, 63, 67, 74, 80
  - (3) 67
  - (4) 67, 86
  - (5) 62, 94
- s 21A 63
- s 22 .... 37, 65
  - (3) 65
  - (4) 13, 67
  - (5) 67
- s 23 6
  - (2) 68
- s 24(5) 74
- s 28 .... 13, 103
  - (1) 11, 70
  - (2) 15
  - (4) 154
  - (6) 13, 16, 64
- s 29(3) 154
- s 32(2), (2A), (2B), (3) 103
- s 32A 37
  - (1) 38, 79
  - (2) 80
  - (4) 38
- s 32B 37, 122
  - (2) 81
- s 34(1)(c) 6
- s 44 43
- s 70(1) 28, 32
  - (2) 15, 71–5

Children and Young Persons (Amendment) Act 1986—

- s 1 157
- s 2 87
- s 3 .... 40, 45, 47, 53, 81, 100
  - (2) 47

Children's Homes Act 1982 152
Civil Evidence Act 1968 ... 54, 88, 194
- s 11 .... 26, 57, 121
Civil Evidence Act 1972 ... 54, 88, 196

Courts Act 1971—

- s 10 89
- s 13(4)(d) 93

Criminal Justice Act 1948—

- s 37(1) 93

Criminal Justice Act 1967—

- s 22(1) 92

Criminal Justice Act 1982—

- s 17 73
- s 20 70

TABLE OF STATUTES

Criminal Justice Act 1982—*contd*
 s 21 69
 s 27 .... 32, 73
Data Protection Act 1984—
 s 21 160–1
Domestic Proceedings and
Magistrates' Courts Act 1978—
 s 10 .... 3, 4
Education Act 1944 30
 s 36 163
 s 37 30
 s 39 .... 30, 163
 s 40(2) 30
 s 76 164
 s 95(2) 30, 57
Education Act 1981—
 s 1 29
Evidence Act 1938—
 s 1 58
Family Law Reform Act 1969—
 s 2(3) 182
 s 7(2) 5, 153
  (3) 188
 s 8 165
Family Law Reform Act 1987 159,
                                  170
 Pt II 109
 s 4 .... 109, 116, 134, 141, 177
 s 7 110
 s 8(1) 28, 34, 37
  (2) 109, 116
  (3) 134
  (4) 177
  (5) 141
 s 9 182
 s 33 157
 Sched 2, para 74 170
   para 75 .... 157, 159
   para 79 .... 110, 177
   para 84 157
Foster Children Act 1980—
 ss 1, 2 16
 s 12 .... 16, 17
  (5) 107
 s 13(2) 14
 s 14(2) 17
Guardianship Act 1973—
 s 1 162
  (3) 117, 166
 s 2(2) 4, 5
 s 6(2) 123
  (3A) 124
Guardianship of Minors Act 1971 ....
                                  199
 s 1 43

Guardianship of Minors Act
1971—*contd*
 s 5 .... 117, 141
 s 9 .... 4, 116, 170
Health and Social Services and Social
Security Adjudicators Act 1983—
 s 4 149
 s 6 168
 s 19(1), (2) 156
  (3), (4) 157
 Sched 1 168
 Sched 2, para 10 27
   para 11 14
   para 14 37
   para 16 103
   para 21 27
   para 48 115
   para 49 149
   para 50 151
   para 51 177
   para 55 139
 Scheds 4, 10 150
Housing (Homeless Persons) Act
1977 108
Interpretation Act 1978—
 s 7 118
Justice of the Peace Act 1949—
 s 3 42
Legal Aid Act 1974 .... 12, 94
 s 2(4) 131
 s 28(6) 73
Legal Aid Act 1982 98
Local Authority Social Services Act
1970—
 s 2 114
 Sched 1 114
Local Government Act 1972—
 s 111 181
Magistrates' Courts Act 1980—
 Pt II 16, 29, 119
 s 22 77
 s 54 120
 s 55 119–20
 s 56 .... 44, 77, 120
 s 57 .... 44, 120
 s 60 157
 s 64 .... 101, 134, 173
 s 81(8) 73
 s 87(4) 89
 s 93 157
 s 95 158
 s 97 122
  (1) 60, 122
  (3) 60
  (4) 57

Magistrates' Courts Act 1980—*contd*
  s 108 182
  s 109(2) 101
  s 111 89
  s 113 92
  s 120 72
  s 121(6) 48, 121
  s 122 119
  s 123 44
  s 127 125
  s 152 119
Marriage Act 1949—
  s 3(1)(*a*), (*b*) 182
  Sched 2 184
Matrimonial Causes Act 1973—
  s 43 .... 3, 4
  s 52(1) 3
Mental Health Act 1983 ...... 72, 113
  s 1(2) 71
  s 26(4) 72

Mental Health Act 1983—*contd*
  s 37 71
    (4) 71
  s 38(2), (5), (6) 71
  s 54(3) 71
  s 69 72
Prosecution of Offences Act 1985—
  s 27 31
Poor Law Act 1930—
  s 73 163
Powers of Criminal Courts Act 1973—
  s 35 86
Rehabilitation of Offenders Act 1974—
  s 4(1) 57
  s 7(2)(*d*) 57
Social Security Act 1986 155

Table of Statutory Instruments

Administration of Children's Homes
Regulations 1951 [SI No 1217] . . . . .
  142, 150, 167
  reg 4 162
  regs 5, 6 164
  reg 11 167
  reg 12(1) 142
Adoption Agencies Regulations 1983
[SI No 1964]—
  reg 7(1)(a) 175
Boarding-out of Children Regulations
1955 [SI No 1377] 56, 122, 143,
  154, 163
  regs 6,7 164
  reg 14(2) 143
  reg 19 162
Child Benefit (General) Regulations
1976 [SI No 965] 183
  reg 16(5) 183
    (6)(a), (b) 183
    (8) 183
Children and Young Persons Act 1969
(Transitional Modifications of
Part I) Order 1970 [SI No 1882] . . 6
Children and Young Persons
(Definition of Independent Persons)
Regulations 1971 [SI No 486] . . . 175
Community Homes Regulations 1972
[SI No 319] 149, 163, 167
  reg 5 164
  reg 8 162
  reg 10 167
Crown Court Rules 1971 [SI No
1292]—
  r 7 87
  r 9 . . . . 88, 101
  r 10(2) 101

Crown Court Rules 1971 [SI No
1292]—contd
  r 17 93
  r 21 90
Crown Court (Amendment No 2)
Rules 1976 [SI No 2164]—
  r 8B 88
Data Protection (Subject Access
Modification) (Social Work) Order
1987 [SI No 1904] 161
Emigration of Children
(Arrangements by Voluntary
Organisations) Regulations 1982 [SI
No 13] 141
Justices' Clerks Rules 1970 [SI No
231]—
  r 3 38
Legal Advice and Assistance (No 2)
Regulations 1980 [SI No 1898]—
  reg 8(2) 96
Legal Aid (General) Regulations 1980
[SI No 1894]—
  reg 15(5) 99
Legal Aid in Criminal Proceedings
(General) Regulations 1968 [SI No
1231] 98
Local Authorities and Local Education
Authorities (Allocation of
Functions) Regulations 1951 [SI No
472] 185
Magistrates' Courts (Children and
Young Persons) Rules 1970 [SI No
1792]—
  r 8(2) 48
  r 9 49
  Pt III 31, 44, 65, 76, 152
  Pt IIIA 46, 119–20

Magistrates' Courts (Children and Young Persons) Rules 1970 [SI No 1792]—*contd*
  r 14 .... 34, 64, 76
    (3) 82
    (4) 77
  r 14A 38, 79
    (2) 40, 81
    (4) 39, 42
    (5) 81
    (6) 41
  r 14B 46, 80
  r 15 47
    (1) 83
    (2) 77
  r 16 82
    (1) 45
    (2)(*a*) 48
  r 16(3) 46
  r 17 .... 77, 79
    (1) 37
    (2) 37, 79
  r 18(1), (2) 47
  r 19 45
  r 20(1) 49, 50
    (2)(*a*), (*b*) 50
  r 21(1), (2) 50
  r 21B 120, 123
    (2) 120
  r 21C 122
  r 21E 122–3
  r 22 29
  r 26 .... 35, 37, 78
  r 28(2) 68–9
  Sched 2—
      Form 4 35
      Form 5 35
      Form 7 .... 26, 35, 77
      Form 7A 81
      Form 8 29
      Form 9 12
      Form 10 14
      Form 11 13
Magistrates' Courts (Children and Young Persons) (Amendment) Rules 1984 [SI No 567(L3)] 40
  r 2 41
  r 7 119
Magistrates' Courts (Children and Young Persons) (Amendment) (No 2) Rules 1983 [SI No 1793] . 154

Magistrates' Courts Rules 1968 [SI No 1920]—
  r 13 48
  r 14 ...... 13, 29, 44, 65, 76, 119–20
  r 20 84
  r 67 .... 36, 119
    (1) 60
  r 68 .... 26, 57, 121
  rr 76–81 89
  r 99 35
    (2) 35, 61, 120
    (6) 60
  r 107 60
Rules of the Supreme Court—
  ord 53 94
    r 3(7) 188
  ord 55 .... 128, 172
    r 3(1) 128
      (3) 130
    r 4(1) 128
  ord 56, rr 1, 4A, 5 90
    r 6 90
  ord 59, r 1 91
    (18) 91
    r 2–15 91
    r 14(4) 91
    r 15 91
  ord 62 .... 101, 131
  ord 79, r 9 93
  ord 80, r 2 93
    r 3(8) 128
  ord 90 112
    r 9 128
    r 16 128
      (3) 128
      (6) 129
      (8) 129
  ord 94, r 13 67
Secure Accommodation (No 2) Regulations 1983 [SI No 1808] 151–2
  reg 7 151
Secure Accommodation (No 2) (Amendment) Regulations 1986 [SI No 1591] 153
  reg 4 153
Voluntary Homes (Registration) Regulations 1948 [SI No 2408] .. 150
Voluntary Homes (Return of Particulars) Regulations 1949 [SI No 2092] 150

Abbreviations

In addition to the conventional abbreviations, the following are used throughout the book:

CA	Children Act 1975
CCA	Child Care Act 1980
CYPA 1933	Children and Young Persons Act 1933
CYPA 1963	Children and Young Persons Act 1963
CYPA 1969	Children and Young Persons Act 1969
CYPAA 1986	Children and Young Persons (Amendment) Act 1986
CYPAR	Magistrates' Courts (Children and Young Persons) (Amendment) Rules 1984
CYPR	Magistrates' Courts (Children and Young Persons) Rules 1970
FCA	Foster Children Act 1980
FLRA 1969	Family Law Reform Act 1969
FLRA 1987	Family Law Reform Act 1987
HSSA	Health and Social Services and Social Security Adjudications Act 1983
MCA	Magistrates' Courts Act 1980
MCFR	Magistrates' Courts (Forms) Rules 1981
MCR	Magistrates' Courts Rules 1981
RSC	Rules of the Supreme Court

STOP PRESS

Since this book went to press the Government has announced that the Children and Young Persons Amendment Act 1986 will be implemented on 1 August 1988. On that date the Magistrates' Courts (Children and Young Persons) Rules 1988 will come into force and will govern all juvenile court proceedings. The Magistrates' Courts (Children and Young Persons) Rules 1970 (as amended) will be revoked and reference should be made to the 1988 Rules whenever the CYPR are mentioned in the text.

The new rules provide for parents and grandparents to be accorded party status in care proceedings. Some existing rules of procedure have been amended or clarified. Other provisions remain unchanged. Brief details of any alterations are given in the following table of destinations.

		CARE PROCEEDINGS	
1970 Rules	*1988 Rules*	*Subject*	*New provisions*
r 14	r 14	Notice by person proposing to bring care proceedings	Notice to be served on grandparents, if whereabouts known. Notice to be served on person with whom child has had home for period or periods totalling not less than 42 days instead of single period as before.
—	r 15	Notice to parent or guardian of party status	Notice to be sent whenever separate representation order made (Schedule 2, Form 9).
r 14A	r 16	Appointment and duties of guardian ad litem	Part-time probation officer may be appointed guardian ad litem if not previously concerned with child or family.

STOP PRESS

CARE PROCEEDINGS contd.

1970 Rules	1988 Rules	Subject	New provisions
—	r 17	Application by grandparents to be parties to proceedings	Grandparents may be granted party status if they had a substantial involvement in the child's upbringing at any time before the commencement of proceedings *and* this is likely to be in the interests of the child's welfare. Application on Form 10, Schedule 2.
r 14B	r 18	Rights of parents and guardians	Clarifies when in proceedings parent/guardian may give or call evidence and/or make representations to meet allegations made against them without prejudice to any additional rights party status may confer.
r 14C	r 19	Rights of other persons	Gives any person who has demonstrated an interest in the child's welfare (maintained until the commencement of proceedings) the right to make representations to the court provided that these are likely to be relevant.
r 15	r 20	Adjournment and procedure	Existing provisions extended to cover parents and grandparents with party status. Grandparent, parent and child to cross-examine witnesses and address court in that order unless court agrees to vary order in the interests of justice.
r 16	r 21	Duty of court to explain nature of proceedings: evidence and order of speeches.	
r 17	r 22	Conduct of case on behalf of child	Relative or other person conducting case no longer termed child's 'friend'.

CARE PROCEEDINGS contd.

1970 Rules	1988 Rules	Subject	New provisions
r 18	r 23	Power to hear evidence in the absence of child and to require parent or guardian to withdraw	Extended to cover grandparents and any other person entitled to make representations to the court.
r 19	r 24	Duty of court to explain procedure to child at the end of applicant's case	
r 20	r 25	Consideration of reports	Provides for advance disclosure of written reports to parties and specified persons.
—	r 26	Consideration of reports: secure accommodation	Provides for advance disclosure of written reports to parties and to specified persons.
r 21	r 27	Duty of court to explain manner in which it proposes to deal with case and effect of order	Provides for court to explain the effect of order to parent and to child in simple language suitable to his age and understanding.
—	r 28	Leave of court for withdrawal of discharge proceedings	Child or guardian ad litem can only withdraw application for discharge of care order made by parent on child's behalf with leave and court must consider grounds for application to withdraw and any evidence parent may wish to adduce and should only grant leave if it would be inappropriate to discharge the care order.

ACCESS PROCEEDINGS AND PARENTAL RIGHTS RESOLUTIONS

1970 Rules	1988 Rules	Subject	New provisions
r 21A	r 29	Application and interpretation of rules	
r 21B(1)	r 30	Notice of complaint	Notice to be sent to any guardian or custodian who is not a complainant.
			Provision for notice to be given to person with whom child has had home for specified period varied as in r 14.

STOP PRESS

ACCESS PROCEEDINGS AND PARENTAL RIGHTS RESOLUTIONS contd.

1970 Rules	1988 Rules	Subject	New provisions
r 21C	r 31	Appointment and duties of guardian ad litem	Provision for part-time probation officer to be appointed guardian as in r 16.
r 21D	r 32	Evidence of guardian ad litem	
r 21B(2)	r 33	Rights of persons other than parties	Provision for interested person to make representations to the court as in r 19.
r 21D	r 34	Evidence and procedure generally	Provides for advance disclosure of written reports to parties and specified persons.
r 21E	r 35	Power of court to hear evidence in the absence of child, etc.	

PROCEEDINGS UNDER THE CYPA 1963, s 3

1970 Rules	1988 Rules	Subject
r 22	r 36	Notice of complaint and restrictions on adjudicating justice

SCHEDULE 2 — FORMS (as reproduced in Appendix 1)

Form 7	Form 7	Notice of care proceedings
Form 4	Form 4	Summons — care proceedings and proceedings in respect of supervision order
Form 5	Form 5	Summons for attendance of parent or guardian
Form 8	Form 11	Notice to parent under r 36
Form 9	Form 12	Authority to remove to a place of safety
Form 10	Form 13	Warrant to search for or remove a child or young person
Form 11	Form 18	Order for removal of foster child or protected child to a place of safety

Chapter 1

Introduction

On 31 March 1985 there were 72,782 children in the care of local authorities in England and Wales. Of these 31,545 were committed to care by care orders made under the Children and Young Persons Act 1969; 2,199 were committed to care under an interim care order, remanded in care in criminal proceedings or detained in care after arrest; 7,707 were committed to care in matrimonial, guardianship or wardship proceedings; and 31,331 were in care under the provisions of s 2 of the Child Care Act 1980 because, for a variety of reasons, their parents were unable or unavailable to care for them. (These statistics are taken from *Children in Care in England and Wales*, March 1985, HMSO.) The statistics do not show how many of this last group are also the subject of resolutions under the CCA, s 3, vesting all parental rights and duties in the local authority.

Because compulsory removal or detention in care involves an important interference with the personal liberty and rights of both the parent and child, it has been recognised that a firm statutory framework is required to govern the exercise of such powers, together with judicial safeguards to prevent abuse. The complexity of the legislation and the need to ensure that the interests of all parties are adequately represented means that the lawyer has an important role to play in this field. This book aims to provide a practical guide to the subject, concentrating on those areas where legal expertise is most likely to be required.

1 What are care proceedings?

For the purpose of this book care proceedings are:
    (*a*) Proceedings under the Children and Young Persons Act 1969, s 1;

(b) Proceedings to vary or discharge a care order (CYPA 1969, s 21) or a supervision order (CYPA 1969, s 15);
(c) An application to a juvenile court to confirm a resolution under the CCA, s 3 after parental objection; and
(d) An application to determine a s 3 resolution (CCA, s 5(4)).

There are other proceedings under the child care legislation which may involve a child in care eg an application for an access order by a parent (CCA, s 12C) or an application by a local authority for authority to keep a child in care in secure accommodation (CCA, s 21A); these proceedings are dealt with in Part IV.

The main statutory provisions which create machinery for admitting children into the care of a local authority on a long-term basis or for an indefinite period are the CYPA 1969, s 1 and the CCA, ss 2 and 3.

The Children and Young Persons Act 1969, s 1

This gives a juvenile court power to make a care order committing a child to the care of a local authority, provided that the court is satisfied that one of the grounds set out in s 1(2)(a)–(f) has been proved and that the child is in need of care or control which he is unlikely to receive unless an order is made. The grounds in s 1(2) relate either to the child's present condition—eg he has been ill-treated or neglected, or is beyond the control of a parent—or to the potential risk to which he may be exposed, where, for example, another child in the same family has been ill-treated, or a person convicted of an offence against another child is coming to live in the same household.

The Child Care Act 1980, ss 2 and 3

Section 2 places a duty on local authorities to receive into care any child under the age of seventeen who has no parent or guardian, or whose parent or guardian is unable to provide proper care for one or more of the reasons specified in s 2(1). Section 3 of the Act gives a local authority power to pass a resolution assuming parental rights and duties in respect of a child received into care under s 2 on a number of specified grounds. The effect of a s 3 resolution is to deprive a parent of his parental rights, including the right to remove the child from care. He does, however, have the right to object to a resolution, whereupon it will lapse unless confirmed by a juvenile court. A parent may also apply to the juvenile court for a resolution to be discharged.

INTRODUCTION 3

To avoid confusion proceedings under the CYPA 1969 will be referred to throughout the book as 'care proceedings', unless the context indicates otherwise, and proceedings under the CCA will be termed 's 3 proceedings'. Care proceedings will be covered in detail in Part I and s 3 proceedings in Part II. Part III will deal with children in the care of voluntary organisations; Part IV will cover the respective rights and duties of the local authority, parent and child while the child is in care; and Part V will discuss proposed reforms of child care law. For the sake of brevity the term 'he' will be used throughout the book and includes 'she' unless the context indicates otherwise.

2 Can care orders be made in other proceedings?

Children can be committed to the care of local authorities or placed under their supervision in other proceedings which are outlined below. These are outside the scope of this book, however, since committal to care is the by-product of such proceedings and not their purpose.

Matrimonial proceedings

In divorce, nullity and judicial separation proceedings the court can commit to the care of a local authority any child of the family who is under the age of seventeen if there are exceptional circumstances which make it impracticable or undesirable to place him in the care of either parent or any other person (Matrimonial Causes Act 1973, s 43). A 'child of the family' in divorce, nullity or judicial separation proceedings means a child of both parties or any other child who has been treated by both parties as a child of their family (but not a child who is boarded-out with the parties by a local authority or voluntary organisation) (Matrimonial Causes Act 1973, s 52(1)). There is no statutory definition of 'exceptional circumstances' but it has been held that the courts must look at what is best in the circumstances and not consider what may be perfect and ideal; the intention of the statute being that children shall remain with their parents if at all possible (*G* v *G* (1962) 106 SJ 858).

The magistrates' court has a similar power in matrimonial proceedings to commit to the care of a local authority any child of the family who is under the age of seventeen, provided there is no custody order made by a court in England and Wales already in force and the child is not already in care, whether under the CCA, s 2, or by virtue of a care order under the CYPA 1969 (Domestic

Proceedings and Magistrates' Courts Act 1978, s 10). A 'child of the family' in matrimonial proceedings in the magistrates' court has the same meaning as in divorce proceedings.

The powers and duties of the local authority in relation to a child committed to care in matrimonial proceedings are set out in the CCA, Part III, which applies to all children in care. The CCA, s 24 (which provides for the emigration of children in care) and s 28 (which relates to the after-care of children in care) do not apply to children committed to care in matrimonial proceedings. If a child is committed to care by an order under the Matrimonial Causes Act 1973, s 43, the local authority must exercise its statutory powers and duties subject to any directions the court may give. A magistrates' court has no power to restrict the local authority in any way when committing a child to care. An order will remain in force until the child reaches the age of eighteen unless revoked before then.

For a full treatment of care orders in matrimonial proceedings see David Salter *Humphreys' Matrimonial Causes*, 16th ed (1984, Longman) and *Magistrates' Court: Domestic Proceedings* by Janet Carter, 1st ed (1987, Longman).

Guardianship

A court may make an order committing a child under the age of seventeen to the care of a local authority where a parent (including the natural father of an illegitimate child) has applied for custody under the Guardianship of Minors Act 1971, s 9, and there are exceptional circumstances making it impracticable or undesirable to entrust the child to either parent or to any other person (Guardianship Act 1973, s 2(2)). The provisions of the CCA, Part III will then apply as if the child were in care under s 2 of that Act, with the exception of ss 24 and 28. The order will terminate on the child's eighteenth birthday.

The High Court, county court and the magistrates' court all have concurrent jurisdiction in guardianship proceedings but only the High Court can issue directions restricting a local authority's exercise of its statutory powers in relation to a child in care. It may for example make an order for access when committing a child to care.

The power to commit a child to care under the Guardianship Act 1973, s 2(2) may become more important when the CA 1975, Sched 3, para 75 is brought into force, since this will remove the court's power to grant custody to a person other than a parent in proceedings under the Guardianship of Minors Act 1971, s 9. If a court considers both parents to be unfit to care for the child, and there is no one willing to apply for a custodianship order (see Custodianship, below), it will have little option but to commit the child to care.

Wardship

A ward of court under the age of seventeen years may be committed to care if there are exceptional circumstances making it impracticable or undesirable for the child to be, or to continue to be, in the care of either of his parents or any other person (Family Law Reform Act 1969, s 7(2)). The court also has an inherent jurisdiction to place a ward of any age in the care of a local authority and can use this power to commit a ward who has attained the age of seventeen (*Re SW (A Minor) (Wardship: Jurisdiction)* [1986] 1 FLR 24). As in guardianship proceedings the CCA, Part III will apply, with the exception of ss 24 and 28, although a local authority must exercise its powers in relation to a child committed to care in wardship proceedings subject to any directions given by the court.

Wardship jurisdiction, and therefore committal to care, terminates on the child's eighteenth birthday, unless determined earlier by court order.

Custodianship

Under the CA 1975, s 33 a person who is not the natural parent of a child may apply for a custodianship order granting him legal custody, provided he satisfies certain conditions. The Guardianship Act 1973, s 2(2) (see above) applies to such applications. The court therefore has power to commit a child to care instead of making a custodianship order in exceptional circumstances. There is also an additional power to make a care order on the revocation of a custodianship order. A custodian, parent or guardian, or a local authority, may apply for the order to be revoked and the court must make a care order if, as a result of revocation, there will be no person having legal custody of the child, or there will be such a person but the court does not consider it desirable for the child to be in the legal custody of that person (CA 1975, s 36).

Custodianship orders and care orders on revocation can be made in respect of any child under the age of eighteen. The local authority will have the same powers as it does in respect of a child committed to care in guardianship proceedings.

Adoption

A court which refuses to make an adoption order in respect of a child under the age of sixteen may make an order committing the child to the care of a local authority, if there are exceptional circumstances making it impracticable or undesirable to place him in the care of either parent or any other person (Adoption Act 1976, s 26). The local authority will have the same powers as it does in respect of a child committed to care in guardianship proceedings.

For adoption law generally, the reader is referred to Josling and Levy *Adoption of Children* 10th ed (1985, Longman).

Criminal proceedings

Care orders can be made in criminal proceedings in respect of any child or young person who has been found guilty of an offence which, if committed by an adult, would be punishable by imprisonment (CYPA 1969, s 7(7)). Note, however, that the court should not make a care order unless the seriousness of the offence warrants it *and* it is satisfied that the child is in need of care and control which he is unlikely to receive without an order (CYPA 1969, s 7A). A child or young person must also be remanded to care if he has been charged or convicted of an offence or committed to the Crown Court for trial or sentence and bail has been refused, unless, in the case of a young person over the age of fourteen, the court certifies that he is too unruly to be committed safely to care (CYPA 1969, s 23).

In the CYPA 1969 the term 'child' applies to juveniles under the age of fourteen and 'young person' to those between the ages of fourteen and seventeen. The wording of both s 7 and s 23 originally envisaged that the age of criminal responsibility would be raised from ten years to fourteen years and that no criminal proceedings would be brought against any child under that age. This reform has not been implemented and the wording of the sections has therefore been amended so that the provisions relating to care orders in criminal proceedings apply to children between the ages of ten and fourteen as well as to young persons (CYPA 1969, s 34(1)(*c*), and Children and Young Persons Act 1969 (Transitional Modifications of Part 1) Order 1970 (SI No 1882)).

A care order cannot be made in respect of any young person over the age of seventeen unless the proceedings were commenced when he was under that age *and* the court agrees to continue hearing them (CYPA 1963, s 29). Care orders made in criminal proceedings terminate when the young person reaches the age of eighteen, or, if the order was made after his sixteenth birthday, nineteen.

Subject to certain variations a local authority has the same powers and duties in relation to a child committed to care whether a care order is made in criminal proceedings or in civil proceedings under the CYPA 1969, s 1. Criminal proceedings must not be confused with care proceedings brought on the offence ground (CYPA 1969, s 1(2)(*f*)) see pp 30–32.

3 When will a lawyer be involved?

A lawyer may be called upon to advise and represent the child, his parents or the local authority in proceedings to take or retain a child in care. He may be asked to advise on the respective rights of the parties while the child is in care; for example, can the local authority change the child's religion? Who must consent to essential medical treatment? Can the authority deny a parent access? He may be required to act in access proceedings or on an application to place or keep a child in secure accommodation. Finally, he may be required to represent the parties in proceedings to terminate compulsory care.

All cases involving children require special skills and techniques. In care proceedings it is essential that the lawyer not only adopts a sensitive approach but that he also has a sound knowledge of the law and procedure. He must have a clear idea from the outset exactly whom he is representing; this is not always apparent in care cases.

Part I

The Children and Young Persons Acts 1933–1969

Chapter 2

Detention in a place of safety

There are several overlapping statutory provisions which authorise the detention of a child in a place of safety for varying periods. Unless detention is for a short period, or a child requires medical treatment, a place of safety will usually mean a community home provided or controlled by a local authority or an approved local authority foster home. It can also be a police station, hospital, surgery or any other place willing to receive a child (CYPA 1933, s 107). Local authorities are obliged to make accommodation available in community homes for children removed to a place of safety and as a matter of good practice they should supervise any child detained in a place of safety within their area even if the child is not detained in local authority accommodation (CCA, s 73(1)). A place of safety order is often a prelude to care proceedings under the CYPA 1969, s 1 although it is possible for the child to be released or received into care under the CCA, s 2 when the order expires.

1 Place of safety order

The CYPA 1969, s 28(1) enables any person to apply to a single justice for authority to detain a child under the age of seventeen and take him to a place of safety if the applicant has reasonable cause to believe that:
    (*a*) any of the conditions set out in the CYPA 1969, s 1(2)(*a*)–(*e*)—ie the grounds for bringing care proceedings—are satisfied in respect of the child (see pp 20–32); or
    (*b*) a court would find it probable that he will be ill-treated or neglected (within the meaning of s 1(2)(*a*)) because this has happened to another child who is or was a member of the same household; or

(c) the child is about to leave the United Kingdom in contravention of the CYPA 1933, s 25 (which regulates the sending abroad of juvenile entertainers).

Note that a place of safety order can be sought even if a child is temporarily in a safe place such as a hosptial (*H v Sheffield City Council* (1982) JSWL 303). It would not be appropriate, however, to prevent the removal of a child in voluntary care under the CCA, s 2. In that case the appropriate action would be for the local authority to pass a resolution assuming parental rights under the CCA, s 3 or to make the child a ward of court (*Essex CC v TLR and KBR (minors)* (1979) 9 Fam Law 15).

An application can be made to a single justice out of court hours and a record of all adjudications arising from such applications must be kept by the clerk to the justices whether an application is made in court hours or otherwise.

The authority to remove the child to a place of safety will be issued in Form 9 (CYPR, Sched 2) which is reproduced in Appendix 1. Any person can apply for a place of safety order and if the application is made on behalf of a local authority, the order will name the individual social worker who actually made it. A person who detains a child in a place of safety other than a community home provided or controlled by a local authority can recover the cost of the child's maintenance from the local authority within whose area the child resided immediately before his removal to the place of safety (CCA, s 73(2)).

The power to detain lasts for twenty-eight days, beginning with the day on which the order is made, unless a shorter period is specified. It does not authorise the applicant to enter premises to search for the child and its use is therefore confined to circumstances in which the child's whereabouts are known and it is easy to gain access to him. The reasons for the child's detention in a place of safety should be explained to his parents or guardian, and to the child himself if he is capable of understanding, as soon as practicable after removal.

A local authority should apply for a place of safety order in respect of a child who is a ward of court only in the most extreme circumstances and it must then apply to the High Court for directions at the next sitting. In all other cases an emergency application should be made to the wardship court or outside court hours to the duty judge (*Practice Direction* [1988] 1 WLR 475). A local authority can apply for an order under s 28(1) even though a juvenile court has only a few days earlier discharged a care order in respect of the same child (*R* v *A Justice for Lincoln (Kesteven), ex parte M* [1976] 1 All ER 490). The authority cannot, however, apply for an extension of its authority to detain a child in a place of safety, and any attempt to detain a child indefinitely by releasing him for short periods between applications under s 28(1) could be an abuse of process (see Lord Widgery CJ in *R* v *A Justice for Lincoln (Kesteven), ex parte M*, above, at p 495). If a local authority seeks to detain a child in care after the expiry of a place of safety order it should commence care proceedings under the CYPA 1969, s 1 or apply for an order under s 28(6) which empowers a juvenile court or a single justice to make an interim care order or to order the early release of any child detained under s 28. If the child's release is not ordered and an interim care order is made, the child (or his parent or guardian on his behalf), may apply to the High Court (CYPA 1969, s 22(4)) or to the juvenile court (CYPA 1969, s 21(2)) for its discharge.

There is no right of appeal against a place of safety order. A parent or guardian can in theory apply for an interim care order under s 28(6) but if the object of this application is to obtain a refusal from the justices together with a direction that the child be released the application is likely to be treated as an abuse of process and fail (*Nottinghamshire CC* v *Q* [1982] 2 All ER 641). An interim care order under s 28(6) can last a maximum of twenty-eight days from the date of the order if made by a juvenile court, and a maximum of twenty-eight days from the date the child first came into legal custody (ie was removed to a place of safety) if made by a single justice.

2 Place of safety warrant

The CYPA 1933, s 40 enables any person acting in a child's interest to apply on oath to a single justice for a warrant authorising a police officer to search for a child under the age of seventeen and to remove him to a place of safety where there are reasonable grounds to suspect that:

(*a*) the child has been or is being assaulted, ill-treated, or neglected in any place within the jurisdiction of the justice, in a manner likely to cause him unnecessary suffering; or

(*b*) any offence mentioned in the CYPA 1933, Sched 1 has been or is being committed in respect of the child (see Appendix 3 for the relevant offences).

The applicant must give evidence on oath of the facts giving rise to his suspicions. The law provides that certain situations will automatically give reasonable grounds to suspect that an offence is being committed against the child or that he is being ill-treated. Thus the supervisor of a child placed under a supervision order in care proceedings brought under s 1(2)(*a*), (*b*), (*bb*) or (*c*) of the CYPA 1969 (the 'abuse' grounds) can apply for a warrant if there has been a refusal to permit visits by the supervisor or a medical examination as required by the order (CYPA 1969, s 14(A) inserted by the HSSA, Sched 2, para 11).

Similarly, any refusal to allow a local authority to visit a privately fostered child or a child under the age of sixteen placed with prospective adopters, or to inspect the premises where such a child lives, will provide reasonable grounds for suspicion (FCA, s 13(2), Adoption Act 1976, s 37(1)). Refusal to allow an inspector authorised by the Secretary of State to enter any community home, voluntary home, or place where a child is boarded out by a local authority, voluntary organisation or by private arrangement will also give grounds for suspicion (CCA, s 75(3)).

The warrant will be issued in Form 10 (CYPR 1970, Sched 2), which is reproduced in Appendix 1. It must be addressed to a named police officer who may be accompanied when he executes it by the applicant (unless the court otherwise directs) and by a medical practitioner (if the court so directs). The child need not be named although he must be identifiable (eg 'the male child between the ages of one and five years at present residing at 22 Acacia Avenue, Bidminster'). The warrant may authorise the police officer to search for the child, but to remove him only if he is being or has been ill-treated, neglected or assaulted or is the victim of any of the specified offences. Alternatively it can authorise the child's removal whatever the circumstances. In either case it will authorise entry into any house, building or other place named in the warrant, using force if this is necessary.

The child can only be detained in a place of safety for the period specified in the warrant, which cannot exceed twenty-eight days (CYPA 1963, s 23(1)). If he is not released or received into care under the CCA 1980, s 2 during that period, he must be brought before a juvenile court which may either order his release or make an interim care order (CYPA 1963, s 23(3), (5)). A child who is under the age of five or is incapacitated by illness or accident need not be brought before the court when an application is made under the CYPA 1963, s 23. The local authority in whose area a place of safety is situated is responsible for bringing before a juvenile court any child detained there under a warrant unless some other person or body agrees to do so (eg the police or the local authority in whose area the child ordinarily resides). For this reason a local authority must be notified whenever a child is detained in a place of safety within its area which it has not itself provided.

3 Detention by a police officer

The CYPA 1969, s 28(2) authorises a police officer to detain a child under the age of seventeen in a place of safety if he has reasonable cause to believe that:

  (a) any of the conditions set out in the CYPA 1969, s 1(2) (a)–(d) is satisfied; or
  (b) a court would find it probable that the child will be ill-treated or neglected (within the meaning of s 1(2)(a)) because this has happened to another child who is or was a member of the same household; or
  (c) the child is of compulsory school age but is not receiving efficient full-time education because he is in the charge of a vagrant who takes him from place to place.

It should be noted that a police officer cannot detain a child under s 28(2) on suspicion of committing an offence or for truancy (unless this arises from the vagrancy of the person in charge of the child).

Section 28(2) only authorises a police officer to detain a child, not to enter premises to search for him. The officer must, as soon as practicable, inform the child and his parents of the reason for detention and must ensure that an officer who is not below the rank of inspector, or the officer in charge of the police station, enquires into the circumstances of the detention as soon as possible. The senior officer may then either order the child's release or make arrangements for his detention in a place of safety. If the child is to be detained both he and his parents should be informed of their right to apply to a justice for his early release.

An application to a justice may be made by a parent or guardian on the child's behalf (CYPA 1969, s 70(2)), but it should be borne in mind that the Legal Aid Act 1974 makes no provision for legal aid to cover such an application. If an application is made to a justice he must order the child's release unless he considers that the child ought to be detained in his own best interests. The police should be notified of the hearing of an application for a child's release and should be given an opportunity to be heard, otherwise a justice may not have all the information necessary to decide what is in the child's best interests (*R* v *Bristol Justices, ex parte Broome* [1986] 1 WLR 352).

If the child's release is not ordered or no application is made he may be detained in a place of safety for a maximum period of eight days, including the day on which his detention began. If the police or local authority wish to detain the child beyond this period proceedings should be commenced under the CYPA 1969, s 1 or an interim care order should be sought under the CYPA 1969, s 28(6).

4 Removal of a foster child

The Foster Children Act 1980, s 12 enables a local authority to apply to a juvenile court for an order authorising the removal of any child fostered by private arrangement (as defined in s 1 of that Act) to a place of safety if:

 (*a*) he is being kept by or is about to be handed over to a foster parent who is unfit to care for him; or
 (*b*) the foster parent has been disqualified from keeping foster children; or
 (*c*) a requirement imposed by the local authority regarding the premises has not been kept; or
 (*d*) the premises or the environment in which the foster parent lives are detrimental to the child.

The application must be made by way of complaint unless there is imminent danger to the health or well-being of the child, in which case a person authorised to visit foster children (usually a local authority social worker acting under the FCA, s 2) may apply to a single justice for authority to remove the child at once. (For procedure governing applications by way of complaint see the MCA, Part II, and MCR, r 14.)

If a removal order is obtained the local authority should inform the child's parents, guardian or anyone who acts in that capacity. If arrangements cannot be made for them to take over the child's care he may be received into care under the CCA, s 2 even if the statutory grounds for admission into care do not apply, or he is over the age of seventeen.

The order for removal is in Form 11 (CYPR, Sched 2), which is reproduced in Appendix 1. It must state a period not exceeding twenty-eight days, beyond which the child cannot be detained without being brought before a juvenile court. If, therefore, a child is not released into the care of a parent or guardian or received into care under the CCA, s 2, care proceedings must be instituted under the CYPA 1969, s 1 or an interim care order should be sought under the CYPA 1963, s 23. There is a right of appeal to the Crown Court against a removal order (FCA, s 14(2)).

5 Removal of a protected child

The Adoption Act 1976, s 34 enables a local authority to apply to a juvenile court for an order authorising the removal of a protected child from unsuitable surroundings. The grounds for removal and procedure are similar to those for removal of a foster child under the FCA, s 12. A protected child is a child under the age of sixteen who has been placed in the actual custody of prospective adopters.

6 Detention after arrest

The CYPA 1969, s 2(4) enables a justice to issue a warrant for the arrest of any child who is the subject of current or proposed care proceedings to secure his attendance at court. If the child is arrested, but cannot be brought before a court immediately he may be detained in a place of safety for up to seventy-two hours but must be brought before the court which issued the warrant, or if this is not possible, before a single justice, within that period (CYPA 1969, s 2(5)).

There is a similar power to detain in a place of safety a child arrested under a warrant issued to secure his attendance at proceedings to vary or discharge a supervision order (CYPA 1969, s 16(3)).

The power to issue a warrant under the CYPA 1969, s 2(4) or s 16(3) should be confined to cases where a summons has been served on a child a reasonable time before the hearing and he has failed to appear, or to cases where it proves impossible to serve the summons.

7 Medical examination

Parental rights are not transferred when a child is detained in a place of safety under the statutory powers discussed above. A local authority which may be providing accommodation for a child detained in a place of safety cannot therefore give consent to a medical examination; neither can the named individual who obtained the place of safety order or warrant.

A doctor must seek consent from a parent and from the child himself, if he is of an age and understanding to give consent, before carrying out a medical examination. He can only examine the child without parental consent if he has reasonable cause to believe that medical treatment may be needed and the examination is carried out to assess that need and to provide for the child's proper care while detained in a place of safety.

A medical examination without consent for the purposes of obtaining evidence only is unauthorised and could constitute an assault. A medical examination should not proceed on the basis of parental consent if the child is competent to consent but refuses to do so. For a further discussion on consent to medical treatment see p 164.

An interim care order will pass parental rights to a local authority enabling it to give consent to the medical examination and treatment of a child in its care subject to the need to obtain the child's consent in appropriate cases. If therefore a doctor decides that a medical examination or treatment should be carried out but not as a matter of urgency, and the necessary consents are not forthcoming from the parent and/or child, the local authority should consider seeking an interim care order in care proceedings or, if this would be inappropriate, issuing a summons in wardship. All local authorities and regional and district medical and nursing officers were given guidance to this effect by the Chief Inspector of the Social Services Inspectorate of the Department of Health and Social Security in February 1988.

Chapter 3

Care proceedings

1 Who may bring proceedings?

Any local authority or constable who believes that there are grounds for making an order under the CYPA 1969, s 1(3) may institute care proceedings. The term 'constable' applies not only to full-time police officers but also to special constables and members of specialist police forces such as the railway police, the docks police etc. The National Society for the Prevention of Cruelty to Children and its officers are also authorised to bring proceedings but only on the grounds listed in the CYPA 1969, s 1(2)(*a*)–(*d*). An education authority alone may bring proceedings on ground (*e*)—the education ground.

The majority of cases are brought by local authorities, since they have a positive duty to investigate all information they receive about children at risk in their area and must institute care proceedings if there appear to be grounds, unless some other person or organisation is about to do so, or proceedings would not be in the interests of the child or the public. Any other person bringing proceedings must notify the local authority in whose area the child lives and, if the child is over the age of thirteen, a probation officer attached to the appropriate juvenile court. If it is difficult to ascertain where the child usually lives the local authority in whose area the circumstances giving rise to the proceedings arose should be notified.

For the sake of simplicity the reader should assume—in this part of the book—that proceedings are brought by a local authority unless otherwise indicated.

20 THE CHILDREN AND YOUNG PERSONS ACTS 1933–1969

2 Jurisdiction of court

Care proceedings cannot be brought in respect of any child who is over the age of seventeen or who is over the age of sixteen and is or has been married. If a child reaches the age of seventeen after the commencement of proceedings the court may continue to hear the case and may make any order it could have made if he had not attained that age (CYPA 1963, s 29). Care proceedings commence when a child is first brought before a court under the CYPA 1969, s 1 (CYPA 1969, s 2(14)).

Care proceedings can be brought in respect of any child who is present in England or Wales, whether or not he is domiciled there. A care order, however, cannot be made in respect of any child whose parent is entitled to diplomatic immunity (*R* v *Hendon Justices, ex parte D* (1974) 118 SJ 756).

The term child will be used in this part of the book to describe any person under the age of seventeen to whom the Children and Young Persons legislation applies, although the CYPA 1969 draws a distinction between children (under fourteen years) and young persons (fourteen to seventeen years). This terminology is of greater relevance to criminal proceedings.

3 Grounds

The person bringing proceedings must prove not only one of the specific conditions in the CYPA 1969, s 1(2)(*a*)–(*f*), but also that the child is in need of care or control which he is unlikely to receive unless an order (not necessarily a care order) is made under s 1(3) of the Act. This additional requirement is known as the 'care or control test' (see p 32).

The specific conditions as set out in the CYPA 1969, s 1(2) are that:
  (*a*) the child's proper development is being avoidably prevented or neglected, or his health is being avoidably impaired or neglected, or he is being ill-treated;
  (*b*) it is probable that the above condition will be satisfied in his case having regard to the fact that the court or another court has found that that condition is or was satisfied in the case of another child who is or was a member of the same household;
  (*bb*) it is probable that the conditions set out in (*a*) above will be satisfied in his case, having regard to the fact that a person

who has been convicted of an offence mentioned in the CYPA 1933, Sched 1 (see Appendix 3) (including a person who was placed on probation or received an absolute or conditional discharge upon conviction) is or may become a member of the same household as the child;
(c) he is exposed to moral danger;
(d) he is beyond the control of his parent or guardian;
(e) he is of compulsory school age and is not receiving efficient full-time education suitable to his age, ability and aptitude, and any special educational needs he may have; and
(f) he is guilty of an offence, excluding homicide.

These grounds will now be examined in detail.

4 Ill-treatment or neglect

In s 1(2)(a) the condition is a single condition although it offers five alternative grounds. It is sufficient for notice of proceedings to state simply that proceedings are brought under s 1(2)(a) without specifying the particular ground relied upon within that section. Indeed, the grounds are not mutually exclusive and it is always open to a local authority to show that the child's present condition or state of health is caused by a combination of factors all relevant to s 1(2)(a) (*Wooley* v *John and Patricia Haines* (1975), unreported but discussed at (1976) 140 JP 16).

This condition is concerned with existing circumstances and not with future events no matter how imminent. Thus the person bringing the proceedings must prove that the child's development or health is actually suffering in some way or that he is being ill-treated. It is not sufficient merely to produce evidence of parental conduct likely to affect the child's development or health in the future.

A local authority cannot, therefore, bring proceedings on this ground after a child has been in care on a voluntary basis under the CCA, s 2 for a period of time simply to prevent the child's removal into a situation which is potentially harmful (*Essex CC* v *TLR and KBR (Minors)* (1979) 9 Fam Law 15). The appropriate course of action in these circumstances is for the authority to pass a resolution under the CCA, s 3 assuming parental rights over the child or, if there are no grounds for a resolution, to make the child a ward of court.

The relevant time for assessing whether the circumstances described in s 1(2)(a) apply is that point in time immediately before the process of protecting the child was first put into motion (*Re D (A Minor)* [1987] 1 FLR 422). In practice, this means immediately prior to any application for a place of safety order or an interim care order in respect of the child. If, however, the child is not in the care of a parent or guardian at this time because, for example, he is in hospital following non-accidental injury the relevant time will be when his parents last had care and control in the chain of events immediately preceding the issue of a summons (*H* v *Sheffield City Council* (1982) JSWL 303).

Thus s 1(2)(*a*) can apply to a child who has been in care under successive interim care orders and may be restored to health or developing satisfactorily by the time a final hearing takes place. It can also apply to a child who has been placed at home 'on trial' with a parent previously found to be neglectful even though that parent may appear to be managing well by the time of the final hearing. This was the situation in *M* v *Westminster City Council* [1985] FLR 325 and the court was able to rely on evidence of neglect at the time the proceedings were commenced. It was held that present circumstances were relevant but only in the context of what had happened in the past.

The concepts of development, health and treatment are continuing concepts and it is therefore permissible for the court to investigate past events in order to ascertain whether the circumstances described in s 1(2)(*a*) did apply at the relevant time. How far into the past the court should delve is a matter of degree and must depend on the facts of the particular case. In *Re D (A Minor)* (above) the court took into account a mother's behaviour before the child's birth. The mother was a registered drug addict and during pregnancy she took drugs in excess of those prescribed for her in the full knowledge that this could damage her unborn child. The child was born suffering from symptoms caused by withdrawal from narcotics. The child's health was clearly impaired and the cause was the mother's avoidable behaviour during pregnancy. It was held to be immaterial that this circumstance preceded the child's birth. Section 1(2)(*a*) was satisfied even though the child had been in hospital and then in care since birth.

Proper development

The term 'proper development' includes physical, mental and emotional development. The concept is a wide one and the court is expected to look at the present conduct of those caring for the child and its effect on the child's past, present and future development.

The test of whether the harm to the child's development is avoidable is an objective one and it is not sufficient for a parent to argue that he or she is unable to avoid the conduct in question. Expert evidence from, for example, a child psychologist is not essential but it is always open to the court to request evidence of a particular nature if it thinks fit (*F* v *Suffolk CC* (1981) 79 LGR 554) although it may not call witnesses of its own volition.

Health

The term 'health' includes physical and mental health. The Home Office has advised against the use of care proceedings in cases where a child's health is being impaired because a parent refuses to consent to essential medical treatment. The Department of Health and Social Security already has an appropriate procedure to deal with such cases without the need for care proceedings—see Home Office Circular No 63/1968, 5 March 1968, and Ministry of Health Circular F/P9/1B, 14 April 1967.

Ill-treatment

Evidence of a single act of ill-treatment may provide sufficient proof for care proceedings if the consequences are severe. Where injuries are only minor it will usually be necessary to show a persistent pattern of minor, unexplained injuries over a period of time in order to prove ill-treatment. Whatever the case it will be necessary, if there is no direct evidence of ill-treatment, for the person bringing the proceedings to prove that on the balance of probabilities the injuries are non-accidental; medical evidence will usually be the crucial factor.

If the medical evidence supports a finding of non-accidental injury, the application can succeed even if the identity of the perpetrator is unknown or cannot be proved. Where the medical evidence points less clearly to deliberate injury but there is still a pattern of unexplained injuries an application may still succeed under s 1(2)(*a*) on the basis that the child's health is being avoidably impaired or neglected.

Injuries caused by excessive chastisement pose particular problems where the parties involved are from another culture with standards of child care and discipline which may differ considerably from the standard generally acceptable in this country. The approach adopted by the High Court in a recent wardship case (*Re H (Minors) (Wardship: Cultural Background)* [1987] 2 FLR 12) is of some assistance. The court was concerned with two Vietnamese children who were the victims of neglect and excessive chastisement. It was held that in dealing with children of foreign ethnic origins and culture the court should consider the situation against the reasonable objective standards of that culture so long as they did not conflict with the minimal acceptable standards of child care in England.

Sexual abuse
Sexual abuse is a category of ill-treatment which has caused particular concern in recent times due to its apparent increase and the controversy which surrounds the techniques employed in its diagnosis. In cases in which there is no criminal conviction or admission by an adult, abuse may be proved by clinical findings, by express disclosure by the child or by expert interpretation of the child's behaviour. Whilst certain findings, such as the existence of venereal disease or extensive bruising in the genital area, may readily support a diagnosis of sexual abuse, other clinical signs are less obvious and are subject to widely-differing interpretations within the medical profession. This is illustrated in the case of *In Re F (Minors)* (1987) *The Times*, 28 December, in which the medical experts called in wardship proceedings disagreed on a diagnosis of sexual abuse based upon the controversial reflex anal dilation test.

Lawyers who need to know more about the problems surrounding the clinical diagnosis of sexual abuse may find it helpful to refer to the medical publications listed in Appendix 5.

Diagnosis based upon information disclosed or impressions gained during special 'disclosure' interviews with the child may be equally problematic. Interviews are frequently conducted by those with psychiatric rather than forensic skill. Leading questions are often employed as a device to obtain information thereby limiting the evidential value of the interviews (see *Re E (A Minor) (Child Abuse: Evidence)* [1987] 1 FLR 269). The entire process is often recorded on videotape and further controversy surrounds the admission of these video recordings in evidence (see p 59 and also *Re E (A Minor) (Child Abuse: Evidence)* above and *Re M (A Minor) (Child Abuse: Evidence)* [1987] 1 FLR 293). For an interesting survey of judicial attitudes in this area refer to [1987] 1 FLR pp 269–346 in which seven wardship cases involving allegations of sexual abuse are collected together. Each contains judicial comment on the use in evidence of interviews conducted with children at the Child Abuse Clinic of the Great Ormond Street Hospital for

Sick Children in London. The interview technique pioneered at this hospital is now being applied at other centres.

Because of the evidential difficulties local authorities are increasingly resorting to wardship rather than care proceedings in cases of sexual abuse.

Concurrent criminal proceedings

If a parent of a child subject to care proceedings is committed to the Crown Court for trial in criminal proceedings arising out of the same facts, it has in the past been usual practice for the care proceedings to be adjourned until the criminal trial is over (Home Office Circular No 88/1972, 25 April 1972). This may be appropriate in many cases but Home Office Circular No 84/1982, 25 October 1982, now makes it clear that adjournment should not be automatic in all cases. If there is no reason to believe that the care proceedings will prejudice the trial in the adult court they should be allowed to proceed. An obvious example is where the accused intends to plead guilty.

Recent judicial decisions have favoured the continuance of care proceedings even where it has been argued that this would prejudice the position of a parent in criminal proceedings. Thus in *R* v *Exeter Juvenile Court, ex parte H* and *R* v *Waltham Forest Juvenile Court, ex parte B* (1988) *The Times*, 19 February, the President of the Family Division held that the welfare of the child was paramount and was the principle which must guide a court in deciding whether to adjourn. It was vital that care proceedings should proceed with great despatch as any delay involved risk to the child. A similar view was expressed by Bush J in *R* v *Inner London Juvenile Court, ex parte G* (1988) 152 JP 239, but he considered the welfare of the child to be one of the matters to be considered by the court in performing a balancing exercise of a judicial nature. Wherever the emphasis may correctly lie it is clear that a parent seeking an adjournment in these circumstances today faces a harder task than was once the case. If the care proceedings are adjourned the clerk of the juvenile court should inform the Crown Court Listing Office and efforts will then be made to expedite the criminal trial.

An acquittal in the Crown Court need not affect the outcome of the care proceedings. At the criminal court the prosecution must prove guilt beyond all reasonable doubt. In care proceedings it is only necessary to prove the case on the balance of probabilities and even then it is not essential to show who actually caused any nonaccidental injuries. Nevertheless, a conviction in the Crown Court will obviously simplify any subsequent care proceedings as documentary evidence of conviction can then be produced to the juvenile court. A certificate of conviction is admissible as evidence of the commission of an offence but is not conclusive (Civil Evidence Act 1968, s 11).

5 Potential risk

The conditions in s 1(2)(*b*) and (*bb*) deal with potential risk to the child. Condition 1(2)(*b*) covers the situation where the child has not been harmed yet but where this is extremely likely in view of the family history. The court must be satisfied that another child of the same household has been ill-treated or neglected within the meaning of s 1(2)(*a*) and it must then consider what is likely to happen to the child before the court if no order is made (CYPA 1969, s 2(7)).

If a care order was made in respect of the other child in the household, or the person responsible for his ill-treatment was convicted in criminal proceedings, the local authority can produce documentary evidence of the order or conviction to the court (MCR, r 68 and Civil Evidence Act 1968, s 11). In any other case the authority must first ask the court to make a finding that the other child of the household is or was being ill-treated or neglected and it must produce evidence to prove this. The court can make a finding to this effect even if the other child is no longer alive (*Surrey CC* v *S* [1973] 3 All ER 1074).

Care proceedings can be brought under s 1(2)(*b*) simultaneously in respect of several children who are all members of the same household where there is only firm evidence of ill-treatment against one child. The appropriate procedure is to bring that child before the court under s 1(2)(*a*) and the other children under s 1(2)(*b*). The cases will then be heard in the appropriate order.

If the court is asked to make a finding in respect of a child other than the one before the court the standard notice of proceedings (CYPR, Sched 2, Form 7) must be amended accordingly. (See Appendix 1 for a draft form of notice.)

The condition covered by s 1(2)(*bb*) (added by the CA 1975, Sched 3, para 67) enables care proceedings to be brought to protect a child who is likely to be ill-treated or neglected within the meaning of s 1(2)(*a*), because a person who has been convicted of an offence against a child is already, or is likely to become, a member of the same household as the child in question. (See Appendix 3 for the relevant offences.) The section now covers situations where the person convicted of the relevant offence was placed on probation or received an absolute or conditional discharge, such persons being originally excluded from the ambit of the condition (HSSA, Sched 2, paras 10 and 21).

In some cases it may be difficult to prove that a person is likely to join the child's household; admission to the household must be fairly imminent and some evidence of practical arrangements, or at least firm intentions, should be adduced.

The term 'household' is not defined in the Act. Its usual meaning is a group of people sharing a common home and domestic arrangements. However, there are no criteria which are conclusive in themselves and each case must be judged on its facts (*Simmons* v *Pizzey* [1979] AC 37). Thus a 'household' may remain the same even if its locality and the identity of some of its members has changed provided that there are important common features. In the context of s 1(2)(*b*) the important factor is the identity of the persons comprising the household rather than its location (*R* v *Birmingham Juvenile Court, ex parte N (An Infant)* [1984] 2 All ER 688).

6 Exposure to moral danger

The term 'moral danger' in s 1(2)(*c*) often has a sexual connotation although it can apply equally well to criminal behaviour, drug addiction, acts of violence, and any other kind of harmful influence. It cannot, however, apply to an immigrant wife under the age of sixteen who has sexual relations with her husband, provided she was validly married abroad (*Alhaji Mohamed* v *Knott* [1968] QB 1). In cases involving allegations of sexual abuse it is not unusual for proceedings to be brought on this ground and also under s 1(2)(*a*).

The person bringing proceedings must not only prove that the child is exposed to moral danger but also that he is in need of care or control which he is unlikely to receive unless an order is made. If it is the behaviour of those in charge of the child which creates the moral risk then it will obviously be easy to satisfy the care or control test at the same time as proving exposure to moral danger. The test will also be satisfied if those caring for the child are fully aware of his undesirable activities but cannot or will not take any action. If the parents were totally unaware of the moral danger to which the child has been exposed, the court will have to consider whether they will be likely to exercise sufficient control in the future. Failure to do so in the past will obviously be a relevant factor.

7 Beyond control

For the purpose of s 1(2)(*d*) it does not matter whether a child is beyond the control of his parent or guardian because he is unable to accept any discipline or because his parent is incapable of exercising any. In either case he is clearly in need of control which he is unlikely to receive unless an order is made. Thus in cases under s 1(2)(*d*) the same evidence is usually sufficient to prove the specific ground on which the proceedings are brought and to satisfy the care or control test.

A parent is not defined in the CYPA 1969 but has generally been taken to mean natural and adoptive parents but not the putative father of an illegitimate child. This will change when s 8(1) of the FLRA 1987 is implemented. The term 'parent' will then include a putative father if there is in force an order giving him the right to actual custody of the child. Actual custody in this context means actual physical possession of the child.

A guardian, although not defined in the CYPA 1969 is defined in the CYPA 1933, s 107(1) as 'any person who, in the opinion of the court . . . has for the time being the charge of or control over [a] child or young person'. This could presumably include a stepparent, and, in certain circumstances, the putative father of an illegitimate child although it is unlikely that the term will be so interpreted once the FLRA 1987, s 8(1) is implemented. The term control is defined in the context of the phrase 'care or control' to include discipline (CYPA 1969, s 70(1)). In this context its generally accepted meaning is the degree of discipline and supervision necessary for a child's proper upbringing.

A parent or guardian who is unable to control a child can ask the local authority to bring care proceedings. It is often best to make an informal approach to the local authority before following the procedure laid down in the CYPA 1963, s 3. If this fails, the parent or guardian should send a written notice to the local authority requesting it to bring the child before the court under the CYPA 1969, s 1. The appropriate authority is the one in whose area the child resides. There is no prescribed form for a notice under s 3; it is sufficient for a parent simply to state in the form of a letter that he is unable to control his child and requests the local authority to take proceedings under the CYPA 1969, s 1. (See Appendix 2 for a draft letter.)

Notice should be sent, wherever possible, by recorded delivery, although this is not a statutory requirement. If the local authority refuses to bring proceedings, or fails to act within twenty-eight days of the date notice was given (ie the date it would have arrived in the ordinary course of the post, unless the contrary is shown), the parent may apply to the juvenile court by way of complaint for an order directing the authority to bring care proceedings.

Proceedings are commenced by summons issued on the complaint of the parent or guardian. Procedure is governed by the MCA, Part II and MCR, r 14. Assistance by way of representation is available under the legal advice and assistance scheme and those not eligible under the scheme on financial grounds may still qualify for legal aid under the civil legal aid scheme. The CYPA 1963, s 3(3) states that the child shall not attend the hearing although there is nothing to prevent either party calling him as a witness. If the parents are living apart the parent making the application must send the other parent a notice informing him or her of the time and place of the hearing, and of his or her right to be heard (CYPR, r 22). Notice should be in Form 8 (CYPR, Sched 2), reproduced in Appendix 1. At the hearing the local authority has a duty to provide the court with information of the child's home surroundings, his school record, and his health and character.

The court hearing the application cannot determine whether the child is beyond control, only whether there is sufficient evidence to require the local authority to bring proceedings, and, if so, whether it should be required to do so. A local authority may be able to justify its refusal to act, even where there is sufficient evidence, on the ground that proceedings would be contrary to the interests of the child or the public. If the authority is ordered to bring proceedings the resulting case should be heard by a different bench.

8 The education ground

Only an education authority can bring proceedings under s 1(2)(*e*), although evidence of school non-attendance may be produced, if relevant, in proceedings brought on any other ground. The child must be of compulsory school age (five to sixteen years). A child is considered to have 'special educational needs' if he has a learning difficulty for which he requires special educational provision. The terms 'learning difficulty' and 'special educational provision' are extensively defined in s 1 of the Education Act 1981.

If a child is not a registered pupil at any school, or is not attending regularly, an education authority may, instead of, or in addition to, bringing proceedings under the CYPA 1969, s 1, prosecute a parent in the magistrates' court under the Education Act 1944. A parent may be prosecuted if he fails to comply with a school attendance order requiring him to register his child as a pupil at a named school (Education Act 1944, s 37) or if the child fails to attend regularly a school at which he is a registered pupil (Education Act 1944, s 39).

Before deciding whether to prosecute a parent, an education authority must consider whether to bring care proceedings instead of, or in addition to, a prosecution (Education Act 1944, s 40(2)). It is often easier to bring care proceedings if a parent has already been convicted of an offence under the Education Act, since s 1(2)(*e*) will be deemed to be satisfied if:
- (*a*) a parent has failed to comply with a school attendance order; or
- (*b*) the child is not regularly attending a school at which he is a registered pupil within the meaning of s 39 of the Education Act; or
- (*c*) the person in charge of the child is an habitual wanderer who takes the child from place to place.

A certificate of conviction under ss 37 or 39 of the Education Act will therefore provide the necessary evidence to satisfy s 1(2)(*e*). A certificate giving particulars of attendance and signed by a headteacher will also be admissible as evidence of non-attendance (Education Act 1944, s 95(2)). It is, however, always open to a parent to adduce evidence that the child is receiving efficient full-time education despite non-attendance at school. An authority is unlikely to prosecute a parent if this has had little effect in respect of other children in the same family (*Re DJMS (A Minor)* [1977] 3 All ER 582).

In addition to proving the education ground an education authority must, of course, satisfy the care or control test (see p 32). In *Re DJMS (A Minor)* (above) the Court of Appeal decided that care or control 'applied not only to the physical well-being of a child but also to his proper education'. Thus a child who is being kept away from school but has an otherwise excellent home could still be in need of care or control.

9 The offence condition

A child over the age of ten, who is alleged to have committed an offence (other than homicide), may be brought before a juvenile court under the CYPA 1969, s 1 as an alternative to criminal proceedings. In practice this provision is seldom used. This may be because a local authority or police officer who elects to bring proceedings under s 1(2)(*f*) not only has to prove beyond all reasonable doubt that the child has committed the alleged offence but also that the care or control test is satisfied—thereby assuming a double burden of proof.

The lower age limit of ten applies to care proceedings brought on the offence ground because a child below that age cannot be found guilty of an offence (CYPA 1933, s 50). The alleged offence must not have been the subject of previous care or criminal proceedings, and, if it is a summary offence, it must have been committed not more than six months before the commencement of proceedings (CYPA 1969, s 3(1)). Only a local authority or a constable may bring care proceedings on this ground although the NSPCC may use evidence of an alleged offence, where relevant, in proceedings brought on any other ground, eg as evidence that a child is beyond control or exposed to moral danger. A constable bringing proceedings on the offence ground must first obtain the consent of the Director of Public Prosecutions (Prosecution of Offences Act 1985, s 27).

Special rules of procedure apply to proceedings under s 1(2)(*f*) (see Chapter 4). The court cannot find the offence condition satisfied unless it would have found the child guilty of an offence in criminal proceedings (CYPA 1969, s 3(3)). The hearing is therefore divided into two distinct parts. First, the person bringing proceedings must prove that the child has committed the alleged offence in accordance with the rules of procedure governing criminal proceedings. Then if this is proved, the court must inform the child before going on to consider whether the care or control test is satisfied. Once the offence is proved the proceedings become civil, and procedure is governed by the CYPR, Part III which applies to care proceedings generally. Despite the special procedure it is, of course, possible for the same facts to satisfy the offence condition and the care or control test. It may, for example, be clear from the circumstances of the offence that it was committed because the child was not adequately supervised or controlled at home.

The court has certain additional powers of disposal if the offence condition is satisfied. If the child is over the age of fourteen it may bind him over in a recognisance not exceeding £50 and for a period not exceeding one year to keep the peace or be of good behaviour (CYPA 1969, s 3(7)). It may order the parent or guardian of the child to pay up to £1,000 in compensation to the victim of the offence unless satisfied that the parent or guardian cannot be found or that such an order would not be reasonable having regard to all the circumstances of the case, in which case a compensation order can be made against the child (CYPA 1969, s 3(6) as amended by the CJA 1982, s 27). A compensation order cannot be made against a parent or guardian unless he has been given an opportunity of being heard or has been required to attend court and has failed to do so (CYPA 1969, s 3(6A)). A parent or guardian has a right of appeal to the Crown Court against a compensation order (CYPA 1969, s 3(8)).

If the court finds the offence condition proved, but is not satisfied that the child is in need of care or control, it cannot make an order under the CYPA 1969, s 1(3) although it can still make a compensation order. A child may appeal to the Crown Court against a finding of guilt if no order is made under s 1(3). Note that if the offence ground is proved and the care or control test satisfied, the court can make a care order however trivial the offence. By contrast, a care order can only be made in criminal proceedings if the court is of the opinion that this is appropriate because of the seriousness of the offence and that the child is in need of care or control which he is unlikely to receive unless a care order is made.

10 Care or control test

The term 'care' includes protection and guidance, and 'control' includes discipline (CYPA 1969, s 70(1)). There will obviously be some overlap between the evidence which establishes the primary ground in s 1(2)(*a*)–(*f*) and that which satisfies the care or control test. A neglected or ill-treated child is clearly in need of care and a child who commits an offence will often lack control. Nevertheless the court must consider the two issues separately as far as possible; it does not necessarily follow that a child is in need of care or control because the primary ground is satisfied. In considering the care or control test the court is concerned with what is likely to happen in the future if an order is or is not made, and evidence of past behaviour and events will be relevant only insofar as it bears upon this.

A solicitor representing a child in the proceedings could in certain cases argue that the care or control test is not satisfied because the child or his parents are prepared to co-operate with the local authority voluntarily. This might arise, for example, if the parents are prepared to place the child in care voluntarily under the CCA, s 2 or to submit to supervision, so that the child will receive the care or control he needs without an order being made. This argument may be particularly persuasive if the authority has offered very little assistance or support to either parent or child before resorting to proceedings. If, on the other hand, the authority has been working with the family for some time with little success it will be easy for it to argue that an order is essential. Voluntary co-operation can, after all, be withdrawn at any time.

Chapter 4

Procedure

1 Commencing proceedings

A person bringing care proceedings must send a notice to the clerk of the juvenile court specifying the ground on which the proceedings are brought and the names and addresses of the persons or bodies to whom a copy of the notice must be sent in accordance with CYPR, r 14. These are as follows:

(a) the child, unless this is inappropriate having regard to his age or understanding;

(b) any parent or guardian of the child if his or her whereabouts are known—'parent' at present includes natural or adoptive parents but not the father of an illegitimate child; when the FLRA 1987, s 8(1) is implemented it will include the natural father of an illegitimate child who has the right to actual custody by court order (actual custody in this context means actual physical possession): 'guardian' means any person having for the time being charge or control over the child;

(c) any foster parent or person with whom the child has had his home for a period of six weeks or more, ending not more than six months before the date of the application, if his or her whereabouts are known: this means a person who has had actual physical possession of the child for the requisite period whether or not that possession is shared with one or more persons (Balcombe LJ in *Re S (A Minor) (Care Proceedings: Wardship Summons)* [1987] 1 FLR 479 at p 488);

(d) the appropriate local authority, ie the local authority in whose area the child habitually resides, or, if he does not appear to reside in the area of a local authority, the authority in whose area the circumstances giving rise to proceedings arose, unless in either case proceedings are brought by that authority; and (*e*) the probation officer for the area for which the court acts, if the child is over the age of thirteen.

The notice should specify the date, time and place of hearing unless a summons is to be issued to secure the attendance of any party notified. Notice should be in Form 7 (CYPR, Sched 2), which is reproduced in Appendix 1.

A summons may be issued to secure the attendance of the child (CYPA 1969, s 2(4)), although this will not be necessary if he is already in the care of the local authority, under a place of safety order or an interim care order, since the authority will be able to ensure that he attends. A separate summons may be issued to secure the attendance of a parent or guardian or a joint summons may be issued to parent and child (CYPR, r 26). The summons will be issued in Form 4 or 5 (CYPR, Sched 2), whichever is appropriate. Both forms are reproduced in Appendix 1.

A single justice or a justice's clerk may issue a summons to a child and/or parent. Procedure for issue of a summons varies from court to court. The summons can be served personally, by post or left with another person at the usual or last known address of the person to whom it is addressed (MCR, r 99). A single justice may issue a warrant for a child's arrest if it is proved on oath that the summons cannot be served or that it was served a reasonable time before the hearing but the child has failed to appear. The warrant may be endorsed as to bail, but if it is not the child can be detained in a place of safety for up to seventy-two hours after arrest, although he must be brought before the court which issued the warrant or a justice within that period (CYPA 1969, s 2(5)). A warrant for the arrest of a parent or guardian may be issued in similar circumstances.

It should be noted that if the summons has not been served by personal delivery to the person to whom it is directed a warrant will not be issued unless it is proved that the summons came to his knowledge. For this purpose any letter or communication written by him or on his behalf which reasonably infers knowledge will be admissible as evidence (MCR, r 99(2)).

2 Which court?

Care proceedings may be commenced in any juvenile court although the case must subsequently be remitted to a juvenile court acting for the area in which the child resides, unless it is dismissed for lack of evidence (CYPA 1969, s 2(11)). In *R* v *Manchester Justices, ex parte Bannister* [1983] 4 FLR 77 it was held that a child resides where it eats, drinks and sleeps. Thus a baby made the subject of a place of safety order shortly after birth took the residence of its foster parents and not its natural mother with whom it had never lived.

If proceedings are commenced in a court which does not act for the area in which the child resides the usual procedure is for that court to hear sufficient evidence to satisfy it that proceedings are properly brought and then to remit the case, after making an interim care order if necessary. If an interim order is made the clerk of the court of remission will be duly informed and the case will be listed for hearing in that court before the expiry of the interim order. If no order is made the local authority in whose area the child resides must be informed of the case. It is then under a duty to bring the child before the appropriate court within twenty-one days.

If proceedings are brought under s 1(2)(*f*) (the offence condition) the first court may determine guilt before remitting the case and its finding will be binding on the court of remission (CYPA 1969, s 3(5)). No other finding will be binding on the court of remission and it must hear the evidence in full before reaching a decision.

Before remitting a case a court must inform the child (unless his age and understanding make this impracticable), and any parent or guardian who is present, that it proposes to remit the case, and it must hear any representations they wish to make on this point.

3 Who must attend?

The *child* must be brought before the court unless he is under the age of five, when the court may direct under the CYPA 1969, s 2(9) that he 'shall be deemed to have been brought before the court', provided it is satisfied either that his parent or guardian is present or that notice of proceedings was served on any parent or guardian a reasonable time before the hearing. Service may be proved by evidence on oath or by producing to the court a copy of the notice, endorsed with a certificate of service by post in Form 145 (MCR, r 67).

The person bringing proceedings in respect of a child under the age of five should apply for a direction under s 2(9) at the commencement of proceedings. Any parent or guardian present will be given an opportunity to be heard on the matter and once a direction is given it will apply throughout the proceedings even if the case is remitted to another court under the CYPA 1969, s 2(11).

If a child is over the age of five but is unable to attend court because of illness or accident the court cannot proceed with the full hearing in his absence but it can make an interim care order. Further interim orders can always be made in the absence of a child under five and in the absence of a child of any age if he is legally represented and the court so directs (CYPA 1969, s 22 as amended by the HSSA, Sched 2, para 14 and see also *Northamptonshire CC v H* (1987) *The Times*, 7 November).

A *parent or guardian* should be required to attend unless it is unreasonable to expect him to do so (CYPA 1933, s 34). Most courts will expect a parent or guardian to attend and the rules of procedure envisage this. A summons or warrant may be issued to secure attendance (CYPR, r 26). The term parent does not include the father of an illegitimate child at present but it will include a natural father who has the right to actual custody by court order once the FLRA 1987, s 8(1) is implemented. A guardian is defined in the CYPA 1933, s 107(1) as 'any person who, in the opinion of the court . . . has for the time being the charge of or control over [a] child or young person'. In certain circumstances this could include the father of an illegitimate child.

4 Parties

The parties to the proceedings are the applicant (local authority, police, or NSPCC) and the child, although the rules of procedure do allow a parent or guardian to participate in the hearing.

The child may be legally represented but, if he is not, the court must allow a parent or guardian to conduct the case on his behalf unless:
  (*a*) the parent or guardian has requested the local authority to bring proceedings under the CYPA 1963, s 3(1) (ie because the child is beyond control); or
  (*b*) the child otherwise requests; or
  (*c*) the court has made an order for separate representation under the CYPA 1969, s 32A (CYPR, r 17(1)).

A relative or some other responsible person may also be permitted to conduct the case on the child's behalf unless a guardian ad litem has been appointed under the CYPA 1969, s 32B or the child otherwise requests (CYPR, r 17(2)).

5 Conflict of interest

If there is, or may be, a conflict of interest between a parent or guardian and the child on any matter relevant to the proceedings, the court may make an order that the parent shall not be treated as representing the child or authorised to act on his behalf (CYPA 1969, s 32A(1)). This power may also be exercised before the hearing by a single justice or a justice's clerk (CYPA 1969, s 32A(4) and Justices' Clerks Rules 1970, r 3). In deciding whether to make an order, the court must act in the best interests of the child so far as its powers permit. There is no requirement that parents be given an opportunity to make representations before an order for separate representation is made but they will receive notice of the order (*R* v *Plymouth Juvenile Court, ex parte F and F* [1987] 1 FLR 169).

6 Appointment of a guardian ad litem

If an order for separate representation is made the court may appoint a guardian ad litem to represent the child and it must do so if this appears to be in the child's interests (CYPR, r 14A). This power is also exercisable by a single justice or a justices' clerk before the hearing. In reaching a decision the court will take into account the age of the child and his ability to participate in the proceedings on his own behalf and express his views to the court.

If the child is young the court should bear in mind that his solicitor may not be able to carry out the necessary close investigation of the facts and may therefore have to support the making of a care order without the independent view of a guardian ad litem (*R* v *Plymouth Juvenile Court, ex parte F and F*, above). A decision not to appoint a guardian may be challenged by judicial review but only if it can be argued that no reasonable court would have failed to make an appointment.

The court may decide not to appoint a guardian ad litem but may still appoint a solicitor to represent the child. Whilst a parent will receive formal notice of the appointment of a guardian, there is no formal requirement that he be notified of the appointment of a solicitor by the court.

7 Legal representation

It is generally accepted that children who are the subject of care proceedings should be legally represented and that, wherever possible, representation should be by a solicitor with relevant knowledge and experience. The Law Society has therefore set up a Child

Care Panel of solicitors with the relevant expertise (see Appendix 4 for address). All solicitors joining the panel are required to complete an approved training course which will normally be followed by an interview. They must hold a current practising certificate and have not less than eighteen months' previous advocacy experience in the juvenile court. Panel members are normally required to give an undertaking to conduct personally all cases referred to them. Membership is subject to review after three years.

The initial choice of solicitor to represent the child will be made by the parent or guardian unless an order for separate representation has already been made. The choice does not have to be made from the Child Care Panel although this is obviously advisable. A solicitor who is consulted by a parent in these circumstances should make it clear that he is accepting instructions to represent the child. If an order for separate representation is subsequently made, the parent will be obliged to seek legal representation elsewhere. An older child may be capable of appointing a solicitor himself and the choice will then be his.

If an order for separate representation is made and a guardian ad litem appointed, consideration must be given at the time of appointment as to whether the child should be legally represented. The guardian may then be directed to appoint a solicitor for the child (CYPR, r 14A(4)). If an order for separate representation is made but no guardian ad litem appointed the court may appoint a solicitor to represent the child itself, if he is not already represented. Appointment will be from the Child Care Panel. Some courts adopt this practice even if an order is made for the appointment of a guardian. This is to ensure that the child is represented at an early stage in the proceedings although it may take some time for the case to be allocated to a named individual on the local Guardian ad Litem Panel.

The child's solicitor and the guardian ad litem must act together in considering how to present the child's case. The solicitor should accept instructions from the guardian unless, having taken into account the guardian's views, he considers that the child wishes to give conflicting instructions and is of an age and understanding to do so. This will not only apply to the conduct of the care proceedings but to any decision as to whether an appeal should be made to the Crown Court. It is the solicitor's responsibility to reconcile the recommendations of the guardian with the statutory powers of the court (*M* v *Berkshire CC* [1985] 1 FLR 257, CA). Thus a solicitor who endorsed the making of a care order when the guardian was actually recommending a care order followed by early rehabilitation of the child was not failing to follow instructions.

Parents are not parties to the proceedings and therefore have no right to legal representation. A juvenile court does, however, have an inherent right to regulate its own proceedings and this includes a discretion to allow a parent to be legally represented (*R* v *Gravesham Juvenile Court, ex parte B* [1982] 4 FLR 312). If a separate representation order is made a parent has the right to apply for legal aid which presupposes a right to legal representation in these circumstances. Once the CYPAA 1986, s 3 is implemented a parent or guardian will automatically be made a party to the proceedings as soon as an order for separate representation is made.

8 The role of the guardian ad litem

If the court decides to appoint a guardian ad litem in an appropriate case it must select an individual from the panel maintained by the local authority for the area which it serves. Members of the panel will usually have a social work qualification plus relevant experience. Appointment to the panel may be for a period not exceeding three years although any member may be re-appointed. Membership may also be terminated at any time if the local authority considers that the member is unable or unfit to carry out his functions as a guardian ad litem. There is no upper age limit but appointment or re-appointment over the age of 65 years is discouraged. A guardian ad litem must have no conflict of interest. Thus the court may not appoint any person who is a member, officer or employee of the local authority which is a party to the proceedings. Neither may it appoint any person who is or may have been a member, officer or employee of a local authority or voluntary organisation and who has in that capacity been directly concerned with arrangements for the child's care, accommodation or welfare. A serving probation officer may not be appointed guardian ad litem in care proceedings (CYPR, r 14A(2) as substituted by the CYPAR, r 2).

A guardian ad litem may be appointed before the hearing of the care proceedings by a single justice or a justice's clerk. When the appointment is made the justice or justice's clerk must consider whether the child should be legally represented and may direct the guardian ad litem to instruct a solicitor to represent the child. The court may revoke the appointment of a guardian ad litem at any time and substitute another appointment.

The guardian ad litem's duties as laid down in the CYPR, r 14A(6) (as substituted by the CYPAR, r 2) are:

1 So far as reasonably practicable, to investigate all circumstances relevant to the proceedings and for that purpose to interview such persons, inspect such records and obtain such professional assistance as he considers appropriate;
2 To regard as the first and paramount consideration the need to safeguard and promote the child's best interests until he reaches adulthood and to take into account the wishes and feelings of the child having regard to his age and understanding, and to ensure that his wishes and feelings are made known to the court;
3 Unless a solicitor has already been instructed to represent the child or the court has given a direction that a solicitor be instructed, to obtain the views of the court as to whether the child should be legally represented and, unless the court directs otherwise, to instruct a solicitor to represent the child;
4 To consider how the case should be presented on the child's behalf, acting in conjunction with the child's solicitor when one has been appointed, and to give instructions to the solicitor unless the solicitor considers, having taken into account the views of the guardian ad litem, that the infant wishes to give instructions which conflict with those of the guardian ad litem and that he is able, having regard to his age and understanding, to give such instructions on his own behalf;
5 To seek the views of the court in any case where difficulties arise in relation to the performance of his duties;
6 To make a written report to the court as soon as practicable;
7 To perform such other duties as the court may direct;
8 At the conclusion of the case to consider, acting in conjunction with the child's solicitor, whether it would be in the child's best interests to appeal to the Crown Court and if it is so considered to ensure that notice of appeal is duly given.

A guardian ad litem has no statutory right of access to the records maintained by a local authority or any other agency in a particular case. Local authorities and other agencies (such as Area Review Committees) are nevertheless expected to allow the guardian access as an officer appointed by the court (Local Authority Circular LAC (86) 2, 31 January 1986, para 15).

42 THE CHILDREN AND YOUNG PERSONS ACTS 1933–1969

Note that if a guardian refers a case to the court because difficulties have arisen, the court's power to give directions before hearing is exercisable by a single justice or a justices' clerk (CYPR, r 14A(4)).

The DHSS publish a *Guide for Guardians ad Litem in the Juvenile Court* (1984) which discusses the guardian's functions in detail.

9 The juvenile court

The provisions governing the constitution of the juvenile court for Inner London can be found in the CYPA 1933, Sched 2, Part II, and for all other areas in the Juvenile Courts (Constitution) Rules 1954. A juvenile bench in the Inner London area should consist of three justices including a chairman who may be a metropolitan stipendiary magistrate. If it is impossible to constitute a full bench, but an adjournment would not be in the interests of justice, a stipendiary magistrate may sit alone or a lay chairman may sit with one other justice.

Outside the Inner London area a juvenile bench may be comprised of two or three justices, although in special circumstances where it is impossible to constitute a full bench, a juvenile court justice who is also a stipendiary magistrate may sit alone.

Normally the bench should include a member of each sex although this requirement can be relaxed in special circumstances where it would be inexpedient in the interests of justice for there to be an adjournment. The bench must not include a justice who is a member of the local authority which is party to any proceedings before it (Justice of the Peace Act 1949, s 3).

Section 47 of the CYPA 1933 stipulates that the only persons permitted to be present when a juvenile court is sitting are:
   (*a*) members and officers of the court;
   (*b*) the parties to the proceedings, their solicitors and counsel, witnesses, and any other person directly connected with the case (which would, presumably, include a parent);
   (*c*) any person specially authorised by the court, eg trainee social workers, researchers, etc; and
   (*d*) bona fide representatives of the press (although any reports of the case in the press or on radio or television must not reveal the name or address of the child, his school, or any other particulars likely to lead to his identification, unless reporting restrictions have been relaxed to avoid causing him injustice (CYPA 1933, s 49 and CYPA 1963, s 57(4));

publication in contravention of this provision is an offence punishable on summary conviction with a fine not exceeding £2,000 (CYPA 1933, s 39(2))).

10 The hearing

There are two parts to the hearing:
  (*a*) The applicant must prove one of the primary grounds in s 1(2)(*a*)–(*f*), and satisfy the care or control test.
  (*b*) The court must consider what order, if any, to make, if it finds the case proved.

In addition, if proceedings are brought under s 1(2)(*f*), the court must determine the question of guilt before considering whether the care or control test is satisfied.

11 The welfare principle

Every court dealing with a child has a general duty to have regard to the child's welfare and it must in a proper case take steps to remove him from undesirable surroundings and secure that proper provision is made for his education and training (CYPA 1969, s 44).

It is not clear whether s 1 of the Guardianship of Minors Act 1971, which makes the welfare of the child the first and paramount consideration in proceedings concerning his custody, upbringing and property, applies to care proceedings. In *Re D (A Minor) (Justices' Decision: Review)* [1977] 2 WLR 1006, Dunn J took the firm view that it did not although it was right for justices to consider the child's welfare once they were satisfied as to the primary ground under s 1(2)(*a*) and that the child was in need of care or control. Ewbank J took a different view in *R* v *Birmingham Juvenile Court, ex parte P and S* [1984] FLR 343 and stated that in care proceedings, as in other cases involving the custody and upbringing of a child, the welfare of the child was the paramount consideration. It should be noted that he was concerned with the making of an interim care order under the CYPA 1969, s 2(10) (see p 63) and not a final order.

In *R* v *Exeter Juvenile Court, ex parte H* and *R* v *Waltham Forest Juvenile Court, ex parte B*, both reported at (1988) *The Times*, 19 February, the President of the Family Division stressed that the welfare of the child was paramount when the court was considering whether or not to adjourn care proceedings on the application of a parent facing concurrent criminal proceedings. Bush J in a similar case (*R v Inner London Juvenile Court, ex parte G*, (1988) 152 JP 239) did not consider the welfare of the child to be the paramount consideration but one of the matters to be considered by the court at all stages of the decision making process.

What emerges from the more recent decisions is a general acceptance that the welfare of the child is a consideration for the court throughout the proceedings, and especially in matters where the court has a wide discretion, such as whether or not to grant an adjournment. Nevertheless, the courts must work within the statutory framework imposed by Parliament and cannot make a care order, even if the welfare of the child requires this, unless the statutory grounds are satisfied. The welfare of the child may then become the paramount consideration (Ormrod LJ in *Re C (A Minor) (Justices' Decision: Review)* [1981] 2 FLR 62). It may therefore be true to say that juvenile courts always act in the best interests of the child so far as their powers permit (Ormrod LJ in *Re H (A Minor) (Wardship: Jurisdiction)* [1978] 2 All ER 903 and approved by Lord Roskill in *A v Liverpool City Council* [1982] AC 363 at p 379B).

12 Order of evidence and speeches

Proceedings are civil (except in relation to the offence condition, s 1(2)(*f*)) and procedure is governed by the CYPR, Part III. Rule 14 of the MCR governs the order of evidence and speeches as in proceedings by way of complaint, and ss 56, 57 and 123 of the MCA apply (subject to the provisions of the CYPA 1933 and 1969), enabling the court to disregard any defect in process and to dismiss the case if both parties or just the applicant fail to attend.

Justices have an inherent jurisdiction to regulate their own procedure subject to the proviso that they do not contravene any statutory provision, regulation or rule binding upon them (*Croydon LBC v N and Others* [1987] 2 FLR 61 and see also *Simms v Moore* [1970] 2 QB 327) and *M v Westminster City Council* [1985] FLR 325). The inherent jurisdiction of the court has been invoked to allow a parent to cross-examine (*R v Milton Keynes Justices, ex parte R* [1979] 1 WLR 1062, decided before the amendment of CYPR, r 14), to allow a parent to be legally represented (*R v Gravesham Juvenile Court, ex parte B* [1983] 4 FLR 312), and to authorise the disclosure of a guardian ad litem's report to an independent social worker instructed by a parent (*R v Sunderland Juvenile Court, ex parte G* (1987) *The Times*, 15 December).

If the child is present at the hearing, the court (usually through the clerk to the justices) must inform him of the general nature of the proceedings and the grounds on which they are brought in language he can understand. If this is impracticable in view of his age and understanding, or because he is not present at the hearing, the information should be given instead to any parent or guardian present (CYPR, r 16(1)).

The applicant, who may be represented by solicitor, counsel or a duly authorised officer, will then call his evidence and may first address the court. The child, or the person conducting the case on his behalf, may cross-examine any of the witnesses called by the applicant in the usual way. The applicant may then re-examine any witnesses on matters arising out of cross-examination and members of the bench may put additional questions, if any.

If, after hearing the applicant's evidence, the court considers a prima facie case has been made out, it must tell the child (or the person conducting the case on his behalf) that he may call witnesses and give evidence or make a statement himself (CYPR, r 19). The applicant will have made out a prima facie case if sufficient evidence has been adduced at this stage (and not challenged or undermined in cross-examination) for the court to find the case proved.

The child (or his representative) may make a submission of no case to answer at the conclusion of the applicant's evidence. If the submission is unsuccessful the child cannot then give or call any further evidence. A parent cannot make a submission on his own behalf as he is not a party to the proceedings (*M* v *Westminster City Council*, above). This will change when the CYPAA 1986, s 3 is implemented provided that there is a separate representation order in force (see p 46). The power to dismiss an application on a submission of no case to answer should only be exercised in exceptional circumstances; if, for example, an applicant has no case in law or his evidence cannot be believed (*R* v *Chertsey Justices, ex parte E* [1987] 2 FLR 415). As a general proposition, it is preferable for a court to hear all the evidence before coming to a conclusion as to what is best for a child and whether the necessary grounds have been proved (*M* v *Westminster City Council*, above).

If a prima facie case has been made out, and no submission is to be made, the child or his representative may then address the court whether or not any evidence is to be called. The applicant may cross-examine any witnesses for the child in the usual way and may, with leave of the court, call evidence in rebuttal at the end of the child's case, if a new issue has been raised which could not have been foreseen.

A parent or guardian (or their legal representative) may also cross-examine any witness in the proceedings with regard to allegations made against him. Rule 14B of the CYPR provides for this to take place at the conclusion of all the evidence and before the closing speeches. Most courts, however, use their inherent jurisdiction to control their own procedure to allow cross-examination to take place at an earlier and more convenient stage in the proceedings. A parent will usually cross-examine each witness, as to relevant matters, after the conclusion of the evidence-in-chief and any cross-examination by the other party to the proceedings. This will allow the parent to deal with allegations arising out of both the evidence-in-chief and any prior cross-examination.

At the conclusion of evidence for the child, any guardian ad litem appointed may give evidence to the court whether or not he has already been called as a witness (CYPR, r 16(3)). A parent or guardian must then be given an opportunity to give or call evidence to meet any allegations made against him in the course of the proceedings. The court must then allow any foster parent or other person entitled to receive notice of the proceedings under the CYPR, r 14 to make representations although the rules of procedure do not state whether such a person is entitled to remain in court throughout the proceedings, or entitled to legal representation. This may be a matter for the court's discretion although it is clear that a foster parent or person entitled to notice has no right to legal aid. Following this, and if an order has been made for separate representation, a parent or guardian may make representations to the court.

After this the child or his representative may address the court unless he has already done so. Either party may then, with leave, address the court a second time, although the second speech of the child or his representative must be delivered before the second speech, if any, of the applicant. Leave to deliver a second address cannot be granted to one party and refused to the other. After the closing speeches the court must decide whether it finds the case proved, and it may retire to do so. If the court finds the case proved it will inform the child and any parent or guardian present before going on to consider any reports submitted.

The special rules of procedure which apply when the court is asked to find the offence condition satisfied are dealt with below (pp 48–49). The rules governing procedure generally will require modification when the CYPAA 1986, s 3 is implemented, as a parent will then be a full party to proceedings once a separate representation order is made. This will, presumably, allow him to participate fully in the proceedings and he will no longer be limited to meeting allegations made against him. Section 3(2) of the CYPAA 1986 also permits grandparents to apply to be made parties to care proceedings in circumstances yet to be specified and further amendment of the rules may be necessary, in due course, to regulate the extent to which grandparents will be permitted to participate.

13 Exclusion of the child or parent

If the court considers that all or any part of the evidence should not be given in the child's presence it may exclude him from the courtroom, unless he is conducting his own case or the evidence in question relates to his own character or conduct (CYPR, r 18(1)). The court may also require a parent or guardian to withdraw from the courtroom while the child is giving evidence or making a statement, provided that it then informs the person excluded of the substance of any allegations made against him by the child (CYPR, r 18(2)). Although the justices may hear evidence in the child's absence they have no power to see the child privately at any stage in the proceedings (*Re T (An Infant)* (1974) 118 SJ 78).

14 Exclusion of witnesses

In civil proceedings there is no requirement that witnesses be excluded from court prior to giving evidence. This is a matter entirely within the court's discretion although witnesses are likely to be excluded if either party to the proceedings or a parent objects to their presence.

Expert witnesses are usually allowed to remain in court during the testimony of other experts in their field, and often throughout the hearing, if it is important that they hear all the evidence.

15 Adjournment

The court can adjourn the proceedings at any stage and may either fix a date, time and place for the resumed hearing or leave this to be determined at a later date (CYPR, r 15). When adjourning proceedings the court can make an interim care order and, if it does so,

48 THE CHILDREN AND YOUNG PERSONS ACTS 1933–1969

a date for the resumed hearing must be fixed on adjournment. See p 63 for the maximum duration of an interim care order. In other cases when a date is not fixed on adjournment the hearing cannot be resumed unless the court is satisfied that both parties have been given adequate notice of the resumed hearing date.

The court is not obliged to adjourn if a child is made a ward of court after the commencement of proceedings in the juvenile court, especially if the final hearing is imminent or has actually commenced (*Re S (A Minor) (Care Proceedings: Wardship Summons)* [1987] 1 FLR 479). For criteria for adjournment when there are concurrent criminal proceedings see p 25.

A case which is adjourned part-heard must be resumed before the same bench, although it can be resumed in the absence of one member of the original bench provided that he or she then takes no further part in the proceedings and the regulations governing the constitution of the court are not breached (MCA, s 121(6)). This does not apply to a case remitted to another court under the CYPA 1969, s 2(11) after the offence condition has been found proved.

16 Proving the offence condition

If proceedings are brought under the CYPA 1969, s 1(2)(*f*) the court must first determine whether or not the offence condition is satisfied before considering any other matter relevant to the proceedings. The rules of procedure normally applicable to criminal proceedings will govern this part of the hearing. The applicant must prove beyond all reasonable doubt that the child has committed the alleged offence, and in addition, if the child is under the age of fourteen, he must prove that the child knew that what he was doing was wrong. Order of evidence and speeches is laid down in the MCR, r 13 and follows that of a summary trial in the magistrates' court with minor variations. The court must explain to the child the substance of the alleged offence in simple language that he can understand and must ask him whether or not he admits the offence (CYPR, r 16(2)(*a*)). If the child does not admit it, the applicant must call evidence to support the allegation and he may address the court before doing so. The child or person representing him may cross-examine any of the witnesses in the usual way. A child who is not represented will often make assertions instead of putting questions in cross-examination. If this is the case the court may put questions to any witness on his behalf and may question the child to clarify any point arising out of his assertions (CYPR, r 8(2)). If the court finds that the applicant has made out a prima facie case it must inform the child of his right to call evidence, and to give evidence or make an unsworn statement himself (CYPR, r 9). He should be told that an unsworn statement will not carry as much weight as evidence on oath. At the conclusion of the evidence for the defence the applicant may call evidence in rebuttal. The child, or the person representing him, may either address the court at the beginning of his case or after the court has heard the evidence, if any, in rebuttal. Either party may apply for leave to address the court a second time and leave cannot be granted to one party and refused to the other. If leave is granted the applicant must address the court before the child or his representative does so.

If the court finds the offence condition satisfied it must inform the child before going on to consider whether the care or control test is also satisfied. Once the offence condition is proved the proceedings become civil again and the usual rules of procedure and evidence apply.

17 The report stage

If the court finds the case proved it must then consider any reports available before deciding what order, if any, to make. If further reports are required the case can be adjourned and an interim care order made (CYPR, r 20(1) and CYPA 1969, s 2(10)).

The local authority or education authority bringing the proceedings must provide the court with a report on the child's home surroundings, school record, health and character unless this is unnecessary because, for example, the court already has this information (CYPA 1969, s 9(1)). If further information is required the court may ask the local authority to provide this (CYPA 1969, s 9(2)). In some areas arrangements have been made for the probation service to provide reports on the home circumstances of children over the age of thirteen, thereby relieving the local authority of this duty. Medical and psychiatric reports may be provided where necessary and details of the child's school record may be given in a separate school report. If an order for separate representation has been made and a guardian ad litem appointed, the guardian's written report will be considered at this stage (CYPR, r 20(1)). The guardian ad litem may also make oral representations to the court. If no guardian ad litem has been appointed but the child's solicitor has obtained a report from an independent social worker this may be submitted to the court at this stage.

50 THE CHILDREN AND YOUNG PERSONS ACTS 1933–1969

The court need not read the reports aloud and it may require the child or his parent or guardian to withdraw from the courtroom while the reports are being considered (CYPR, r 20(1)). If, instead, the bench retires to consider reports it must not seek additional information from a social worker (or any other person who has written a report) in the privacy of the retiring room (*R* v *Aberdare Justices, ex parte Jones* [1973] Crim LR 45). If a report is not read aloud, or is considered in the child's absence, he must be told the substance of any part of the report bearing on his character or conduct which materially affects the way the court intends to deal with the case, unless this is impracticable having regard to his age and understanding (CYPR, r 20(2)(*a*)). A parent or guardian must in similar circumstances be told the substance of any part of the report which appertains to his character or conduct, or to the character, conduct, home surroundings or health of the child (CYPR, r 20(2)(*b*)). If the child or his parent or guardian then wish to call further evidence to refute any allegation made in a report the court may adjourn the proceedings to enable them to do so, provided that it considers that the further evidence will be material. If necessary the person who made the report which is being challenged may be required to attend the adjourned hearing.

Before the court finally disposes of the case it must inform the child (if he is of sufficient age and understanding), his representative, and any parent present, of the manner in which it proposes to deal with the case and it must allow them to make representations (CYPR, r 21(1)). It must explain to the child the general nature and effect of any order made, unless this is impracticable having regard to his age and understanding, or, in the case of an order requiring a parent or guardian to enter into a recognisance (see p 72), this appears to be undesirable (CYPR, r 21(2)).

A guardian ad litem should be permitted to see any reports to be submitted to the court prior to the hearing (Local Authority Circular No 20/1976, para 27). The court must provide a copy of the guardian ad litem's report to all parties to the proceedings and to any parent or guardian who attends or requests a copy (or to their representatives) in advance of the hearing (*R* v *Epsom Juvenile Court, ex parte G* [1988] 1 WLR 145). If the child is not legally represented, however, he need not be given a copy of the report unless the guardian ad litem thinks it desirable.

The guardian's report is confidential and may only be disclosed to third parties with the leave of the court (*R* v *Sunderland Juvenile Court, ex parte G (A Minor)* (1987) *The Times*, 15 December). The court will only authorise disclosure to an expert witness, such as an independent social worker, if satisfied that the evidence of that witness may assist the court in the particular case.

There is no express requirement for the child or parent to be provided with a copy of any report prepared by the local authority or probation service. Nevertheless, it has been usual practice for the legal representatives of the child and parent to be supplied with a copy when proceedings reach the report stage, if not earlier. In *R v West Malling Juvenile Court, ex parte Kendall* [1986] 2 FLR 405, it was held that a father was entitled to advance disclosure of both the guardian ad litem's report and the local authority's report so that his legal advisers could prepare a proper case to refute allegations in those reports.

18 Withdrawal of application

An application for a care order cannot be withdrawn without the leave of the court. If the court refuses to grant leave and the local authority then declines to call any evidence in support of the application the court should still be prepared to hear the evidence of the guardian ad litem who may take a different view (*R v Birmingham Juvenile Court, ex parte G, R v Birmingham Juvenile Court, ex parte R* (1988) *The Times*, 25 May). It follows from this decision and other recent decisions on the withdrawal of applications for the discharge of care orders (see p 81) that there should be some enquiry into the merits of the case whenever leave is sought to discontinue proceedings.

Chapter 5

Evidence

The law of evidence is complex and cannot be dealt with in great depth in a work of this scope. This chapter will therefore cover those aspects most relevant to care proceedings. Readers should refer to the standard works on the law of evidence and to *Stone's Justices' Manual*, Vol 1, Part II—Evidence for a full treatment of the subject.

Standard of proof
The burden of proof in care proceedings must be discharged by the applicant who must adduce sufficient evidence to prove the case. The civil standard of proof applies; the case must therefore be proved on the balance of probabilities. On the simplest level this means that the court must find it more likely than not that the facts are as alleged by the applicant. Different degrees of probability may apply, however, depending on the nature of the allegation. Thus in a wardship case, *In Re G (A Minor)* (1987) *The Times*, 30 July, it was held that a more stringent degree of probability was required to satisfy a court that a father, rather than any other person, had been guilty of sexual misconduct towards his daughter.

1 The nature of evidence

Evidence can be defined as information which establishes or disproves a fact or point in question. It may be communicated to the court through the oral testimony of a witness, via a document produced in court or in the form of real evidence (see below).

In civil proceedings formal admissions of fact may be made by either party and no evidence need be called to prove those facts (*Berkhamsted Rural District Council* v *Duerdin-Dutton* (1964) 108 SJ 157). It is unclear to what extent this principle applies in care

EVIDENCE

proceedings in which, at present (and until the implementation of the CYPAA 1986, s 3), the child is the only party to the proceedings other than the local authority. A parent is not therefore in a position to make a formal admission of fact. In the Government's *Review of Child Care Law* (DHSS, September 1985) the view was taken that an ability to agree an issue was neither 'desirable in principle or necessary in practice' (para 16/37).

The rules of evidence which govern civil proceedings in the magistrates' court generally also apply to care proceedings except when the offence condition must be proved (see p 48). To be admissible, evidence must be confined to fact and not opinion unless the witness is an expert (see below). Evidence must not include hearsay or privileged information, but as always there are exceptions to these general rules.

2 Relevance

Evidence must be relevant. To be so it must relate directly to the facts in issue in a case or be relevant to those facts in that it tends to prove or disprove them in some way. Thus evidence that a father was having incestuous relations with two sisters of a child before the court under the CYPA 1969, s 1(2)(*a*) and (*c*) was held to be relevant in *R* v *Lincoln (Kesteven) County Justices, ex parte M (A Minor)* [1976] 1 All ER 490.

Evidence that a person has acted in a similar way in the past or that a similar situation has arisen previously ie similar fact evidence, is relevant and admissible. Character evidence, including evidence of previous convictions, will nearly always be relevant in relation to a parent or guardian of a child involved in care proceedings. Evidence of the bad character of other witnesses will only be relevant if the witness puts his own character in issue or it is elicited in cross-examination.

3 Expert opinion

Only an expert may give his opinion in evidence although a witness as to fact who is also an expert in the relevant field eg a social worker, may be asked to express an opinion. In cases of doubt it is for the court to decide whether a witness is an expert or not after considering his qualifications and experience.

An expert witness may refer to tables, charts and reference works when giving evidence. An expert may be called to give an opinion based on examinations or interviews he has actually carried out or he may be asked to express an opinion on the evidence before the court within his particular area of expertise.

The court cannot summon expert witnesses of its own volition although it may suggest to either party that the opinion of a particular type of expert be sought. The court cannot compel a parent to be seen or examined by an expert. A parent who wishes to instruct an expert to examine or interview a child would, presumably, have to obtain the consent of the local authority, if the child is the subject of an interim care order, and the guardian ad litem if there is an order for separate representation.

The role of the independent social worker as an expert witness in care proceedings has become less prominent since provision was made for the appointment of a guardian ad litem. This accords with practice in the higher courts (see *Practice Direction (Minor: Independent Reporter)* [1983] 1 WLR 416) and is in keeping with the general view that children should be seen by as few different experts as possible. It is still permissible for a parent to call an independent social worker as a witness but the court may refuse to hear him if it considers that he has no relevant evidence to give (*R* v *Sunderland Juvenile Court, ex parte G (A Minor)* (1987) *The Times*, 15 December). Confidential reports, such as the report of the guardian ad litem, can only be disclosed to an independent social worker with the consent of the court (*R* v *Sunderland Juvenile Court, ex parte G*, above).

Solicitors requiring an expert opinion may find it useful to consult the Register of Expert Witnesses maintained by the Law Society (see Appendix 4 for address). Most fields of expertise are covered.

4 Hearsay evidence

The Civil Evidence Acts 1968 and 1972, which considerably dilute the effect of the hearsay rule in civil proceedings, do not yet apply to civil proceedings in the magistrates' court (*R* v *Wood Green Crown Court, ex parte P* [1982] 4 FLR 206). Hearsay evidence (ie evidence of facts which are not within the knowledge of a witness but have been communicated to him by someone else) is not therefore admissible unless it falls within one of the following exceptions:

(*a*) statements by deceased persons;
(*b*) statements forming part of the res gestae of the case (ie statements which were made contemporaneously with or

shortly after any act or occurrence in issue in the proceedings so as to form part of the same transaction);
(c) statements in public documents;
(d) confessions or admissions against interest by a party to the proceedings; or
(e) admissions by any person concerned with or having control over the child, eg a parent or guardian (*Humberside CC* v *DPR (An Infant)* [1977] 1 WLR 1251) but not allegations made to a third party against any person having control of the child (*Re S (Care Proceedings: Evidence)* [1980] 1 FLR 301).

A social worker could, therefore, give evidence of a parent's admission that he had ill-treated a child but he could not repeat in evidence a statement made by one parent alleging that the other had ill-treated the child. The only person who could repeat this statement is the person to whom it was made. A social worker cannot give evidence of facts known to a previous social worker, even if these are recorded in the case records, unless the facts are also within his own knowledge. The same applies to statements made to a previous social worker which may be admissible if that worker gave evidence.

Hearsay evidence which does not fall within one of the above categories may nevertheless be admissible as evidence that a particular statement was made but not as evidence of its truth. For example, a witness may, in certain circumstances, give evidence of a previous statement made out of court by another witness in order to attack that witness's credibility.

5 Privilege

Certain information is by its nature privileged and protected from disclosure in legal proceedings. Communications between a person and his legal adviser have absolute privilege which can only be waived by the client. This also applies to communications between a legal adviser and a third party for the purposes of litigation. Communications between other professional groups and their clients are not similarly protected. There is privilege against self-incrimination. This means that a witness does not have to answer a question or produce any document which might expose him or a spouse to a criminal charge.

Certain documents have been held to be privileged because there is a public interest in maintaining their confidentiality. This has been held to apply to the records kept by local authorities under the Boarding-out of Children Regulations 1955 (SI No 1377) (*Re D* [1970] 1 WLR 1109) and to certain documents kept by the probation service (*Re M (Minors)* (1986) 16 Fam Law 336). Documents disclosing the identity of informants in child abuse cases are similarly protected (*D v NSPCC* [1978] AC 171). It has been held that a local authority's case records also fall within this category except insofar as the authority has itself waived its privilege by producing any part of its records in evidence (*In Re S (Minors) (Wardship: Police Investigations)* [1987] 3 WLR 847).

Privilege on public interest grounds is not absolute and must be claimed and justified in each case. The correct procedure before a court can decide whether or not a document is privileged is for the party requiring disclosure to show that the document is relevant to the proceedings and for the party opposing disclosure to specify its grounds for objection (*R v Greenwich Juvenile Court, ex parte Greenwich London BC* (1977) 7 Fam Law 171). In general, a local authority should consider how much it may safely disclose rather than how much it may be entitled to conceal since its main aim should be to assist the court in reaching a decision which is in the best interests of the child (per Peter Pain J in *R v Greenwich Juvenile Court*, above). This view expressed some time ago is very much in keeping with current policy on access to information generally (see p 160).

6 Oral testimony

In care proceedings all oral evidence must be given on oath or affirmation. Any person who cannot appreciate the obligation this imposes is not a competent witness. This also applies to a person who is incapable of understanding questions or giving a proper answer by reason of mental incapacity or permanent or temporary disability.

The child and his parents are competent and compellable witnesses for the applicant. A child can only give evidence if he appreciates the meaning of the oath and is of sufficient intelligence to testify. There is no legal requirement for a child's evidence to be corroborated in civil proceedings but greater weight will obviously attach to evidence which is corroborated.

Any witness may refresh his memory from notes or records, with the leave of the court, provided that these were made by him, or made by someone else and read over to him, at a time when he had a clear recollection of the facts recorded. A witness who refers to case records when testifying must submit them to examination by any other party to the proceedings and runs the risk of being cross-examined on their contents.

A witness cannot be asked in examination-in-chief about any previous statement made out of court which is inconsistent with his testimony unless he has been declared a hostile witness by the court. A hostile witness can be cross-examined by the party calling him. Any witness can be asked about a previous inconsistent statement in cross-examination and if he denies it, evidence may be called to prove that it was made. Previous consistent statements made by a witness prior to the hearing are only admissible if they form part of the res gestae of the case (see p 54) or to refute a suggestion in cross-examination that a witness has recently concocted his evidence.

Any witness, whether attending on a summons (see p 60) or otherwise, who refuses to give evidence or produce any document which is not privileged may be committed to prison for a term not exceeding one month or be fined up to £1000 or both (MCA, s 97(4)).

7 Documentary evidence

There are specific statutory powers to admit certain types of documentary evidence in care proceedings. Thus, evidence of a person's physical or mental state of health may be given by certificate signed by a registered medical practitioner (CYPA 1963, s 26). The certificate must be confined to fact and any opinion or speculation as to how an injury may have been caused will be inadmissible.

A headteacher's certificate is admissible as evidence of school attendance (Education Act 1944, s 95(2)). A certificate of conviction is evidence that an offence has been committed (Civil Evidence Act 1968, s 11 and MCR, r 68). Note that s 4(1) of the Rehabilitation of Offenders Act 1974 does not apply to care proceedings. Evidence may therefore be adduced of a conviction which would otherwise be spent (Rehabilitation of Offenders Act 1974, s 7(2)(*d*)).

Other types of documents may be admissible provided that they are relevant, do not contain hearsay and are not privileged. The best evidence rule dictates that any document produced in evidence must be an original although the court can accept a copy if it is satisfied that the original has been lost or destroyed. If an original document is in the possession of one party to proceedings and the other retains a copy, he should serve notice requesting production of the original. If the recipient fails to comply with the notice, secondary evidence ie the copy is admissible. It is also admissible if the original document is in the possession of a third party who refuses to produce it and cannot be compelled to do so on the grounds of privilege.

Section 1 of the Evidence Act 1938 applies in the juvenile court and provides that a statement of facts in a document is admissible provided that:

    (*a*) the maker of the statement had personal knowledge of the facts; and
    (*b*) he is called as a witness in the proceedings; and
    (*c*) direct oral testimony of the facts would be admissible; and
    (*d*) he is not 'a person interested' in the proceedings.

The general effect of this provision is to allow certain reports to be read by the court before a witness gives evidence. A witness could also use the report to refresh his memory and he could be cross-examined on it. The document must be confined to fact; hearsay and opinion will be inadmissible.

There is further provision for a statement to be admissible in the absence of the maker if he is dead, unfit to attend, overseas or impossible to trace. The court may also admit a statement in his absence if satisfied that undue delay or expense would otherwise be caused. The court has the power to admit a certified copy of a document on similar grounds.

These provisions could, for example, allow statements of fact in a child's medical or school records to be admitted in evidence if the doctor or teacher who recorded the facts was no longer available to give evidence for one of the reasons specified. Statements of fact recorded by a previous social worker in the case records of a social services department would not usually be admissible under these provisions as the maker would normally be a person interested in the proceedings.

8 Real evidence

A witness may produce real evidence in the course of his testimony. This may take the form of a material object, a photograph or anything else which the court is invited to observe directly. Thus a parent might produce in court a door knob which he alleges caused an accidental injury to the child. A doctor may produce photographs and x-rays to illustrate injuries sustained by the child. A police officer may produce photographs of the child's home to illustrate its state of neglect. The person responsible for taking the photographs (or x-rays) must be called as a witness to testify as to their authenticity unless this is agreed between the parties.

A person's appearance may constitute real evidence. The court could, for example, be asked to observe injuries or scars on the child's body. The court could also be asked to view the site where an injury occurred although the expense of leaving the courtroom is unlikely to be justified where a photograph or detailed description would suffice.

9 Tape and video recordings

A tape recording properly authenticated can be admissible in evidence. A social worker or police officer could, for example, produce in evidence a tape recording of an interview with a parent during which the parent made an informal admission of ill-treatment, provided that the court could be satisfied that the tape was original, authentic and had not been tampered with in any way. In these circumstances the tape would not be real evidence but analogous to a documentary record of the interview.

Video recordings, used more frequently in the investigation of child abuse, pose greater problems. A video recording can constitute real evidence where, for example, a witness has filmed an incident involving a parent and child. In these circumstances the videotape may be admissible in evidence in the same way as a photograph (*J Barber & Sons* v *Lloyd's Underwriter and Others* (1986) LSG 3253). More often, however, the subject of the video recording will be an interview with the child during which incidents of abuse, sexual or otherwise, are disclosed. The person conducting the interview may seek to produce the recording as evidence that certain informal admissions were made by the child which support a diagnosis of sexual abuse. Even if no admissions are made, the child's reactions and demeanour during the interview may be capable of interpretation by an expert.

Grave concern has been expressed about the interviewing techniques employed in the diagnosis of sexual abuse (see p 24) and judicial opinion has varied as to the evidential standing and value of video recordings made of such interviews. Thus, in *Re E (A Minor) (Child Abuse: Evidence)* [1987] 1 FLR 269, Ewbank J doubted the evidential standing of a videotape recording of an interview of this nature, although he was more concerned about the evidential value of the interview itself. In *Re M (A Minor) (Child Abuse: Evidence)* [1986] 1 FLR 293, Latey J expressed the view that all such interviews should be recorded on videotape and that such evidence should then be available to the court in the interests of justice. In this way the court would be able to observe gestures, body movements, vocal inflection and intonation and also hear the precise questions and answers, all of which may play an important part in interpretation.

It seems likely that video recordings will be used more commonly in evidence, particularly in sexual abuse cases, once the problems surrounding interviewing techniques are resolved and the use of leading and hypothetical questions eliminated. In some areas efforts are being made to overcome these difficulties by ensuring that all 'disclosure' interviews are conducted by medical and social work agencies together with the police.

10 Witness summons

A single justice or a justices' clerk may issue a summons to secure the attendance of any relevant witness who may be able to give material evidence or produce a document material to the proceedings (CYPA 1969, s 2(6) and MCA, s 97(1)). Application may be made on the appropriate form by the applicant in person or by a solicitor on his behalf (MCR, r 107). Procedure on issue varies from court to court. The summons will be issued in Form 136, MCFR and must be served personally on the proposed witness, either by delivering it to him or by leaving it with another person at his usual or last known address (MCR, r 99(6)). The witness must be offered a reasonable sum of money to cover the cost and expenses of attending court, at the time the summons is served—this is known as 'conduct money'. There is no scale of payment laid down in the MCR.

If a witness fails to attend after the service of a witness summons the court may issue a warrant for his arrest, if satisfied on oath that:
    (*a*) he is a material witness;
    (*b*) he has been duly served with the summons;
    (*c*) conduct money has been paid or tendered;
    (*d*) there is no just cause for his failure to attend (MCA, s 97(3)).

Service may be proved by a declaration in Form 142 (MCFR), sworn before a justice of the peace, solicitor, justices' clerk or county court registrar (MCR, r 67(1)). If the summons was not

EVIDENCE

served by personal delivery to the person to whom it is directed a warrant will not be issued unless it is proved that the summons came to his knowledge. For this purpose any letter of communication written by him or on his behalf which reasonably infers knowledge will be admissible as evidence (MCR, r 99(2)).

A warrant may be issued at first instance instead of a witness summons if the court is satisfied by evidence on oath that a summons is unlikely to secure the attendance of the witness.

11 Advance disclosure of evidence

There is no provision for advance disclosure of evidence in care proceedings. This means that a parent may not know in advance the exact nature of any allegations made against him. The child (and his legal representative) will be in a better position if a guardian ad litem has been appointed, as the guardian will have access to all the relevant information.

In *R v West Malling Juvenile Court, ex parte Kendall* [1986] 2 FLR 405 the Divisional Court held that a father was entitled to advance disclosure of the social enquiry report and guardian ad litem's report, which contained serious allegations against him. The rules of natural justice required a parent to know the allegations made against him with sufficient particularity to enable his advisers to present his case properly. A similar argument can be put forward for advance disclosure of evidence generally and it is likely that the proposed reform of child care law will make provision for this (see Chapter 21). Advance disclosure of reports only may be of limited value to a parent as often the reports are only ready at a comparatively late stage in the proceedings.

Chapter 6

Orders

A care order is just one of the options available to the court if it finds a case proved under the CYPA 1969, s 1(2)(*a*). There are a number of alternative orders the court can make and it may, if it thinks fit, make no order at all, although this would be unusual. The court cannot make more than one order under the CYPA 1969, s 1(3), except in the case of a mentally-disordered child, who may be committed to hospital and made the subject of a care order.

1 Care order

A care order commits a child to the care of the local authority in whose area he habitually resides (see *R* v *Manchester Justices, ex parte Bannister*, cited at p 35). If he does not habitually reside in any particular area he will be committed to the care of the authority in whose area the circumstances giving rise to the proceedings arose (CYPA 1969, s 20(2)(*a*)).

If a child is already in the care of a local authority (by virtue of a care order or otherwise) the care order will name that authority even though the child is actually residing in another area (CYPA 1969, s 20(2A)). This would presumably apply where a child has been in care under an interim care order and has been placed by the local authority in accommodation outside its own area.

A local authority has a right of appeal to the Crown Court against an order committing a child to its care on the ground that the child resided in the area of another local authority at the relevant time and should have been committed to the care of that authority (CYPA, s 21(5) and see p 94).

The order gives the local authority the same powers and duties as the child's parent would have had but for the order, subject to certain restrictions (CCA 1980, s 10(2)). For example, the authority cannot consent to the child's adoption or change the child's religion and there are limitations on its power to restrict the child's liberty (see p 150). Part III of the Child Care Act 1980 applies to children committed to care by a care order as it does to children received into care voluntarily, although a care order does give a local authority some additional powers and duties (see Part IV). The child cannot be removed from care, although the local authority can place him in the charge of a parent, guardian, relative or friend for a fixed or indeterminate period (CCA, s 21(2)). Note, however, that if the care order was made after the offence condition was found proved and the child is found guilty of a further offence punishable by imprisonment in an adult, the court may direct the local authority not to release the child into the charge of a parent, guardian, relative or friend for an initial period of up to six months (CYPA 1969, s 20A and see p 180).

A care order will cease to have effect if the child is adopted or an order is made under the Adoption Act 1976, s 18 or s 55 which effectively frees the child for adoption (CYPA 1969, s 21A). In all other cases the order will remain in force until the child attains the age of eighteen, or nineteen if the order was made after his sixteenth birthday (CYPA 1969, s 20(3)). An order which would ordinarily terminate on a child's eighteenth birthday may in certain circumstances be extended (see Chapter 7). Either the local authority or the child may apply for the early discharge of a care order and the court on discharging it may make a supervision order. A parent or guardian, or independent visitor appointed under the CCA, s 11 (see p 175) may apply for an order to be discharged on the child's behalf.

2 Interim care order

An interim care order is a care order which lasts for twenty-eight days or such shorter period as specified in the order starting with the day on which the order is made (CYPA 1969, s 20(1)). Thus a twenty-eight day order will last for a full twenty-seven days after the day on which it is made and the child must be brought back before the court on the twenty-eighth day (*R* v *Birmingham Juvenile Court, ex parte P and S* [1984] FLR 343).

An interim order can be made by a juvenile court at any stage in care proceedings when it is not in a position to decide what order, if any, to make (CYPA 1969, s 2(10)). It seems that a court may also make an interim care order before the commencement of care proceedings in respect of a child who has been detained in a place of safety (CYPA 1963, s 23(5) and CYPA 1969, s 28(6)). In certain circumstances this power is also exercisable by a single justice, although an interim order made by a single justice can only last a maximum of twenty-eight days from and including the day on which the child was first detained in a place of safety (CYPA 1969, s 20(1)(*b*)). It is not clear whether much use is made of this power to prolong the effect of a place of safety order. In 1985 an interdepartmental group set up by the Department of Health and Social Security to consider child care law found no reason to suppose that such orders were made (*Review of Child Care Law* DHSS, September 1985, para 17.5). Whatever the case, only one interim order can be made under the CYPA 1963, s 23(5) or the CYPA 1969, s 28(6). If further interim orders are necessary care proceedings must be commenced and orders sought under the CYPA 1969, s 2(10). In most cases a local authority which has decided to institute care proceedings but is not yet in a position to proceed with the full hearing will issue notices in accordance with the CYPR, r 14 and seek an interim order under s 2(10) at the first hearing.

Procedure

There are no statutory criteria to guide a court in making an interim order. The only requirement in the CYPA 1969, s 2(10) is that the court is not in a position to make a final order. As a consequence courts have varied widely in the procedure followed and evidence required on interim applications. Recent cases have clarified the position.

If, therefore, an application is unopposed or a parent only wishes to make representations to the court, it is not incumbent on the court to insist that evidence is called provided that it has before it sufficient, reliable material:
   (*a*)   to decide that it is not in a position to make a final order; and
   (*b*)   to exercise its discretion in a judicial manner (*R* v *Croydon Justices, ex parte N* [1987] 1 FLR 252).

Some courts interpret the need for reliable information to mean that formal evidence on oath should be heard, at least on the first occasion an application comes before it, whether opposed or unopposed.

A court must hear formal evidence in support of an application which is opposed and the child and parent(s) must be given an opportunity to cross-examine witnesses, give or call evidence in rebuttal and/or make representations to the court (*R* v *Croydon*

Justices, ex parte N, cited above and *R v Birmingham City Juvenile Court, ex parte Birmingham City Council* (1987) *The Times*, 3 September, CA). Nevertheless, proceedings are interlocutory and evidence and cross-examination should be limited to essential issues (Neill LJ in *R v Birmingham City Juvenile Court, ex parte Birmingham City Council*, cited above).

Procedure on an opposed application is governed by the CYPR, Part III insofar as the rules are applicable to interim applications. Order of evidence and speeches is governed by the MCR, r 14 as in the full hearing (see p 44). The court cannot make an interim order in the absence of the child unless he is under the age of five or unable to attend because of illness or accident although it can direct that he need not attend on return hearings for further interim orders if he is legally represented (CYPA 1969, s 22 as amended and *Northamptonshire CC v H* (1987) *The Times*, 6 November).

Further interim orders can be made by any juvenile bench which sits for the same area as the court which made the original order (CYPA 1969, s 22(3)). An analogy cannot be drawn between renewed applications for interim care orders and successive applications for bail in criminal proceedings when the court is confined to considering new evidence that has arisen since the last hearing (*R v Birmingham Juvenile Court, ex parte P and S*, above and *R v Nottingham Justices, ex parte Davies* [1980] 2 All ER 775). A court hearing a second or subsequent application for an interim order, where circumstances have not changed, may take notice of the fact that a previous court has heard evidence and made an order but should still hear evidence itself and allow a parent and child to cross-examine and give evidence if the application is opposed (*R v Birmingham Juvenile Court, ex parte P and S* and *R v Birmingham City Juvenile Court, ex parte Birmingham City Council*, both cited above).

Evidence

It is for the applicant to make out the case for an interim care order on the balance of probabilities. See Chapter 5 for the rules governing admissibility of evidence.

The evidence adduced by the applicant must satisfy the court that it is not in a position to make a final order and must enable it to exercise its discretion to make an interim order judicially (*R v Croydon Justices, ex parte N*, cited above). The court will usually want to be satisfied that the proceedings are properly brought. In practice this will mean producing some evidence in support of one of the primary conditions in the CYPA 1969, s 1(2). Section 44 of the CYPA 1933 requires the court to have regard to the welfare of the child; in *R v Birmingham Juvenile Court, ex parte P and S* (cited above), Ewbank J said that this should be the paramount consideration for the court. Whatever the case, the evidence should clearly show that it would be in the child's interests for an interim order to be made at that stage.

Evidence that the child would not be properly cared for or would be at risk of further injury if returned home will be relevant. The court will also need to know whether any investigations into the alleged abuse are continuing and whether there are criminal proceedings pending which could delay a final hearing in the juvenile court.

The court should always take into account the need for care proceedings to be dealt with expeditiously. It will usually be in the interests of the child for a decision to be made about his future as soon as possible and local authorities have a duty to conduct the proceedings so as to obviate the need for successive adjournments and interim orders.

Powers and duties of the local authority

A local authority has the same powers and duties in relation to a child committed to care by an interim care order as it does when a care order has been made, although it cannot require a parent to contribute to the child's maintenance (CYPA 1933, s 86). An interim order may commit a child to the care of the local authority in whose area he habitually resides or the authority in whose area the circumstances giving rise to the proceedings arose (CYPA 1969, s 20(2)(*b*)).

An interim order must contain a provision requiring the local authority to whose care a child is committed to bring him before a specified court on the expiry of the order, or on such earlier date as the court may require, unless the court has directed that he need not attend because he is under the age of five or he is legally represented or he is unable to attend by reason of illness or accident. If a local authority wishes to discontinue the proceedings or does not propose to seek any further interim orders it cannot simply allow the current interim order to lapse but must instead bring the child before the court on the due date (unless his attendance is not required) and make the appropriate application to the court. An application under the CYPA 1969, s 1 should only be withdrawn with the leave of the court.

Discharge of interim order

There is no appeal against an interim order but it can be discharged in two ways:
  (a) by the High Court, Queen's Bench Division, on the application of the child, or his parent or guardian on his behalf under the CYPA 1969, s 22(4); or
  (b) by the juvenile court on the application of the child, or his parent or guardian on his behalf, or the local authority under the CYPA 1969, s 21(2).

Procedure on application to the High Court is governed by the RSC, Ord 94, r 13. Application is by summons on notice and must be supported by evidence on affidavit. (See Appendix 1 for the form of summons.) The summons should be served on the local authority to whose care the child is committed, and the person or body bringing the proceedings in which the interim order was made (if different), at least forty-eight hours before the hearing, which will take place before a judge in chambers. Legal aid is available under the civil legal aid scheme although application will have to be made for an emergency certificate, since in the ordinary course of events an interim order will have expired before a legal aid certificate is issued. An applicant who is unable to obtain legal aid but cannot afford legal representation may be represented by the Official Solicitor. The High Court is unlikely to discharge the order unless the applicant can show an error or the wrongful exercise of a discretion by the juvenile court (*Re Jarvis* [1984] FLR 350n) or the decision is plainly wrong (*R v Birmingham Juvenile Court, ex parte P and S*, cited above). If the High Court dismisses the application the local authority responsible for the child's care cannot place him in the charge of a parent, relative or friend while the interim order is still in force without the court's consent.

For procedure on application to the juvenile court under the CYPA 1969, s 21(2), see pp 76–85. If the juvenile court refuses to discharge an interim care order no further applications may be made without the consent of the court (CYPA 1969, s 21(3)). There is a right of appeal to the Crown Court against a juvenile court decision refusing to discharge an interim care order but this is largely academic since the interim order is likely to expire before any appeal will be heard in the Crown Court (CYPA 1969, s 21(4)).

Certificates of unruliness

Under the CYPA 1969, s 22(5) a juvenile court may commit a child over the age of fourteen to a remand centre instead of making an interim care order if he is of so unruly a character that he cannot be safely committed to local authority care. Since at present no remand centres exist to accommodate children committed under this provision the power exists in law only. By contrast boys over the age of fifteen years (but not girls under the age of seventeen years) who are certified unruly in criminal proceedings may be committed to prison or to adult remand centres which are effectively prison establishments (CYPA 1969, s 23(2)).

3 Supervision order

A child may be placed under the supervision of the local authority in whose area he resides (or will reside) or any other local authority which agrees to supervise him. A child of thirteen or over may be placed under the supervision of a probation officer. A child under the age of thirteen may only be placed under the supervision of a probation officer if a probation officer is already or has in the past been involved with a member of the same household and the local authority so request. The purpose of this provision is to prevent, wherever possible, more than one social work agency from becoming involved with the same family. The probation officer appointed must be assigned to the court for the petty sessional area in which the child resides or will reside. It is not necessary to obtain a child's consent to a supervision order.

An order may last for a maximum of three years and if it is made in care proceedings it cannot extend beyond the child's eighteenth birthday. Either the supervisor or the child may apply for the order to be varied or discharged and the court can make a care order on discharge (CYPA 1969, s 15(1)). (See Chapter 7 for procedure on application to vary or discharge a supervision order.)

A supervisor has a duty to advise, assist and befriend the child (CYPA 1969, s 14). To enable him to do this the order may require the child:
    (*a*) to maintain contact with his supervisor, keep him informed of any change of address or job, and receive home visits from him (CYPA 1969, s 18(2)(*b*) and CYPR, r 28(2)). (This requirement is usually included in all supervision orders as a matter of course);
    (*b*) to reside with a named individual provided that that person consents (CYPA 1969, s 12(1));

(c) to be medically examined in accordance with arrangements made by his supervisor (CYPA 1969, s 18(2)(b) and CYPR, r 28(2));
(d) to receive treatment for a mental condition either as the patient of a specified doctor, or as an out-patient at a specified place, or as an in-patient in a hospital or mental nursing home (CYPA 1969, s 12(4)); or
(e) to participate in a scheme for intermediate treatment as directed by his supervisor (CYPA 1969, s 12(2)).

The court may only impose a *mental treatment requirement* ((d) above) if:
(a) it is satisfied on the evidence of a doctor having special experience in the diagnosis and treatment of mental disorder that the child's condition requires and will respond to treatment but does not warrant the making of a hospital order (evidence may be by certificate under CYPA 1963, s 26); and
(b) arrangements have been or can be made for the necessary treatment; and
(c) the child consents to the order if he is over the age of fourteen.

A supervision order cannot be varied to include a mental treatment requirement if it has been in force for more than three months unless it is in substitution for an existing treatment requirement.

The term *intermediate treatment* ((e) above) covers a wide range of activities, some of which may require the child to live away from home for limited periods. Since 30 September 1983 each local authority has been obliged to provide approved facilities for intermediate treatment either on its own or in conjunction with another local authority. Facilities can be provided directly by the authority itself or by other bodies such as the police, the probation service or voluntary agencies. Activities may be purely recreational or geared towards training and community work (CYPA 1969, s 19 as amended by the CJA 1982, s 21).

Although the court must decide whether to include an intermediate treatment requirement in a supervision order it is left to the supervisor to decide whether and to what extent the child should participate in any scheme. Thus a supervision order containing an intermediate treatment requirement may authorise a supervisor to direct the child:

(a) to live in a specified place or places for a period or periods not exceeding ninety days; and/or
(b) to report to a specified person or persons on a day or days specified and not exceeding ninety days in total; and/or
(c) to participate in specified activities on a day or days specified and not exceeding ninety days in total (CYPA 1969, s 12(2) as amended by the CJA 1982, s 20).

The court may specify shorter periods than the statutory limits for intermediate treatment if it wishes to do so. Any day on which a child fails to comply with a supervisor's directions can be disregarded for the purposes of computation. An intermediate treatment requirement takes effect subject to any requirement for treatment for a mental condition. Note that a juvenile court can impose certain other requirements in a supervision order made in criminal proceedings, including a night curfew.

A supervision order, whatever requirements it contains, gives a supervisor no power to enter the child's home without consent, or physically to remove a child to any place. If the child fails to comply with any requirement contained in the order the supervisor's only remedy, if the order was made in care proceedings, is to apply to the court under the CYPA 1969, s 15(1) for the order to be discharged and a care order substituted or if the situation warrants it to apply for a place of safety order under the CYPA 1969, s 28(1). The court has additional powers to deal with the breach of a supervision order made in criminal proceedings.

To ensure that all parties are clear exactly what requirements an order contains a copy of the order must be sent to the following (CYPA 1969, s 18(3));
(a) the child;
(b) his parent or guardian, if he is under the age of fourteen;
(c) his supervisor;
(d) the local authority in whose area he resides or will reside, if not appointed supervisor;
(e) the person with whom the child must reside if the order contains a residence requirement;
(f) the person responsible for the child's treatment or in charge of the place where he is to receive treatment if the order contains a mental treatment requirement; and
(g) the justices' clerk for the petty sessional area in which the child resides or will reside if the court which made the order falls within a different area.

4 Hospital and guardianship orders

A hospital order is an order committing a mentally-disordered child to hospital for treatment as an in-patient. A guardianship order enables a child to be treated in the community, but vests all parental powers in the person appointed guardian (usually the local authority) so that the child's interests are protected and he receives the treatment he requires.

Before a court can make either order two doctors (one of whom must have special experience in the diagnosis and treatment of mental disorders) must verify that the child is suffering from a mental disorder sufficiently severe to warrant an order, and the court must be satisfied that this is the most suitable way of dealing with the case (Mental Health Act 1983, s 37). A hospital order cannot be made unless the court is satisfied that arrangements have been made for the child to be admitted to a specified hospital within twenty-eight days. The child may then be detained in a place of safety until admission (Mental Health Act 1983, s 37(4)). Mental disorder includes mental illness, psychopathic disorder, subnormality and severe subnormality. Each of these terms is defined in the Mental Health Act 1983, s 1(2).

Medical evidence may be written or oral. If it is written and the child is legally represented a copy must be supplied to his solicitor or counsel. If he is not represented the court should explain the substance of the report to any parent or guardian present. In either case the child or his representative may require the doctor who wrote the report to attend court to give oral evidence and may also call evidence to rebut anything contained in the report (Mental Health Act 1983, s 54(3)).

If the evidence gives the court reason to suppose that a hospital order may be appropriate but it is not prepared to make a full hospital order, for whatever reason, it may make an interim hospital order (CYPA 1969, s 2(10)). An interim order can initially be made for a period of twelve weeks and is thereafter renewable for periods of up to twenty-eight days but the order cannot last for more than six months in all (Mental Health Act 1983, s 38(5)). The court can renew an interim order or replace it with a hospital order in the absence of the child provided that he is legally represented and his solicitor or counsel is given an opportunity to be heard (Mental Health Act 1983, s 38(2) and (6)).

Both hospital and guardianship orders last initially for six months but may then be renewed for a further period of six months and thereafter annually without a court order. The person in charge of the child's treatment, whether under a hospital or guardianship order, may at any time discharge the order. In addition a hospital order may be discharged by the hospital managers and a guardianship order by the local authority. The child's nearest relative, as defined in the Mental Health Act 1983, s 26(4) (usually his father or mother), has no power to discharge either a hospital or a guardianship order but can apply to a Mental Health Review Tribunal for the child's release during the first six months of the order in the case of guardianship, and during the second six months of detention in the case of a hospital order; in both cases applications can be made thereafter at yearly intervals (Mental Health Act 1983, s 69). The child has a similar right to apply to a tribunal and there is provision for automatic referral to a tribunal where a hospital order is renewed and more than one year has elapsed since the case was last considered by a tribunal. Assistance by way of representation under the Legal Advice and Assistance Scheme is now available for representation at Mental Health Review Tribunals.

The court can make a care order and a hospital order at the same time. The local authority will then be responsible for visiting the child in hospital and will be his nearest relative for the purposes of the Mental Health Act 1983.

5 Recognisance by parent

The court can order the child's parent or guardian to enter into a recognisance to take proper care of him and exercise proper control over him. The recognisance cannot be for an amount exceeding £1000 and may not last more than three years or until the child's eighteenth birthday, whichever is the sooner.

A parent cannot be bound over without his consent and there is therefore no right of appeal against a recognisance order. A recognisance cannot be forfeited except by court order on complaint. (See the MCA, s 120 for procedure.)

6 Recognisance by child

If the court finds the offence condition satisfied in the case of a child over the age of fourteen it may order him to enter into a recognisance to keep the peace or to be of good behaviour. The recognisance cannot be for an amount exceeding £50 and may not last for longer than one year (CYPA 1969, s 3(7)). An order cannot be made without the child's consent and there is therefore no right of appeal. The court cannot make a recognisance order where it finds the offence condition but not the care or control test satisfied.

7 Compensation order

If a court finds the offence condition satisfied it may order the child's parent or guardian to pay compensation to any person who has suffered personal injury, loss or damage to property as a result of the offence. A compensation order cannot be made unless the parent or guardian has been given an opportunity to be heard or has been required to attend the proceedings but has failed to do so. The term 'guardian' in this context refers only to a person appointed by deed, will or court order (MCA, s 81(8)). The child may be ordered to pay the compensation if his parent or guardian cannot be found or if it would be unreasonable in the circumstances of the case to require his parent or guardian to pay (CYPA 1969, s 3(6) as amended by the CJA 1982, s 27). No compensation can be ordered for loss or damage arising out of a motor accident unless the relevant offence is theft and the damage is to the stolen vehicle (Powers of Criminal Courts Act 1973, s 35). Provided that the offence condition is proved the court can order compensation whether or not the care or control test is satisfied. It may also make a compensation order in addition to any other order available in care proceedings.

The compensation awarded cannot exceed £2000, and in making an order the court must have regard to the means of the person against whom the order is made insofar as they appear or are known to the court. Any person ordered to pay compensation may appeal to the Crown Court within twenty-one days of the order. Legal aid is available under the criminal legal aid scheme (Legal Aid Act 1974, s 28(6)).

A child who is ordered to pay compensation but fails to do so may be made the subject of an attendance centre order (CJA 1982, s 17). Alternatively, the court may order a parent or guardian, if he so consents, to enter into a recognisance to ensure that the child pays the sum due or it may order the parent or guardian to pay the sum ordered or any balance outstanding instead of the child. Before an order can be made the court must enquire into the defaulter's means in his presence on at least one occasion, and it must be satisfied that he has or has had the means to pay, but has refused or neglected to do so.

Chapter 7

Variation and discharge of care and supervision orders

1 Grounds for variation or discharge

Care order
The local authority to whose care a child is committed may apply to the juvenile court for a care order, due to expire on the child's eighteenth birthday, to be extended for a further year if:
  (*a*) the child is accommodated in a community home or a home provided by the Secretary of State; and
  (*b*) it is in the interest of the child or the public for him to continue to live there beyond the age of eighteen because of his mental condition or behaviour (CYPA 1969, s 21(1)).

The court cannot extend the order unless the child is present at the hearing.

Either the local authority or the child may apply to the juvenile court for a care order to be discharged and the court may on discharging it make a supervision order (CYPA 1969, s 21(2)). A parent, guardian or independent visitor appointed under the CYPA 1969, s 24(5) may apply for discharge on the child's behalf (CYPA 1969, ss 24(5), 70(2)). The applicant must satisfy the court that it is appropriate for the order to be discharged *and* that the child will still receive the care or control he needs after discharge, whether by means of a supervision order or otherwise.

If the court refuses to discharge an order no further application for discharge can be made for three months unless the court consents.

Supervision order
Either the supervisor or the child may apply to the juvenile court for a supervision order to be varied or discharged and the court may on discharging it make a care order (CYPA 1969, s 15(1)). A parent or

guardian may apply for variation or discharge on the child's behalf (CYPA 1969, s 70(2)).

The court can vary a supervision order by changing the supervisor, extending or reducing the duration of the order, cancelling any requirement contained in the original order, or inserting a new requirement in addition to or in substitution for an existing one. (See p 68, above for requirements that may be included in a supervision order.) The court has additional powers to vary supervision orders made in criminal proceedings which do not apply in care cases.

The court cannot make an order varying or discharging a supervision order or substituting a care order, unless it is satisfied that the child is unlikely to receive the care or control he needs if an order is not made (eg when making a care order), or that he is likely to continue receiving the care or control he needs notwithstanding the order (eg when discharging a supervision order or cancelling a mental treatment requirement) (CYPA 1969, s 16(6)).

If the court dismisses the application for variation or discharge no further application can be made for three months unless the court consents.

Mental treatment requirement—Special provisions apply to the inclusion or variation of mental treatment requirements. Thus a supervision order cannot be varied to include a mental treatment requirement more than three months after the date of the original order unless the new requirement is in substitution for an existing one (CYPA 1969, s 15(1)). Even within the three month period the court cannot insert a treatment requirement into an existing order unless satisfied on medical evidence that the child is suffering from a mental condition which requires and will respond to treatment and that arrangements have been or can be made for him to receive the necessary treatment (CYPA 1969, s 16(6)(*c*)). The court must obtain the consent of a child over the age of fourteen before it can vary a supervision order to include a treatment requirement or vary an existing treatment requirement unless the only effect of variation is to terminate or reduce the duration of treatment (CYPA 1969, s 16(7)).

The doctor in charge of the child's treatment has a duty to report in writing to the child's supervisor if he is unwilling to continue treating the child or believes that:

(*a*) treatment should continue beyond the period specified in the order; or

(b) different treatment is needed; or
(c) the child is not susceptible to treatment; or
(d) further treatment is unnecessary (CYPA 1969, s 15(5)).

The supervisor must then refer the matter to the juvenile court which may cancel or vary any treatment requirement without formal application for variation.

2 Procedure

The same rules of procedure (ie CYPR Part III and MCR, r 14) apply to applications to vary or discharge care/supervision orders as they do to care proceedings generally, subject to certain variations.

Which court?

Proceedings to vary or discharge a supervision order must be commenced in a juvenile court acting for the petty sessions area named in the order. This will be the court for the area in which the child resided or was about to reside at the time the order was made even if for some reason he was not placed under the supervision of his own local authority.

Application to discharge or extend the duration of a care order must be made to a juvenile court which acts for the area of the local authority to whose care the child is committed. If the child lives outside this area proceedings can also be commenced in a juvenile court acting for the area in which the child lives, although this is not the usual practice.

Commencing proceedings

The applicant must send to the clerk of the court a notice specifying the nature of the proceedings and the names and addresses of the persons to whom copy notices have been sent in accordance with the CYPR, r 14.

If the application is by the child (or a parent or guardian on his behalf) copy notices should be sent to:
  (a) the local authority named in the supervision order or the authority to whose care the child is committed;
  (b) any foster parent or person with whom the child has lived for a period of six weeks or more ending not more than six months before the date of the application, if his or her whereabouts are known;
  (c) any parent or guardian whose whereabouts are known unless he or she has made the application on the child's behalf; and

(*d*) the child's supervisor if the application is for the discharge or variation of a supervision order and the supervisor is not the local authority named in the order.

If the application is by the local authority or supervisor copy notices should be sent to:
(*a*) the child, unless this is impracticable in view of his age and understanding;
(*b*) any parent or guardian whose whereabouts are known; and
(*c*) any foster parent or other person with whom the child has lived for a period of six weeks or more ending not more than six months before the date of the application, if his or her whereabouts are known.

If the application is to discharge a care or supervision order the respondent in the proceedings (ie the local authority or supervisor if the application is by the child, and the child if the application is by the local authority or supervisor) must also be sent a notice requiring him to inform the clerk of the court as soon as practicable (and in any event not later than fourteen days after receipt of the notice), whether or not the application will be opposed (CYPR, r 14(4)). The court must usually order separate representation and appoint a guardian ad litem in all unopposed applications to discharge a care or supervision order and this provision is designed to give the court advance notice of such cases. The rules do not provide for a notice to be sent to a parent or guardian in the case of a child who is too young to be sent notice of proceedings.

Notice of proceedings is in Form 7 (CYPR, Sched 2), suitably amended. (For the usual form of notice see Appendix 1.) There is no prescribed form for the additional notice required under CYPR, r 14(4). Most juvenile courts have a standard form of notice for this purpose.

Who must attend?

The child—Although the juvenile court can make certain orders in the child's absence, he must presumably attend the hearing if he is the applicant in the proceedings unless a parent, relative or friend is conducting the case on his behalf or he is legally represented (CYPR, r 17 and MCA, s 22). An unrepresented applicant who fails to attend runs the risk that his application will be dismissed (CYPR, r 15(2) and MCA, s 56).

The child must attend the hearing of an application to extend a care order beyond the age of eighteen since the court cannot make an order in his absence. However, he is not required to attend the hearing of an application by the local authority to discharge a care order although in certain circumstances his presence will obviously be desirable. If the child is over the age of fourteen and the court intends to substitute a supervision order containing a mental treatment requirement for an existing care order, the child must be present since a treatment requirement cannot be imposed without his consent.

The court can do any of the following in the child's absence:
(*a*) discharge a supervision order;
(*b*) cancel any requirement contained in a supervision order;
(*c*) reduce the duration of the order or any requirement it contains;
(*d*) change the supervisor named in the order; or
(*e*) change the local authority or petty sessions area named in the order.

If a supervision order is to be varied in any other way (eg by extending its duration or by inserting a new requirement), or if the court is to be asked to make a care order on discharge, the child must attend the hearing and a summons can be issued to secure his attendance (CYPA 1969, s 16(2)). If the child does not then appear at the hearing, and service can be proved, a warrant may be issued for his arrest (CYPA 1969, s 16(2), (5)). A warrant may also be issued if the summons cannot be served. After arrest a child may be detained in a place of safety for up to seventy-two hours although he must be brought before the court or a justice within that period and may then be released or committed to care by an interim care order (CYPA 1969, s 16(3), (4)). (For procedure on issue of a summons or warrant see p 35 above, for form of summons see Appendix 1.)

Parent—A parent or guardian does not have to attend proceedings to vary or discharge a care order or supervision order if the child is not brought before the court although this is often desirable. If the child is to be brought before the court, for example in proceedings to vary a supervision order, the court can require a parent or guardian to attend unless it would be unreasonable to expect him to do so, and it may issue a summons to secure his attendance (CYPA 1933, s 34 and CYPR, r 26). If the summons cannot be served or a parent fails to attend, and service can be proved, the court may issue a warrant for his arrest. (For procedure on issue of a summons and warrant see p 31, for form of summons see Appendix 1.)

A parent or guardian applying for variation or discharge of a care or supervision order on the child's behalf will normally be expected to attend the hearing, even if legally represented. In most cases his attendance will be required in any event to give evidence in support of the application.

Local authority or supervisor—The local authority responsible for the child's care or supervision may be represented at the proceedings by a solicitor or counsel, or by a duly authorised officer. Very often the social worker in charge of the case will also attend. If the child is supervised by a probation officer then he should attend and may be legally represented.

Representation

The parties to the proceedings are the child and the local authority/ supervisor. The child may be legally represented but if he is not the court must allow a parent or guardian to conduct the case on his behalf unless the child otherwise requests or the court has made an order for separate representation (CYPR, r 17). A relative, friend or some other responsible person may also be allowed to conduct the child's case unless a guardian ad litem has already been appointed to represent his interests (CYPR, r 17(2)).

A parent or guardian will usually select a solicitor to represent the child unless the child has been granted legal aid and is old enough to exercise his own right of choice or the court has made an order for separate representation. If the whereabouts of the parents are unknown the court itself may appoint a solicitor when granting legal aid.

An order for separate representation can be made where there is, or may be, a conflict of interest between a parent or guardian and child on any matter relevant to the proceedings (CYPA 1969, s 32A(1)). The court may then appoint a guardian ad litem to represent the child and should do so if this appears to be in the child's interests; the guardian ad litem may then instruct a solicitor to represent the child in court (CYPR, r 14A).

A parent can only challenge a court's exercise of its discretion to appoint a guardian ad litem if he can show that no reasonable court would have acted in the same manner (*R* v *Plymouth Juvenile Court, ex parte F and F* [1987] 1 FLR 169). In reaching a decision, courts should bear in mind that a solicitor acting for a young child may not be able to carry out the necessary close investigation of the facts and circumstances and would benefit from the independent view of a guardian.

Unopposed applications
If an application to discharge a care or supervision order made in care proceedings is unopposed, the juvenile court must make an order that a parent or guardian shall not be treated as representing the child or authorised to act on his behalf unless an order is unnecessary to safeguard the child's interests (CYPA 1969, s 32A(2)).

A care or supervision order is made in care proceedings if it is made under the CYPA 1969, s 1(3) (care proceedings), or s 15(1) (a care order made on the discharge of a supervision order), or s 21(2) (a supervision order made on the discharge of a care order), provided that in the case of substitute orders the original order was made in care and not criminal proceedings. An order for separate representation will have effect for the purpose of any appeal to the Crown Court arising out of the proceedings.

The term 'unopposed' has no statutory definition and there are no statutory guidelines to indicate when an application may be deemed to be unopposed. Where the application is made by a local authority/supervisor the court is advised to consider it unopposed unless notified to the contrary by the child within fourteen days of the service of notice of proceedings (Local Authority Circular No 20/1976, 22 October 1976). Nevertheless some juvenile courts prefer to wait until the first hearing to ascertain the position and will then adjourn the proceedings if necessary. Where the application is by the child (or a parent or guardian on his behalf) arrangements have been made in most areas for the local authority/supervisor to advise the court as soon as possible whether the care/supervision order is one to which the separate representation provisions apply and whether the application is unopposed and, if so, why.

An order for separate representation will not invalidate an application for discharge made by a parent or guardian on the child's behalf. The court will still hear the application in the usual way although the parent or guardian will not be treated as authorised to act on the child's behalf. He may still, however, participate in the proceedings to the limited extent permitted by the CYPR, r 14B. Thus at the conclusion of the evidence and before the closing speeches he may give or call evidence to refute any allegations made against him, he may cross-examine witnesses on such allegations, and he may make representations to the court. He may be legally represented for this purpose and can apply for legal aid.

When the CYPAA 1986, s 3 is implemented a parent will be a party to an application for discharge if a separate representation order is made. The rules of procedure will then, presumably, be amended to permit parents to participate fully in the proceedings.

An order for separate representation may be made by a juvenile court at the hearing, in which case an adjournment will be necessary, or it can be made by a single justice or a justices' clerk before the hearing. In unopposed applications a guardian ad litem must at the same time be appointed unless this is not necessary to safeguard the child's interests (CYPA 1969, s 32B(2)). There are unlikely to be many cases in which the appointment of a guardian ad litem is unnecessary once an order for separate representation has been made. A notice of the appointment of a guardian ad litem in Form 7A (CYPR) must be sent to the guardian ad litem, the applicant and all those entitled to notice of proceedings under the CYPR, r 14(2) (CYPR, r 14A(5)). This is not the case where an order for separate representation is made but no guardian ad litem is appointed although it has been suggested judicially that this would be good practice (*R* v *Plymouth Juvenile Court, ex parte F and F*, above). The court is not obliged to hear representations from a parent when deciding whether to make a separate representation order but it must act in the child's best interests so far as its powers permit.

Role of the guardian ad litem
The statutory provisions governing the appointment and duties of a guardian ad litem are the same as in proceedings under the CYPA 1969, s 1 and are more fully discussed at pp 40–42.

Withdrawal of application
An application for discharge cannot be withdrawn without the leave of the court. If the application was made by a parent on the child's behalf and an order for separate representation has been made, the court should not allow a guardian ad litem to withdraw the application without considering what material there is to justify withdrawal (*R* v *Wandsworth Juvenile Court, ex parte S* [1984] FLR 713). The court should never reach a decision on withdrawal without giving a parent the opportunity to be heard (*R* v *Poole Juvenile Court, ex parte P* [1988] 1 FLR 8 and *R* v *Southwark Juvenile Court, ex parte C* [1988] 1 FLR 8). In practice, this will usually involve an inquiry into

the merits of the case for discharge of the order (per Ackner LJ in *R v Wandsworth Juvenile Court*, cited above, at p 717).

The hearing

As in proceedings under the CYPA 1969, s 1, the hearing is divided into two parts:
 (a) the applicant must prove that it is appropriate for the order to be discharged/varied and that the care or control test will be satisfied; and
 (b) the court must then consider any reports submitted before making an order.

Proceedings are civil, and the same rules of evidence and procedure apply as in proceedings under the CYPA 1969, s 1 (see pp 43–47). The applicant, whether the local authority/supervisor or the child, will present his case first. If the child is the respondent and is present at the hearing the court must inform him in simple language of the nature of the proceedings. If this is impracticable having regard to his age and understanding, or he is not present in court, the relevant information should be given instead to any parent or guardian present (CYPR, r 16).

If a guardian ad litem has been appointed he may be called as a witness for the child and will then give the results of his investigation as evidence whether or not he has also prepared a written report. The guardian ad litem may also give evidence at the close of evidence for the parties whether or not he has already been called as a witness. After this and before the final speeches a parent or guardian may call or give evidence to refute any allegations made against him in the proceedings and if an order for separate representation has been made he may make representations to the court. A foster parent or other person entitled to be given notice of the proceedings under the CYPR, r 14(3) will also be given an opportunity to make representations to the court.

A submission of no case to answer may be made at the conclusion of the applicant's case but the court should only exercise its power to dismiss an application in exceptional circumstances. An application with no basis in law or supported by evidence which cannot be believed could fall into this category (*R v Chertsey Justices, ex parte E* [1987] 2 FLR 415). The prevailing view is that it is preferable in most cases for a juvenile court to hear all the evidence before coming to a conclusion as to what is best for a child (Butler Sloss J in *M v Westminster City Council* [1985] FLR 325).

The court has a general duty to have regard to the welfare of the child and it must in a proper case take steps to remove him from undesirable surroundings and to secure that proper provision is made for his education and welfare (CYPA 1933, s 44). Nevertheless it can only make an order for variation or discharge if the applicant can prove on the balance of probabilities that this would be appropriate and will also satisfy the care or control test. The court is not concerned to decide whether the primary condition under the CYPA 1969, s 1(2) upon which the order was made still applies. There can be lesser or different reasons for allowing the original order to continue; the only relevant matter is whether discharge is in the child's interests (*R* v *Chertsey Justices, ex parte P*, cited above).

If at any stage in the proceedings the court considers that it is likely to vary or discharge a supervision order but before doing so it needs further information which can only be obtained if the child is detained in care, it may adjourn the proceedings and make an interim care order (CYPA 1969, s 16(4)).

Adjournment

There is a general power to adjourn proceedings at any stage (CYPR, r 15(1)). Adjournment can be to a fixed date or to a date to be determined. If no date is fixed the hearing cannot be resumed unless the court is satisfied that both parties have been given adequate notice of the resumed hearing date. For procedural requirements when a case is adjourned part-heard see p 48.

An application for adjournment may be made to allow other proceedings involving the child to take precedence and to avoid a conflict of jurisdiction. A parent may, for example, be applying for revocation of a care order on a child's behalf at the same time as the local authority is seeking an order freeing the child for adoption in the High Court. This was the position in *R* v *Tower Hamlets Juvenile Court, ex parte London Borough of Tower Hamlets* [1984] FLR 907 and the juvenile court's decision not to adjourn the application for discharge of a care order was quashed by an order of certiorari. It was held that the magistrates could not hear the application for discharge without the leave of the High Court while adoption proceedings were pending.

It is for the court and not the local authority to consider whether proceedings should be adjourned in these circumstances. In deciding whether or not to exercise its discretion the welfare of the child will be a major consideration for the court. In *C* v *Berkshire CC*

[1987] 1 FLR 210 it was held to be the paramount consideration. If adoption proceedings have already started the court will have to consider the effect of any delay in making long-term decisions for the child's future.

Conflict may also arise if a parent is seeking discharge of a care order at the same time as the local authority is applying for the discharge of an existing access order, often as a first step towards adoption. Although both applications are heard in the juvenile court they are governed by different rules of procedure and carry a right of appeal to different appellate courts. It may therefore be difficult for the applications to be heard together even though most of the evidence will be common to both. In these circumstances the court may have to decide which application should proceed first.

Reports

If the court finds the case proved it must then consider any reports submitted. The report stage is often of less significance in proceedings for variation or discharge of an order than it is in proceedings under the CYPA 1969, s 1. The court will usually have heard the views of the social worker or probation officer in charge of the case in evidence, and would not have found the case proved unless satisfied on the balance of probabilities that it is appropriate to vary or discharge the order. Nevertheless the information contained in a report may affect the court's exercise of its discretion when making an order. It may, for example, after reading the reports, decide to make a supervision order on discharging an existing care order. The court will consider the guardian ad litem's written report at this stage in the proceedings. As with any other report it may well contain information which the rules of evidence would prevent the writer giving as sworn evidence.

The procedure governing the consideration of reports is laid down by the MCR, r 20 as in proceedings under the CYPA 1969, s 1 (see pp 49–51). The court need not read any report aloud and it may require the child or a parent or guardian to withdraw from the courtroom while a report is being considered. The court must provide a copy of the guardian ad litem's report to both parties to the proceedings or to their legal representatives and to a parent or guardian who attends or requests a copy in advance. If the child is not legally represented he does not have to be given a copy of the report unless the guardian ad litem considers this to be desirable. The report should be available before the hearing (*R* v *Epsom Juvenile Court, ex parte G* [1988] 1 WLR 145).

Local authorities have no express duty to provide social enquiry reports under the CYPA 1969, s 9 in discharge or variation proceedings but it is usual for them to do so. A parent is entitled to advance disclosure of the reports of both the guardian ad litem and the local authority so that his solicitors can prepare a proper case to refute any allegations made against him in the reports (*R v West Malling Juvenile Court, ex parte Kendall* [1986] 2 FLR 405). A guardian ad litem should be permitted to see any reports to be submitted to the court prior to the hearing (Local Authority Circular No 20/1976, para 27).

Chapter 8

Appeals

There are two routes of appeal against a juvenile court's decision in care proceedings. One is to the Crown Court as of right and thereafter to the Divisional Court on a point of law only. The other is by way of case stated on a point of law from the juvenile court direct to the Divisional Court. In both cases appeal lies from the Divisional Court to the Court of Appeal, Civil Division, and thereafter to the House of Lords, but only with leave.

1 Crown Court

Right of appeal

A child may appeal to the Crown Court as of right against:
  (a) any order made under the CYPA 1969, s 1(3) (care, supervision, hospital or guardianship orders) other than a parental binding over (CYPA 1969, s 2(12));
  (b) a finding that the offence condition is satisfied in a case where the court makes no order (because the care or control test is not satisfied), provided that the child did not admit the offence (CYPA 1969, s 3(8));
  (c) a compensation order made under the Powers of Criminal Courts Act 1973, s 35 (CYPA 1969, s 3(8));
  (d) an order made under the CYPA 1969, s 21(1) extending a care order beyond the age of eighteen (CYPA 1969, s 21(4));
  (e) the dismissal of an application to discharge a care order including an interim order (CYPA 1969, s 21(4));
  (f) a supervision order made on the discharge of a care order (CYPA 1969, s 21(4));
  (g) the dismissal of an application to discharge a supervision order (CYPA 1969, s 16(8));

APPEALS

(h) a care order made on the discharge of a supervision order (CYPA 1969, s 16(8));
(i) an order varying or discharging a supervision order, unless it was made or could have been made in the child's absence (see Chapter 7) or required his consent, which he gave; and
(j) an order authorising a local authority to keep him in secure accommodation (CCA, s 21A).

When CYPAA 1986, s 2 is implemented a parent will have a separate right of appeal to the Crown Court in respect of (a), (d), and (e) to (i) above if an order for separate representation has been made. At present a parent has an independent right of appeal against a compensation order made under the CYPA 1969, s 3(6).

Who can appeal?

If no order for separate representation has been made a parent or guardian may give notice of appeal on the child's behalf (*B and Another* v *Gloucestershire CC* [1980] 2 All ER 746) even if the child was legally represented in the juvenile court by a solicitor appointed independently of the parents (*Southwark London BC* v *C (A Minor) and Another* [1982] 2 All ER 636; *C (Minors)* v *Martin and Another* [1982] 2 All ER 636). Great care should be exercised, however, in advising a parent to appeal against a care order in the case of a child who has been in and out of care as this may delay any treatment the child may need (per Lord Ormrod in *Wheelhouse* v *Woodward (formerly Wheelhouse)* (1982) 12 Fam Law 180).

If an order for separate representation has been made but no guardian ad litem appointed, the child's solicitor should consider the question of appeal and lodge notice of appeal, if appropriate, unless the child is of sufficient age and understanding to give instructions on his own behalf (*R* v *Plymouth Juvenile Court, ex parte F and F* [1987] 1 FLR 169).

If an order for separate representation has been made and a guardian ad litem appointed the guardian must decide whether to lodge an appeal on the child's behalf unless the child is competent to give instructions. A parent cannot appeal on the child's behalf in these circumstances (*AR* v *Avon CC* [1985] 2 All ER 981).

Procedure

Notice of appeal in writing must be given to the clerk of the juvenile court within twenty-one days of the juvenile court's decision (Crown Court Rules 1971, r 7). The Crown Court may extend this period, whether or not it has already expired, on written application specifying the grounds on which an extension is sought. The Crown Court Rules do not require a notice of appeal in care proceedings to specify the grounds of appeal although this is the usual practice. (See Appendix 1 for a draft notice of appeal.)

The appeal takes the form of a complete rehearing of the case before a judge and justices. Except where facts are admitted witnesses may be recalled and new evidence adduced. It is for this reason that the Crown Court appeal has been described as 'a second trial of the issue without reference to the finding of the juvenile court' (*Review of Child Care Law*, DHSS, para 22.9). Despite the venue, proceedings are civil. Strictly speaking, the Civil Evidence Acts 1968 and 1972 should apply but there are no rules in existence to provide for their application (*R* v *Wood Green Crown Court, ex parte P* [1982] 4 FLR 206). It is usual, therefore, for appeals to be conducted on the basis of the same rules of evidence as apply in the juvenile court.

An order for separate representation made in the juvenile court remains effective for the purposes of any appeal to the Crown Court. The Crown Court has a similar power to order separate representation and appoint a guardian ad litem whenever there is, or may be, a conflict of interest between parent and child on appeal. A parent thus prevented from acting on the child's behalf is still permitted to meet any allegations made against him during the hearing of the appeal by cross-examining any witness, by giving or calling evidence on his own behalf, and by making representations to the court (Crown Court (Amendment No 2) Rules 1976 (SI No 2164), r 8B).

An appellant who wishes to abandon his appeal should give notice in writing to the clerk of the juvenile court not less than three days before the date fixed for hearing, although the Crown Court can grant leave to abandon an appeal within this period (Crown Court Rules 1971, r 9).

Powers of court

The Crown Court may confirm or reverse the juvenile court's decision or it may vary it by substituting any order which the lower court could have made. It can also remit the case to the juvenile court with a direction on how it should be disposed of.

2 Divisional Court

Right of appeal

Any person aggrieved by a decision of the juvenile court may ask the court to state a case for the opinion of the High Court if he considers that the decision is wrong in law or in excess of jurisdiction (MCA, s 111). For example, magistrates who have reached a conclusion without any or sufficient evidence to support it may be asked to state a case. A person aggrieved can be anyone whose legal rights are affected by the decision. It may include not only the parties to the proceedings but possibly a parent or guardian. There is a similar right to apply to the Crown Court for a case to be stated but this is limited to parties to the proceedings (Courts Act 1971, s 10).

An appeal by way of case stated may lie in circumstances in which there is no right of appeal to the Crown Court. A guardian ad litem could, for example, ask the juvenile court to state a case following a successful application for discharge of a care order by a local authority.

A child who applies to the juvenile court to state a case for the opinion of the High Court loses his right of appeal to the Crown Court (MCA, s 87(4)).

Procedure on application

Juvenile court—Application in the juvenile court is governed by the MCR, rr 76–81. Application must be made in writing to the clerk of the juvenile court within twenty-one days of the decision, and must specify the question of law or jurisdiction on which the opinion of the High Court is sought. The applicant must enter into a recognisance before the court (with or without sureties) to prosecute the appeal without delay, to submit to the High Court's decision and to pay any costs ordered on appeal. The justices must state a case within three months of application. There is a prescribed fee for stating a case (50p when the case does not exceed five folios of ninety words, and 5p for each additional folio) but many magistrates' courts waive this. The clerk of the court should submit a draft case to both parties for comment and amendment (if necessary) before the final version is prepared. The High Court will require from the justices only a recital of the facts found and not the evidence heard (*Laird (Inspector of Factories)* v *Simms (Gomersal) Ltd* (1988) *The Times*, 7 March).

The applicant must lodge the original case plus three copies in the Crown Office of the High Court within ten days of receipt, and must serve on the respondent notice of entry of appeal together with a copy of the case, within four days of lodging the appeal (RSC, Order 56, r 6). Service may be effected by post either on the respondent or on his solicitor if they are authorised to accept service on his behalf. Application may be made to the Divisional Court for leave to appeal out of time.

If the justices consider that an application to state a case is frivolous they may refuse to do so but must on request issue to the applicant a certificate of refusal. The applicant may then apply to the Divisional Court for an order of mandamus (see p 94).

Crown Court—Application in the Crown Court must be made in writing to the appropriate officer (usually the Clerk of the Peace) within fourteen days of the decision (Crown Court Rules 1971, r 21). Before a case is stated the applicant may be required to enter into a recognisance to prosecute the appeal without delay. In care proceedings the case should contain all the relevant evidence. It is not sufficient merely to append an order of the Crown Court to the case stated, even if it appears to contain all the relevant facts found by the court and questions of law to be determined on appeal (see Widgery LJ in *Re DJMS (A Minor)*, cited at p 30).

Within ten days of receipt the applicant must lodge in the Crown Office of the High Court the original case, the order or decision appealed against, and the juvenile court order which was the subject of the original appeal to the Crown Court, plus three copies for the use of the court. Application can be made to the Divisional Court for leave to appeal out of time (RSC, Order 56, r 1).

If the Crown Court considers an application to state a case to be frivolous it may refuse to do so but it must, if required, issue to the applicant a certificate of refusal. The applicant may then apply to the Divisional Court for an order of mandamus (see p 94).

The hearing

The appeal is heard by a single judge or, if the court so directs, a Divisional Court of the Family Division (RSC, Order 56, rr 4A, 5). At the hearing counsel for the parties will put forward legal arguments for and against the appeal. There is no rehearing. The justices are not a party to the proceedings but they make representations through counsel acting as amicus curiae.

Powers of the court

The Divisional Court may affirm, reverse or vary any decision of the juvenile court or the Crown Court. It may also remit the case for rehearing if, for example, it considers that evidence was wrongly excluded or that the lower court could not have reached its decision on the evidence submitted.

3 Court of Appeal

From the Divisional Court appeal lies to the Court of Appeal, Civil Division with the leave of either court. For procedure see the RSC, Order 59, rr 1–15 and *Practice Note (Court of Appeal: New Procedure)* [1982] 1 WLR 1312. Application for leave should be made first to the Divisional Court, either at the conclusion of the hearing or ex parte (RSC, Order 59, r 14(4)). If leave is refused application should be made to the Court of Appeal, ex parte at first instance (the court will adjourn the application and give directions for notice to be served on the respondent). Leave to appeal will be granted if:
- (*a*) there is a prima facie case that an error has been made; or
- (*b*) the case involves a point of general principle to be decided for the first time; or
- (*c*) the case raises an important point on which a Court of Appeal ruling would be to the public advantage.

Notice of appeal must be served within four weeks of the date the order of Divisional Court was signed, entered and sealed. This may be a later date than the date on which the order was made. Leave to appeal out of time may be granted. (For a form of notice of appeal see RSC, Order 59, r 3.)

The appeal is by way of rehearing, but usually on documents alone, ie transcripts of evidence in lower courts, judge's notes, etc.

4 House of Lords

Appeal lies to the House of Lords from the Court of Appeal, Civil Division and also direct from the Divisional Court on a point of law of general public importance, eg the construction of a statute or a statutory instrument.

Application for leave to appeal from the Court of Appeal must be made at first instance to the Court of Appeal either at the conclusion of the hearing or ex parte (RSC, Order 59, r 1(18)). If leave is refused application should be made to the House of Lords within one month of the decision appealed against.

An appellant may only apply for leave to appeal direct from the Divisional Court if the judge in that court certifies, either at the conclusion of the hearing or within fourteen days thereafter, that a sufficient case has been made out for appeal to the House of Lords. A certificate will only be granted if both parties consent to the appeal and a point of law of general public importance is involved. If a certificate is granted the appellant has one month in which to apply to the House of Lords for leave to appeal. There is no appeal against refusal to grant a certificate but there is still a right in such a case to apply to the Court of Appeal for leave to appeal in the usual way.

For procedure on application for leave to appeal, and on appeal generally, the reader should refer to Supreme Court Practice 1988, Vol 2, Part 16A. The House of Lords publishes a free booklet, *Form of Appeal, Method of Procedure and Standing Orders*, which offers further guidance.

5 Bail pending appeal

A child committed to the care of a local authority in care proceedings has no specific right to apply for release pending appeal. However, the juvenile court (in common with all magistrates' courts) can grant bail to any person in custody who has given notice of appeal to the Crown Court or has applied to the court to state a case for the opinion of the High Court (MCA, s 113). This power is not limited to criminal proceedings. Thus a child committed to care in criminal proceedings following a finding of guilt may be granted bail pending appeal (*R v P* (1979) 144 JP 39). The same would presumably apply to a child in respect of whom the offence condition (CYPA 1969, s 1(2)(*f*)) has been found satisfied in care proceedings. There are no reported decisions of bail being granted to children committed to care in care proceedings brought on any other ground and it is unlikely that such children would be deemed to be in custody for the purposes of s 113 of the Magistrates' Courts Act 1980.

A child who has given notice of appeal has no right to apply to the Crown Court for bail pending appeal, since the court can only grant bail to an appellant who is in custody pursuant to a sentence imposed by a magistrates' court; a care order made in care proceedings is not a sentence (*R v K* [1978] 1 All ER 180). There is also no right to apply to the High Court, since both its inherent and statutory powers to grant bail are limited to criminal proceedings (Criminal Justice Act 1967, s 22(1)).

A child appealing from the Crown Court by way of case stated may be able to apply for bail, although the position is less clear.

Both the Crown Court and the High Court have power to release on bail 'any person who after the decision of his case by the Crown Court has applied to the court to state a case for the High Court' (Courts Act 1971, s 13(4)(*d*) and Criminal Justice Act 1948, s 37(1)). However, the rules governing application (see Crown Court Rules 1971, r 17 and RSC, Order 79, r 9) are drafted to apply to appellants in criminal proceedings only.

6 Application for judicial review

The Divisional Court of the Queen's Bench Division has supervisory jurisdiction over all inferior courts, which it can exercise by making the prerogative orders of certiorari, mandamus or prohibition.

Any person aggrieved by proceedings in the juvenile court (or in the Crown Court on appeal) may apply to the High Court with leave for one or more of these prerogative orders (either jointly or in the alternative) by way of an application for judicial review. On hearing the application the court may make any of the prerogative orders, or, in an appropriate case, an injunction or a declaration. A person under the age of eighteen may apply only through a next friend (RSC, Order 80, r 2).

Certiorari

This order operates to remove the proceedings to the High Court for review and, if necessary, rehearing. The effect of the order is to declare that an inferior court has acted in excess of its jurisdiction so that any order made is void. Certiorari may be used to quash a final order made by a lower court. The procedure can also be used to quash an interlocutory order or decision. In *R* v *Tower Hamlets Juvenile Court, ex parte London Borough of Tower Hamlets* [1984] FLR 907, for example, certiorari was granted to quash the justices' decision to proceed with the hearing of an application for discharge of a care order when there were adoption proceedings pending in the High Court. Note that the proper course of action where magistrates have reached a conclusion without any or sufficient evidence to support it is to appeal by way of case stated (*R* v *Cardiff Justices, ex parte Salter* [1986] 1 FLR 162).

Prohibition

This is a preventative order which can be made while proceedings are still underway to prevent an inferior court from exceeding its jurisdiction or continuing to do so.

Mandamus

This is a mandatory order directing a court to do something within its power or jurisdiction. It could, for example, be used to compel a juvenile court to hear an application for variation or discharge of a care/supervision order rather than adjourn proceedings or to state a case for the High Court. An application for mandamus to compel a Crown Court to enter and hear an appeal must be made within two months of any refusal to hear the appeal.

Application for leave to apply for judicial review is made ex parte to a Divisional Court of the Queen's Bench Division. It must be accompanied by a statement of the relief sought, the reasons for the application and an affidavit verifying the facts relied upon. If leave is granted to apply for an order of mandamus or prohibition proceedings in the lower court will be stayed pending the outcome of the application. In all cases application for an order must be made within fourteen days of leave being granted. An application for certiorari must be made within three months of the decision complained of unless the Divisional Court has given leave for a late application. Appeal against refusal to grant leave to apply for an order or to make an order on application lies to the Court of Appeal, Civil Division.

For procedure generally on application for judicial review, the reader should refer to the RSC, Order 53. For use of judicial review to challenge the decisions of local authorities in relation to children in their care see p 188.

7 Appeal by the local authority

A local authority to whose care a child is committed by a care order (other than an interim order) may within three months of the date the order was made appeal to the Crown Court on the ground that the child resided in the area of another local authority at the time the order was made and should have been committed to the care of that authority (CYPA 1969, s 21(5)). Notice of appeal must be served on the local authority in whose area it is alleged the child resided at the time the order was made, but the child himself is not a party to the appeal and there is no provision in the Legal Aid Act 1974 for him to be granted legal aid for representation at the hearing.

A local authority may also appeal against a juvenile court's refusal to grant authority to keep a child in care in secure accommodation (CCA, s 21A and see p 153).

A local authority otherwise has no right of appeal to the Crown Court against an order, or the refusal to make an order, in care proceedings, although it does have the same right as the child to appeal to the Divisional Court by way of case stated against a decision of the juvenile court or the Crown Court on appeal, and it can appeal from the Divisional Court with leave to the Court of Appeal, Civil Division and the House of Lords.

Chapter 9

Legal aid and costs

The following sections deal only generally with the availability of legal aid in care proceedings. For detailed guidance on procedure readers are referred to the current edition of *The Legal Aid Handbook*.

1 Legal advice and assistance

Legal advice and assistance, short of representation, is available under the legal advice and assistance scheme (commonly known as the 'green form scheme') to any parent or other person involved in care proceedings provided that he or she satisfies the criteria for financial eligibility. A child is not eligible for assistance under the scheme, although a parent, guardian or person responsible for his care may seek advice on his behalf (Legal Advice and Assistance (No 2) Regulations 1980 (SI No 1898), reg 8(2)).

Under the scheme a solicitor may incur costs and disbursements to the value of £50 without prior approval. Application must be made to the Legal Aid Area Committee for authority to exceed this limit. An assisted person may be required to pay a contribution towards his legal costs based on the level of his disposable income (ie after deduction of tax, national insurance contributions and allowances for dependants). A person in receipt of supplementary benefit will always be entitled to assistance under the scheme without paying a contribution, unless his capital exceeds the statutory limit when he will be outside the scheme altogether. The financial limits for eligibility under the scheme are revised annually.

2 Legal aid in the juvenile court and the Crown Court

A child who is a party to any of the following proceedings may apply to the juvenile court for legal aid under the criminal legal aid scheme:

(a) care proceedings under the CYPA 1969, s 1;
(b) an appeal to the Crown Court against an order made in care proceedings or a finding that the offence condition is satisfied;
(c) an application to discharge a care order;
(d) an appeal to the Crown Court against the dismissal of the above application or a supervision order made on discharge;
(e) an application to extend a care order beyond the age of eighteen;
(f) an appeal to the Crown Court against the extension of a care order;
(g) an application to vary or discharge a supervision order;
(h) an appeal to the Crown Court against the dismissal of the above application or an order for variation or a care order made on discharge;
(i) an application by a local authority for authority to keep a child in care in secure accommodation (see p 150);
(j) an appeal to the Crown Court against an order authorising a local authority to keep a child in care in secure accommodation.

Application for legal aid can be made orally to the court although it is more usually made in writing to the clerk of the juvenile court on a form available from the court. Written application may be made in advance of the hearing. The application will be considered at first instance by the clerk and if he is not prepared to grant legal aid he must refer the application to the court or to a single justice. A parent or guardian may apply on behalf of a child under the age of seventeen. If an order for separate representation has been made a guardian ad litem appointed by the court may apply for legal aid on the child's behalf. Application for legal aid for appeal to the Crown Court should be made initially to the clerk of the juvenile court and then to the Crown Court if refused. A parent of a child under the age of sixteen may be required to furnish a statement of means on a form available from the court. A parent who refuses to do so will be deemed to have sufficient resources to meet all the child's legal costs. The court may also require the child to furnish a statement of means. The court can waive the requirement for a statement of means from any person who appears to be incapable of providing one by reason of mental or physical incapacity. The court can require a statement of means from any person over the age of sixteen who was formerly exempt if he subsequently becomes capable of providing one. The court may also require any applicant to produce evidence of any information disclosed in a statement of means or furnish any additional evidence as may be required.

Legal aid will be granted if this is desirable in the interests of justice and the applicant's means are such that he requires assistance in meeting the cost of representation. Any doubt over whether or not to grant legal aid must be resolved in the applicant's favour. Note that legal aid must be granted to a child who wishes to be legally represented in proceedings to detain him in secure accommodation provided that his means are insufficient to meet the costs of representation. In assessing a child's means the court (or clerk) must take into account the resources and commitments of his parents and any other person having control over him on a permanent basis and not by reason of any contractual arrangement.

Legal aid may be granted subject to the payment of a contribution assessed in accordance with the formula laid down in the Legal Aid in Criminal Proceedings (General) Regulations 1968 (SI No 1231) (as amended). Any contribution assessed will be payable over a twenty-six week period and a legal aid order will not be issued until the first instalment is paid. The order can be revoked if any instalments are not paid although it is possible to seek remission of all or part of any contribution paid at the end of the proceedings, if appropriate.

Legal aid will not extend to counsel's fees unless the proceedings are brought under the CYPA 1969, s $1(2)(f)$ in respect of an indictable offence and the circumstances of the case are extremely grave or difficult. Application for approval to instruct counsel should be made to the appropriate criminal legal aid committee set up under the Legal Aid Act 1982.

Prior approval may be obtained to incur certain costs, for example, in obtaining expert reports or securing the services of an expert witness, from the appropriate criminal legal aid committee. The committee may also authorise any step in the proceedings which is unusual in nature or involves unusually large expenditure. There is, however, nothing to prevent a solicitor who has been refused authority from incurring the expenditure in any event although it may be disallowed on taxation or assessment of his costs.

The usual test applied on taxation is whether in all the circumstances the disbursement is a reasonable one (*Re P* (1979) JSWL 361).

A legal aid order for proceedings in the juvenile court will also cover advice on grounds of appeal, if any, and assistance in the preparation of a notice of appeal or an application to state a case. A further application must be made to the clerk of the juvenile court for legal aid on appeal. A legal aid order for appeal to the Crown Court will cover advice on grounds of appeal, if any, to the Divisional Court and preparation of an application for a case to be stated.

It should be noted that an application for legal aid to appeal to the Divisional Court (and thereafter to the Court of Appeal and House of Lords) must be made under the civil legal aid scheme.

3 Legal aid in the High Court

A child may apply for legal aid under the civil legal aid scheme for representation in the following proceedings:
- (*a*) an application to the High Court to discharge an interim care order;
- (*b*) an appeal to the Divisional Court by way of case stated;
- (*c*) an appeal to the Court of Appeal, Civil Division;
- (*d*) an appeal to the House of Lords; and
- (*e*) an application to the High Court for an order of certiorari, mandamus or prohibition.

Application should be made on Legal Aid Form A1 to the Legal Aid Area Secretary in the case of an appeal, and to the Legal Aid General Secretary for proceedings under (*a*) and (*e*) above. A person of full age and capacity must apply on the child's behalf and will be required to sign an undertaking to pay any contribution which the child could have been required to pay if of full age and capacity before a legal aid certificate is issued. In difficult circumstances the regulations requiring an adult to apply on behalf of a child applicant can be waived (Legal Aid (General) Regulations 1980 (SI No 1894), reg 15(5)).

Legal aid will only be granted if the child's financial resources fall within the prescribed limits and he has reasonable grounds for bringing or taking part in the proceedings. The resources of his parents and any other person having care and control of him on a permanent basis and not by reason of any contractual arrangement must be taken into account, unless there are exceptional reasons not to do so. Any maintenance payments made to the child by court order or under a maintenance agreement must also be taken into account.

4 Legal aid for parents

A parent is not a party to proceedings under the CYPA 1969 and cannot be granted legal aid unless an order for separate representation has been made (*R* v *Worthing Justices, ex parte Stevenson* [1976] 2 All ER 194). Where an order for separate representation is made the court may grant a parent legal aid under the criminal legal aid scheme to take such part in the proceedings as the rules of court allow (CA, s 65). When the CYPAA, s 3 is implemented a parent will automatically become a party to proceedings once a separate representation order is made and will be entitled to apply for legal aid as at present.

Legal aid will only be granted if it is in the interests of justice for the parent to be represented, and his means are insufficient to meet the cost. The court will require a statement of means before it makes a legal aid order and a contribution may be required. Application is made to the clerk of the juvenile court on the appropriate form supplied by the court. The provisions of the criminal legal aid scheme apply to legal aid for parents in care proceedings as they do to legal aid for the child (see p 98).

A parent who wishes to apply to the juvenile court for an order requiring a local authority to institute care proceedings (CYPA 1963, s 3) may apply for assistance by way of representation provided that he is eligible under the legal advice and assistance scheme. Application is made to the appropriate Legal Aid General Committee. If he is not eligible on financial grounds he may still qualify for legal aid under the civil legal aid scheme. Application is made to the Legal Aid General Committee on Form A4.

5 Costs

The juvenile court has no power to award costs to either party in care proceedings under the CYPA 1969 (*R* v *Salisbury and Tisbury and Mere Combined JC, ex parte Ball* [1986] 1 FLR 1). The court can, however, award costs properly incurred in connection with an appeal to the Crown Court to a local authority (or the police or the NSPCC) if the child subsequently abandons the appeal (MCA, s 109(2)). However, a local authority is unlikely to seek an order for costs against a child which will, in any event, be unenforceable in most cases.

A juvenile court can order an unsuccessful party to proceedings under the CYPA 1963, s 3 to pay all or such part of his opponent's costs as the court considers just and reasonable (MCA, s 64). The amount ordered, which may include solicitor's costs and witnesses' expenses, should be stated in any order made by the court including an order dismissing the application.

The Crown Court can make such order for costs between the parties as it thinks just (Crown Court Rules 1971, r 10(2)), including an order for costs against an appellant whose appeal is dismissed for want of prosecution or abandoned without due notice as required by r 9. However, the same considerations apply as in the juvenile court, and a local authority or any other respondent is unlikely to seek an order for costs against a child appellant.

The Divisional Court, Court of Appeal and the House of Lords have a discretionary power to award costs between the parties. If this is exercised costs usually follow the event. The Court of Appeal may award costs 'here and below', ie in the Divisional Court. This may have the effect of reversing any order for costs made in the lower court and as a result a successful party on appeal may recover back any costs already paid. The House of Lords has a similar power to award costs 'here and below'.

For costs in the High Court generally the reader should refer to RSC, Order 62.

Chapter 10

Unauthorised removal from care

1 Absence without leave

A constable may arrest without warrant any child committed to the care of a local authority by a care order (including an interim order) who is absent from the place where the local authority requires him to live. After arrest the child must be returned to the place where he was living, or to any other place the local authority may specify, at the authority's expense (CCA, s 16(1)). The term 'constable' applies not only to a police officer but also to other specialist law enforcement officers, eg railway police, harbour police, etc.

2 Intervention of third party

Any person who knowingly compels, persuades, incites or assists a child committed to care by a care order to abscond or remain absent from the place where he is required to live, without permission, commits an offence punishable on summary conviction by a fine not exceeding £2000 or a term of imprisonment not exceeding six months, or both (CCA, s 16(4)).

A magistrates' court may issue a summons requiring a named person to produce a missing child in care to the court if it is satisfied on oath that there are reasonable grounds for believing that that person can produce the child. Failure to comply with such a summons without reasonable excuse is an offence punishable on summary conviction by a fine not exceeding £400 (CCA, s 16(2)). The court may also issue a search warrant if satisfied by information on oath that there are reasonable grounds for believing that a missing child may be found in specified premises (CCA, s 16(3)).

3 Absence from a place of safety

A constable may arrest without a warrant any child who is absent without consent from a place of safety in which he is detained under the CYPA 1969, s 2(5), s 16(3) or s 28.

If a child is missing from a place of safety the person who applied for a place of safety order under s 28, or the person responsible for making arrangements for detention under s 2(5) or s 16(3), may apply on oath for a summons requiring a named person to produce the child and/or a search warrant (CYPA 1969, s 32(2), (2A), (2B)).

A person who knowingly compels, persuades, incites or assists a child to become absent from a place of safety commits an offence punishable on summary conviction by a fine not exceeding £2000 or a term of imprisonment not exceeding six months or both (CYPA 1969, s 32(3) as amended by the HSSA, Sched 2, para 16).

4 Abduction abroad

A person connected with a child in care under the age of sixteen years who takes or sends that child abroad without the consent of the local authority commits a criminal offence punishable on summary conviction by a term of imprisonment not exceeding three months or a fine of £1000 or both, and on indictment by a term of imprisonment not exceeding three years or a fine or both (Child Abduction Act 1984, s 1(1) and Sched, para 1). A similar offence is committed if the child is not in care but detained in a place of safety and is taken or sent abroad without the consent of a magistrates' court acting for the area in which the place of safety is located. A person connected with a child for the purposes of the Child Abduction Act 1984 includes a parent or guardian, the natural father of an illegitimate child and any person granted custody of the child, whether solely or jointly, by order of a court in England or Wales.

If a child in care is the subject of an order under the Adoption Act 1976, s 18 freeing him for adoption, any consent to the child's removal abroad must come from the adoption agency which applied for the freeing order and not the local authority. If adoption or custodianship proceedings are pending the relevant consent must come from the court in which proceedings are pending (Child Abduction Act 1984, Sched, para 3). If the relevant consents have not been obtained an offence is committed.

Part II

The Child Care Act 1980

Chapter 11

Voluntary reception into care

1 Grounds for admission

A local authority has a duty under the CCA, s 2 to receive into care any child within its area, who is believed to be under the age of seventeen, where it appears to the authority:
- (*a*) that he has no parent or guardian, or has been abandoned by his parents or guardian, or is lost; or
- (*b*) that his parents or guardian are for the time being or permanently prevented by reason of mental or bodily disease or infirmity or other incapacity or other circumstances from providing for his proper accommodation, maintenance and care; and
- (*c*) in either case the intervention of the local authority is necessary in the interests of the child's welfare.

An authority can also receive into care under the CCA, s 2 a child who has been removed from an unsuitable private foster home even if the statutory grounds for admission into care do not apply or the child is over the age of seventeen (FCA, s 12(5)). A similar power exists in relation to children who have been removed from unsatisfactory placements with prospective adopters (Adoption Act 1976, s 34(3)).

The term abandoned as used in s 2 is not defined in the Act. For the purposes of s 3 (see below) a child is deemed to be abandoned if the whereabouts of any parent or guardian remain unknown for more than a year. This definition clearly cannot be extended to s 2, and a child will usually be deemed to be abandoned for the purposes of reception into care if a parent or guardian has left him without indicating his intention to return or making satisfactory arrangements for the child's care.

Section 2 is drafted widely enough to cover almost any situation in which a parent is unable to provide satisfactory care. A local authority has a wide discretion as to what 'other circumstances' come within s 2—it may offer reception into care as a remedy for all manner of social ills, for example, inadequate housing or homelessness. Nevertheless it should be remembered that a local authority has a duty under the CCA, s 1 to make available such advice, guidance and assistance as may promote the welfare of children by diminishing the need to receive them into care. Assistance under the CCA, s 1 can be financial although most local authorities impose a ceiling on the financial aid that may be given and will only offer financial assistance in an emergency and not on a regular basis. Despite these limitations assistance under s 1, eg in the form of a loan to pay off rent arrears or an outstanding electricity bill, may well avert the need to receive a child into care. The Housing (Homeless Persons) Act 1977, by clearly defining the duties of local authorities towards homeless families with children, should also diminish the need to receive children into care as a result of homelessness. Where a family is deemed to be intentionally homeless and thus outside the scope of the Act a local authority does have power to provide alternative housing under the CCA, s 1 but that power is discretionary (*Attorney-General ex rel Tilley* v *London Borough of Wandsworth* [1981] 1 All ER 1162, CA).

2 Duty of a local authority

The local authority for the area in which a child is found to be in need of care is responsible for his reception into care although he may be ordinarily resident elsewhere. However, the local authority in whose area he ordinarily resides may take over his care and should, if it intends to do so, make appropriate arrangements within three months of his admission into care (CCA, s 2(4)). Any dispute between authorities over the question of residence may be referred to the Secretary of State for resolution. A period of residence away from home under the terms of a supervision order, or with foster parents, or at a boarding school or any other institution, is disregarded when determining a child's ordinary residence (CCA, s 2(5)).

Although the grounds for admission into care are reasonably well-defined in the case of the death, illness or incapacity of a parent, problems can arise if an authority refuses to receive a child into care although a parent claims to be unable to provide proper accommodation, maintenance and care. The local authority after investigating the circumstances may have decided that reception into care is inappropriate since the parent is able to provide proper care but is simply unwilling to do so. A parent in such a case could apply to the High Court for an order of mandamus directing the local authority to carry out its statutory duty under the CCA, s 2. However, the wording of s 2 does give the local authority a discretion to decide whether or not it is satisfied that there are grounds for reception into care and the High Court is unlikely to interfere with the exercise of this discretion unless the authority has acted improperly or unreasonably, eg by failing to consider all the relevant facts before reaching a decision or by taking into account irrelevant matters (*Associated Provincial Picture Houses Ltd* v *Wednesbury Corporation* [1948] 1 KB 223).

At the other extreme an authority may exert pressure on a parent to accept reception into care as an alternative to care proceedings under the CYPA 1969, s 1. Such pressure is most improper as the procedure for admission into care under s 2 is entirely voluntary; the local authority is only authorised to *receive* and not to *take* a child into care. If circumstances warrant compulsory removal into care then the appropriate statutory procedure should be used. If a child has been 'received' into care against the wishes of a parent wardship proceedings or an application for judicial review may be appropriate to secure the child's return.

Once a local authority has received a child into care it has a duty to keep him in care so long as he remains under the age of eighteen and his welfare requires it (CCA, s 2(2)). However, it has no authority to keep a child if any parent or guardian wishes to take over his care, and it must, wherever consistent with the child's welfare, endeavour to secure that his care is taken over by a parent or guardian or, where this is not possible, by a relative or friend of the same religious persuasion as the child, or who is willing to bring him up in that faith (CCA, s 2(3)).

The term parent in the Act includes natural and adoptive parents. At present it does not include the natural father of an illegitimate child unless there is in force a court order giving him custody of the child (CCA, s 8(2)). When Part II of the FLRA 1987 is implemented the term parent will also include a natural father if there is in force a parental rights order made under the FLRA 1987, s 4 whereby both parents share actual custody of a child (FLRA 1987, s 8(2)). In this context 'actual custody' of a child means actual physical possession of his person.

A guardian means any person appointed by deed or will or by order of court (CCA, s 87(1)). The term relative includes grandparents, brothers, sisters, uncles and aunts, whether of the whole or half blood (CCA, s 87(2)). It can also include the natural father of an illegitimate child and his relatives within the specified categories although this will no longer be the case once Sched 2, para 79 of the FLRA 1987 is implemented. In the case of an adopted child the term includes any relatives within the defined categories within his adopted family.

The rights and duties of a local authority in respect of a child in care under s 2 are governed by the CCA, Part III and are discussed in detail in Part IV below.

3 Leaving care

A child cannot remain in care under the CCA, s 2 beyond the age of eighteen although a local authority can in certain circumstances continue to provide accommodation and financial assistance beyond that age.

A local authority also ceases to have authority to keep a child in care under s 2 if a parent or guardian wishes to take over his care (CCA, s 2(3)), although a parent or guardian must give at least twenty-eight days' notice of his intention to remove a child who has been in care for the preceding six months unless the authority waives this requirement (CCA, s 13(2)). Failure to give the requisite notice, which may be written or verbal, is a criminal offence punishable on summary conviction by a fine not exceeding £2000 or a term of imprisonment not exceeding three months, or both.

If a local authority does not consider it to be in the child's best interest to comply with a parental request for his return it has a number of options. If the child has been in care for the preceding six months it may pass a resolution assuming parental rights during the requisite twenty-eight day notice period, provided that grounds exist under the CCA, s 3 (see Chapter 12). In the leading case of *London Borough of Lewisham v Lewisham Juvenile Court Justices and Another* [1979] 2 All ER 297, Salmon LJ suggested (obiter) that this would apply even if a parent removed the child without giving the requisite notice or within the notice period but without the consent of the local authority. This was not a unanimous view. If there are no grounds to pass a resolution the authority may make the child a ward of court and seek an order under the FLRA 1967, s 7 committing the child to care.

If notice of intention to remove the child is not required because he has not been in care for the preceding six months the position is less clear. A resolution under the CCA, s 3 can only be passed in respect of a child in care under s 2 of the Act. In such a case it therefore becomes important to determine exactly when care terminates.

In the *Lewisham* case (cited above) it was held that the power of a local authority to retain a child in care does not automatically terminate when a parent communicates his desire for the child's return. Scarman LJ considered that the child remained in care until his parent actually took over his care or demanded his return and indicated a readiness to take over his care immediately. Thus in his view a local authority could swiftly pass a s 3 resolution or institute wardship proceedings between notification of the parent's intention and an actual demand for the child to be handed over. Salmon LJ felt that a resolution passed in such circumstances would be invalid but he did suggest that the authority could possibly delay the return of the child long enough to make it a ward of court. Keith LJ disagreed and considered that an authority had no discretion as to whether or not to return a child once a parent had demanded his return. He did, however, envisage circumstances such as a pending wardship application or a situation of practical impossibility in which no court would order a local authority to return the child to a parent. *Krishnan* v *London Borough of Sutton* [1969] 3 All ER 1367, CA is just such a case. It involved a seventeen-year old in voluntary care and placed with foster parents. When her natural father demanded her return the foster parents refused to hand her over and the court refused to order the local authority to take proceedings against them; a decision, no doubt, influenced by the proximity of the child's eighteenth birthday.

A local authority cannot institute care proceedings under the CYPA 1969, s 1 in order to keep a child in care in these circumstances since the grounds specified in s 1 are unlikely to be satisfied in respect of a child who is already in care. As a last resort, and if no other action is possible in the time available the authority may have no alternative but to hand the child over and rely on its right to apply for a place of safety order (see Chapter 2) should there be evidence of ill-treatment or neglect. This is clearly the least satisfactory course and wardship is to be preferred.

Any interested person including a foster parent may make a child a ward of court and the wardship jurisdiction of the High Court is not ousted by the fact that the child is in care under the CCA, s 2. The welfare of the child is the paramount consideration throughout the proceedings and the court will intervene if there is any danger of care being terminated, when this is not in the child's best interests, even if the parent has not yet taken any positive steps to remove the child (*Re G (Infants)* [1963] 3 All ER 370). Once the child has been made a ward the court can make an interim order prohibiting his removal until the question of his future care has been finally resolved. See p 187 for a general discussion of the relationship between wardship and care and RSC, Order 90 for the procedure governing wardship applications.

If a local authority will not return a child or take steps to obtain authority for his retention in care the parent must take the initiative. Self-help is perhaps the most direct remedy and has received some judicial approval (*B* v *B* (1976) 6 Fam Law 79). However, this may not always be possible because the child's whereabouts have been concealed or because the parent is denied access. In such a case the parent can make the child a ward of court and seek an order for his return in the wardship proceedings although there is a strong likelihood that the court will seek to maintain the status quo pending a full hearing of the case. An application for judicial review, and in particular the prerogative order of mandamus directing the local authority to return the child, could be pursued (see pp 188 and 189). An application for a writ of habeas corpus has been held to be inappropriate in the circumstances (*Re K (A Minor)* (1978) 122 SJ 626).

Chapter 12

Assumption of parental rights

1 Grounds for resolution

A local authority may pass a resolution assuming parental rights and duties in respect of any child in care under the CCA, s 2 if it appears to the authority:
  (*a*) that the child's parents are dead and he has no guardian or custodian; or
  (*b*) that a parent of his,
     (i) has abandoned him, or
     (ii) suffers from some permanent disability rendering him incapable of caring for the child, or
     (iii) while not falling within (ii) above, suffers from a mental disorder (within the meaning of the Mental Health Act 1983) which renders him unfit to have the care of the child, or
     (iv) is of such habits and modes of life as to be unfit to have the care of the child, or
     (v) has so consistently failed without reasonable cause to discharge the obligations of a parent as to be unfit to have the care of the child; or
  (*c*) that a resolution under paragraph (*b*) above is in force in relation to one parent of the child who is or is likely to become a member of the household comprising the child and his other parent; or
  (*d*) that throughout the three years preceding the passing of the resolution the child has been in the care of a local authority, or partly in the care of a local authority and partly in the care of a voluntary organisation.

The grounds for passing a resolution are contained in the CCA, s 3(1). A resolution may be passed by a local authority social services committee which can carry out all the functions of the local authority under the Child Care Act 1980 (Local Authority Social Services Act 1970, s 2 and Sched 1). In exercising its power to pass a resolution the relevant committee should consider whether grounds exist for passing the resolution, the practical consequences of assuming parental rights and the alternatives available (*Re D (A Minor)* (1978) 76 LGR 653). All these matters should be set out in the agenda note placed before the committee and failure to do so could lead to the decision being held to be ultra vires on the basis that the committee did not have before it all the relevant information when making its decision (*Associated Provincial Picture Houses* v *Wednesbury Corporation* [1948] 1 KB 223). The interests of the child should be of paramount importance to the committee when reaching a decision (*M and Another* v *Wigan Metropolitan BC* [1979] 2 All ER 958). Indeed, when reaching any decision relating to a child in care, including whether or not to pass a s 3 resolution, the local authority has a statutory duty to give first consideration to the need to safeguard and promote the child's welfare (CCA, s 18). Local authorities are now expected to give parents an opportunity to make representations to committee members before a resolution is passed (DHSS Circular LAC (84)5—Parental Rights Resolutions). Procedures will vary and some authorities may permit parents to address members at the committee meeting when the resolution is to be considered. Others may only accept a written statement. Whatever procedure is adopted, local authorities should give parents prior notice of the content of the report to be submitted to the committee either in the form of a written statement or a copy of the actual report provided that this would not be contrary to the child's interests.

The local authority also has a statutory duty to ascertain and give due consideration to the wishes of the child so far as practicable and having regard to his age and understanding (CCA, s 18). Older children should be permitted to write or speak to committee members if they so wish (LAC Circular (84)5, para 20).

A child will be deemed to have been abandoned for the purposes of s 3 if after his reception into care the whereabouts of his parents have remained unknown for at least a year (CCA, s 3(8)). It is not essential for a year to have elapsed, however, if the facts clearly suggest abandonment. The other grounds are not defined in the Act and some can be given an extremely wide interpretation. For example, unsuitable habits and modes of life may cover such diverse forms of behaviour as alcoholism, drug addiction, vagrancy, prostitution, recidivism, sexual promiscuity or extreme irresponsibility.

Evidence of a parent's past life will obviously be relevant (*Barker* v *Westmorland CC* (1958) 56 LGR 267) although a parent's life-style or behaviour at the time the resolution was passed (and at the time of any subsequent proceedings) should be of greater importance.

An allegation of consistent failure to discharge the obligations of a parent contemplates a pattern of behaviour over a period of time which may vary in length depending on the nature of the conduct complained of (*M and Another* v *Wigan Metropolitan BC* cited above and *W* v *Sunderland BC* [1980] 2 All ER 514). Parental obligations have been defined as 'the natural and moral duty of a parent to show affection, care and interest towards his child' as well as the duty to maintain him 'in the financial and economic sense' (Pennycuick J in *Re P (Infants)* [1962] 1 WLR 1296). The parent's conduct must be blameworthy to a high degree or display some element of callous or self-indulgent indifference to the child's welfare. It must also be voluntary and not the result of some permanent disability or mental disorder. The test is subjective (*O'D* v *South Glamorgan CC* (Obligation of Parent) (1980) 78 LGR 522) and whether or not a parent's conduct amounts to a consistent failure to discharge his parental obligations is a question of fact and degree depending on the particular circumstances of each case. In assessing whether a parent has reasonable cause for his conduct an objective standard should be applied based on what a reasonable parent would do in all the circumstances (*M and Another* v *Wigan Metropolitan BC*, cited above). Thus a parent who fails to visit his child regularly or places the child in and out of care over a relatively short period may be held to have consistently failed to discharge the obligations of a parent if his behaviour is entirely voluntary, without reasonable cause and has a marked effect on the child's well-being.

The three year ground may apply even if the child has been permitted to live at home for a period or periods of time provided that the intention has always been for him to return to local authority accommodation after such visits. Section 21(2) of the CCA does give a local authority power to place a child in care under the charge or control of a parent, guardian, relative or friend.

Note that if a s 3 resolution is in force in relation to only one parent of a child who has been in care for the preceding six months the other parent must give twenty-eight days' notice in writing of his intention to remove the child from care (CCA, s 13(2) as amended by the HSSA, Sched 2, para 48). The purpose of this provision is presumably to give the local authority sufficient time to pass a resolution assuming the parental rights of the remaining parent, if there are grounds to do so. If the purpose of removing the child is to take him to live in a household comprising both parents then a resolution cannot be passed under s 3(1)(c) during the twenty-eight day period. This is because the wording of the section appears to limit its application to situations in which the child although technically in care is already a member of the same household as the parent who retains parental rights. A resolution can be passed under s 3(1)(c) in these circumstances if the child and parent have already been joined or are about to be joined by the parent divested of parental rights.

Except where s 3 refers to the death of a parent, the term 'parent' includes a guardian appointed by will or court order or any other person who has been granted actual custody of the child by court order (CCA, ss 2(10), 8(2) and 87(1)). It does not include the natural father of an illegitimate child unless he has been granted custody under the Guardianship of Minors Act 1971, s 9 or there is in force a parental rights order made under the FLRA 1987, s 4 (not yet implemented) whereby both parents share actual custody of the child. In this context actual custody of a child means actual possession of his person (CCA, s 8(3) and (4) as amended by the FLRA 1987, s 8(2) (not yet implemented)).

2 Joint exercise of parental rights

A resolution under s 3 will vest in a local authority all those rights and duties which by law a mother and father have in relation to a legitimate child and his property, except for the right to consent to his adoption or an order under the Adoption Act 1976, s 18 or s 55 which will lead to his eventual adoption (CCA, s 2(10)) and the right to determine the child's religion (CCA, s 4(3) and see p 162). The child must be raised in the religious faith of his parents and if there is some disagreement between his parents concerning this the authority should seek guidance by way of wardship proceedings.

A resolution will only assume the parental rights and duties of the parent it names. If that person shared parental rights and duties with another person, eg the other parent or a testamentary guardian, then the local authority will also do so.

This does not mean that the local authority must consult the other parent when exercising its parental powers. It is, in fact, free to exercise its powers in any manner authorised by the CCA, Part III provided that the other parent has not signified disapproval (CA

1975, s 85(3)). If a dispute arises the position becomes more difficult since there is no legal procedure specifically designed to resolve disputes between a local authority and a parent exercising parental rights jointly. Parents in disagreement in similar circumstances may refer the matter to a court for resolution (Guardianship Act 1973, s 1(3)). The obvious remedy for a parent retaining full parental rights if no agreement can be reached is to remove the child from care although he must give twenty-eight days' notice in writing of his intention to do so if the child has been in care for the preceding six months. The local authority can then only prevent the child's removal if there are grounds for passing a resolution under s 3 assuming the parental rights and duties of the remaining parent. If there are no grounds, but the local authority considers that it would be contrary to the child's best interests to be removed from care, its only recourse is to seek the assistance of the High Court in wardship proceedings. The High Court will always exercise its wardship jurisdiction to prevent removal from care if contrary to the child's best interests (*Re S (An Infant)* [1965] 1 All ER 865 and *Re G*, at p 112 above).

If the parent retaining parental rights does not wish to remove the child from care but considers that the local authority is acting in breach or disregard of its statutory obligations he could apply for judicial review. The remedy of wardship would not be available to him unless the local authority consented to the proceedings. It is now clearly established that the High Court will not invoke its jurisdiction in wardship to interfere with the exercise of those powers entrusted to local authorities by statute. For further discussion of these and other remedies see Chapter 20 'Resolution of Disputes'.

3 Termination of a resolution

A resolution under s 3 will cease to have effect:
- (*a*) when the child attains the age of eighteen, although the local authority may continue to provide support and assistance beyond that age (CCA, s 5(1));
- (*b*) if the child is adopted or an order is made under the Adoption Act 1976, ss 18 or 55, which effectively frees the child for future adoption (CCA, s 5(2)(*a*) and (*b*));
- (*c*) if a guardian is appointed under the Guardianship of Minors Act 1971, s 5 (CCA, s 5(2)(*c*));

118   THE CHILD CARE ACT 1980

(d) if the resolution is rescinded by the local authority (CCA, s 5(3));
(e) if the local authority does not apply to a juvenile court under the CCA, s 3(5) within fourteen days of receiving a parent's notice of objection (CCA, s 3(4)) (see below); and
(f) if the resolution is allowed to lapse or is discharged as a result of proceedings under the CCA, s 3(5) or s 5(3) (see Chapter 13).

4 Procedure

A local authority must serve written notice by recorded-delivery post on any person whose parental rights and duties are assumed by a resolution under s 3 unless:
  (a) his whereabouts are unknown; or
  (b) the resolution was passed on the ground that the child's parents are dead and he has no guardian or custodian.

There is no prescribed form of notice but it must inform the person to whom it is directed of his right to object to the resolution and the effect of any objection (CCA, s 3(3)).

A parent who objects to a resolution must serve a counter-notice in writing on the local authority no later than one month after he is served with notice of the resolution. The local authority's notice will be deemed to have been served at such time as it would have been delivered in the ordinary course of the post unless the contrary is proved (Interpretation Act 1978, s 7). There is no prescribed form of counter-notice and it is sufficient for a parent simply to state his objection in the form of a letter. (See Appendix 2 for a draft letter of objection.) However, in DHSS Circular LAC 84(5)—Parental Rights Resolutions—it is suggested that the written notice served by the local authority should contain a simple tear-off strip to be completed and returned if the parents object to the resolution.

An application for judicial review may lie if a local authority has failed to follow the correct statutory procedure in passing a s 3 resolution.

5 Complaint to the juvenile court

A s 3 resolution will lapse fourteen days after the local authority receives notice of objection from a parent, unless the authority applies by way of complaint to a juvenile court having jurisdiction in its area within that period (CCA, s 3(5)). If a complaint is made the juvenile court will issue a summons to the parent which must be served a reasonable time before the hearing date. (For the usual form of summons see Appendix 1.)

If the child's parents are living apart and the local authority is only assuming the parental rights of one parent, it must serve notice of the time and place fixed for hearing on the other parent. Notice must also be given to any foster parent or other person with whom the child has had his home for a period of not less than six weeks ending not more than six months before the complaint was made; this will include any person who has had actual physical possession of the child for the requisite period whether or not that possession has been shared with one or more persons (Balcombe LJ in *Re S (A Minor) (Care Proceedings: Wardship Summons)* [1987] 1 FLR 479 at p 488).

6 The hearing

The usual rules of procedure governing civil proceedings in the magistrates' court apply (MCA, Part II and MCR, r 14) except where these conflict with any rules or enactments regulating the constitution, location or procedure of the juvenile court (MCA, s 152). In addition Part IIIA of the Magistrates' Courts (Children and Young Persons) Rules 1970 (as inserted by CYPAR, r 7) contains procedural rules which relate to specific aspects of proceedings under the CCA. (See p 42 for rules governing the constitution of the juvenile court, persons who may attend hearings and restrictions on the reporting of cases.)

Who must attend?

The local authority is the complainant and the parent the defendant in s 3 proceedings. The local authority may be represented at the hearing by a solicitor, counsel or by a duly authorised officer. The defendant may be represented by solicitor or counsel in which case he will be deemed to be present at the hearing although he does not attend personally (MCA, s 122). The child need not attend the hearing unless his presence is required as a witness.

If the defendant does not attend the hearing and is not legally represented the court can hear the case in his absence provided it is satisfied that the summons was served a reasonable time before the hearing (MCA, s 55). Service may be proved by evidence on oath or by producing to the court a copy of the summons endorsed with a certificate of service in Form 144 or 145 (MCR, r 67(2)). If the summons was not served on the defendant personally, the hearing cannot proceed in his absence unless it is proved that the summons came to his knowledge (MCR, r 99(2)). For this purpose any letter or communication written by or on behalf of the defendant which infers knowledge of the summons will be admissible as evidence of that fact.

If the complainant fails to attend the hearing the court may dismiss the case or exercise its general power to adjourn the proceedings (MCA, ss 55, 56). The same applies if both parties fail to attend (s 57).

Order of evidence and speeches
Procedure at the hearing is governed by the Magistrates' Courts Act 1980, Part II and MCR, r 14 and CYPR, Part IIIA. If the defendant is present, the court should explain to him the nature of the proceedings. The complainant will then call his evidence and may first address the court. The defendant may cross-examine any witness in the usual way. At the conclusion of the complainant's case the defendant (or his solicitor) may address the court whether or not he calls any evidence. At the conclusion of the evidence for the defendant the complainant may call evidence in rebuttal and the defendant (or his solicitor) may then address the court if he has not already done so. Both parties may apply for leave to address the court a second time and leave cannot be granted to one party and refused to the other. If leave is granted the defendant's second speech must be delivered before the complainant's.

A parent who is not a party to the proceedings but has been served with notice of the hearing may meet any allegations made against him by cross-examining any witness and by calling or giving evidence before the defendant's closing speech. Anyone who is entitled to receive notice of the proceedings in accordance with the CYPR, r 21B whether parent, foster parent or person with whom the child has resided for the requisite period may make representations to the court after all the evidence has been called but before the closing speeches (CYPR, r 21B(2)).

Power to adjourn
The court can adjourn the hearing at any time either before or after it has begun to hear the complaint (MCA, s 54). If no date is fixed on adjournment the hearing cannot be resumed unless the court is satisfied that the parties have had adequate notice of the date, time and place of the resumed hearing. If the case is adjourned part

heard it must be resumed before the same bench although it can be resumed in the absence of any member of the original bench provided that he or she takes no further part in the proceedings and the regulations governing the constitution of the juvenile court are not breached (MCA, s 121(6)).

Evidence

The court will not make an order confirming a s 3 resolution unless it is satisfied:
   (*a*)   that the grounds on which the local authority purported to pass the resolution were made out at the time it was passed; and
   (*b*)   that at the time of the hearing there continue to be grounds on which a resolution could be founded (and not necessarily the same grounds relied upon when the resolution was passed (*W v Nottinghamshire CC* [1982] 1 All ER 1)); and
   (*c*)   that it is in the interests of the child for the resolution to be confirmed (CCA, s 3(6)).

The burden of proof is on the local authority and since the proceedings are civil it need only satisfy the court on the balance of probabilities.

The usual rules of evidence governing civil proceedings in the magistrates' court apply (see *Stone's Justices' Manual*, Vol I, Part II—Evidence and Chapter 5 for detailed discussion on evidence in care proceedings, much of which will also apply in proceedings under the CCA, s 3). A certified copy of the resolution should be produced to the court at the commencement of proceedings in case there is any dispute about the date or ground on which the resolution was passed. The court need not hear evidence on admitted facts (*Berkhamsted RDC v Duerdin-Dutton* (1964) 108 SJ 157) and hearsay evidence is inadmissible unless it falls within one of the recognised exceptions to the rule (see p 54). Medical evidence of a person's physical or mental condition may be given in the form of a certificate signed by a registered medical practitioner (CYPA 1963, s 26) and a certificate of conviction is admissible as evidence that an offence has been committed (Civil Evidence Act 1968, s 11 and MCR, r 68).

The child is a competent and compellable witness for either party although his evidence will only be admissible if he fully understands his duty to tell the truth and this must be established by due enquiry before he begins his testimony. The court has power, in special circumstances, to require a parent to leave the court while a child gives evidence or makes a statement but the person so excluded must be told the substance of any allegations made against him by the child (CYPR, r 21E). No witness can be compelled to answer any question which would tend to expose him or his spouse to a criminal charge. Only an expert witness may give his opinion in evidence and he may refer to tables, reference works and any other data for assistance. Any witness may refresh his memory from notes or records provided they were made by him, or by someone else and read over to him, at a time when he still had a clear recollection of the facts recorded. A witness cannot, however, give evidence of facts recorded unless he also has first-hand knowledge of the events referred to in the records. Thus a social worker who has taken over a case from a colleague cannot give evidence from the records kept by his predecessor unless he too had first-hand knowledge of the facts recorded.

A local authority cannot be compelled to produce its entire case file in court (*R* v *Greenwich Juvenile Court, ex parte Greenwich London BC* (1977) 7 Fam Law 171) and may claim privilege for certain documents, eg boarding-out records kept under the Boarding-Out of Children Regulations 1955 (SI No 1377) (*Re D* [1970] 1 WLR 1109). (See p 55 for a general discussion of the doctrine of privilege in juvenile court proceedings.)

A single justice may issue a witness summons to compel the attendance of any reluctant witness who is likely to be able to give material evidence or produce a document which is material to the proceedings (MCA, s 97(1)). If the witness then fails to attend the hearing without cause a warrant may issue for his arrest. (See p 55 for procedure on issue of a witness summons and/or warrant under s 97.)

Separate representation

Under s 7 of the CCA 1980 a juvenile court has power to make a child a party to s 3 proceedings where it considers this to be necessary to safeguard the child's interests. In such a case a guardian ad litem must be appointed unless the court is satisfied that this will not be necessary to safeguard the child's interests. The role and duties of the guardian ad litem are governed by the CYPR, r 21C and are the same as those of a guardian ad litem appointed under the CYPA 1969, s 32B (see pp 40–42).

The guardian ad litem must submit a written report to the court and may in addition (and whether or not he has already been called as a witness) give evidence at the conclusion of the evidence, if any, for the child.

When appointing a guardian ad litem the court must consider whether the child should be legally represented and it may direct the guardian ad litem to instruct a solicitor on the child's behalf. The solicitor so instructed represents the child and not the guardian ad litem. Thus, if any conflict arises between the two, he must take into account the views of the guardian ad litem but should follow the instructions of the child provided that he has satisfied himself that the child is able to give instructions having regard to his age and understanding. This applies not only to the conduct of the case in the juvenile court but also to the decision as to whether or not it would be in the child's interest to appeal to the High Court.

The court has power to exclude the child from court for all or part of the evidence if it is not likely to be in his interest to hear what is said. This power does not extend to evidence relating to the child's character or conduct which must be heard in his presence (CYPR, r 21E).

Reports

A juvenile court can require from a local authority or the probation service an oral or written report on any matter relevant to s 3 proceedings (CCA, s 7(3)). If the report is in writing a copy must be supplied to all parties to the proceedings or their legal representatives either before or during the hearing (Guardianship Act 1973, s 6(2)). In proceedings under the CYPA 1969, s 1 advance disclosure of reports has received judicial support (see *R* v *West Malling Juvenile Court, ex parte Kendall*, above at p 51). All or part of the report may be read aloud and any party to the proceedings may require the author to attend court to give evidence on oath. Any party may give or call evidence on any point raised in a report.

If the child has been made a party to the proceedings and a guardian ad litem appointed, the guardian ad litem will be required to submit a written report to the court. This may be considered without being read aloud but copies must be supplied to all parties or their legal representatives and to any parent who should have been given notice of the proceedings under the CYPR, r 21B. A parent must not disclose the guardian's report to an independent social worker whom he proposes to call as an expert witness without the court's permission (*R* v *Sunderland Juvenile Court, ex parte G (A Minor)* (1987) *The Times*, 15 December). If the child is not legally represented he need not be given a copy of the report unless the guardian ad litem considers this to be desirable but he must be told the substance of any part of the report which bears on his character and conduct unless this is impracticable having regard to his age and understanding. If he then wishes to call further evidence which the court considers to be material an adjournment may be granted.

Note that the court may take account of any statement in a report, whether oral or written, and any evidence given by the author (provided in either case it is relevant to the proceedings), even though it might otherwise be inadmissible as evidence (Guardianship Act 1973, s 6(3A) as amended by the CA 1975, s 90). It is accepted that some hearsay may be included in welfare reports and this is unobjectionable in relation to uncontroversial matters. Otherwise it is important for the author to report his own observations and assessments, and where he must convey the opinion of another he should make this clear, identify his source and give his reasons for agreeing with the opinion (*Thompson* v *Thompson* [1986] 1 FLR 212).

What order?

A juvenile court after hearing a complaint under the CCA, s 3 may either make an order confirming the resolution or may allow it to lapse (CCA, s 3(6)). Either party has the right of appeal to the High Court against the juvenile court's decision (see Chapter 14). If the child has been made a party to the proceedings he also has a right of appeal.

Chapter 13

Application to discharge a s 3 resolution

1 Who may apply?

If a resolution is passed on the ground that a child's parents are dead, and he has no guardian or custodian, any person subsequently claiming to be a parent or guardian may apply for the resolution to be discharged (CCA, s 5(4)(*a*)).

If the resolution is passed on any other ground then only the person divested of parental rights may apply for its discharge (CCA, s 5(4)(*b*)).

2 Grounds for discharge

The juvenile court may discharge a resolution if it is satisfied either that:
  (*a*) there was no ground for passing it; or
  (*b*) it should in the interests of the child be determined.

If a parent alleges that there was no ground for passing the resolution he must apply to the juvenile court for discharge within six months of the date the resolution was passed although the hearing need not take place within that period (MCA, s 127). If there is likely to be any dispute about the date on which the resolution was passed the local authority should be served with notice to produce a certified copy of the resolution.

Note that the CCA, s 5(4) only states the circumstances in which a court may determine a resolution. The power is discretionary. Thus in *K* v *Devon CC* (1987) 17 Fam Law 348, a juvenile court refused to discharge a resolution even though it was satisfied that there was no ground for passing it because it considered that discharge was not in the best interests of the child. A parent who disputes the ground on which a resolution is passed is therefore well advised to object to the resolution within the requisite period rather than rely upon his right to apply for discharge under s 5(4).

3 Procedure

Application is made by way of complaint to the juvenile court having jurisdiction in the area of the local authority which passed the resolution. A parent need not give the authority advance notice of the application, although this may be prudent since the authority may then be prepared to compromise by agreeing to rescind the resolution after the child has been placed at home for a successful trial period.

When making his complaint to the court a parent will have to explain briefly the circumstances of the case and why he now wishes to apply for the resolution to be discharged. It is not necessary to go into the full facts of the case at this stage. The court will then issue a summons for service on the local authority. (For the usual form of summons see Appendix 1.) If the child's parents live apart the parent making the complaint must serve notice of the time and place fixed for the hearing on the other parent if his whereabouts are known.

4 The hearing

Procedure at the hearing follows that of s 3 proceedings except that the parent is the complainant and the local authority the defendant (see pp 118–124 for rules of procedure and evidence). The parent must present his case first and bears the burden of proving, on the balance of probabilities, that the resolution should be discharged. Section 7 of the CCA 1980 which gives the court power to make the child a party to the proceedings and appoint a guardian ad litem and to require reports from the local authority or probation service, applies to applications to discharge a resolution as to s 3 proceedings.

The juvenile court may either discharge the resolution or dismiss the application. Either party has a right of appeal to the High Court against the juvenile court's decision (see Chapter 14).

Chapter 14

Appeals

1 High Court

Right of appeal
There is a right of appeal to the High Court (Family Division) against a juvenile court order made under the CCA, s 3(6) (an order confirming a s 3 resolution) or s 5(4) (an order determining a s 3 resolution), or against the court's refusal to make an order (CCA, s 6). This may be exercised by any party to the proceedings including the child himself or his guardian ad litem if an order has been made under the CCA, s 7(1).

Procedure
Appeal is by originating motion (RSC, Order 55, r 3(1)), and must be entered within six weeks of the decision appealed against. Procedure is governed by the RSC, Order 90, r 16 and Order 55, which governs appeals generally (RSC, Order 90, r 9). Notice of motion should be in the form prescribed in *Practice Direction* [1977] 1 WLR 609, reproduced in Appendix 1. It must state whether the whole or only part of the juvenile court's decision is appealed against and it should set out the grounds of appeal in detail; it is not sufficient to state simply that the finding was against the weight of the evidence.

Notice of motion must be served on the clerk of the juvenile court together with enough copies for him to serve on all parties affected by the appeal (RSC, Order 55, r 4(1)). Personal service is not necessary (RSC, Order 90, r 16(3)).

The appeal is entered by lodging three copies of the notice of motion in the Principal Registry of the Family Division. The appellant must then lodge as soon as practicable thereafter:

(*a*) three certified copies of the order appealed against;

(b) three copies of the clerk's notes of evidence in the juvenile court;
(c) three copies of the justices' reasons for their decision;
(d) three copies of any manuscript document and two copies of any typescript document put in as an exhibit in the juvenile court;
(e) a certificate confirming that notice of motion has been served on the clerk of the juvenile court; and
(f) if notice of motion includes an application to extend the time for appeal, a certificate in duplicate signed by the appellant's solicitor (or the appellant himself if he is unrepresented) setting out the reasons for the delay with the relevant dates.

Note that if the child was made a party to the proceedings in the court below and is affected by the appeal, the notice of motion should be served upon any guardian ad litem already appointed. The notice of motion should show the child as a party to the proceedings in the court below as represented by the guardian ad litem. No further order is required to appoint the same guardian in the appeal proceedings but the guardian must file a written consent to act in the Principal Registry as soon as practicable after the notice of motion has been served. The child's solicitor must file a certificate in accordance with RSC, Order 80, r 3(8) (*Registrar's Direction—10 March 1986*, LSG 23 April 1986 at p 1189).

The clerk of the juvenile court will send direct to the Principal Registry a certificate confirming service on all parties affected by the appeal. If the child is a party this must include the address at which the guardian ad litem was served. If there is any difficulty in obtaining the justices' reasons for their decision or any other documents in connection with an appeal, an application can be made to a single judge of the Family Division for an order for production (*Re B (A Minor)* (1978) *The Times*, 26 October and RSC Order 90, r 16(8)). If the clerk's notes are not available the court may hear and determine the appeal on any other evidence or statement of what occurred in the lower court as appears to be sufficient.

It is obviously desirable that appeals concerning children are heard as soon as possible. It has been stated that twenty-eight days is the maximum period of delay acceptable before the hearing of an appeal against an order transferring care and control of a child (Cumming-Bruce LJ in *Re W and W (Minors)* [1984] FLR 947 and *Hereford and Worcester CC* v *EH* [1985] 2 FLR 976). To achieve this notice of motion should be followed by an early application for an expedited hearing (*R* v *Slough Justices, ex parte B* [1985] 1 FLR

384). Counsel are required to make themselves available for the early hearing of an appeal in these circumstances and should note this requirement when first accepting instructions in a case (*Re W and W (Minors)*, above).

The court can confirm or reverse the decision of the juvenile court. It is not bound to allow an appeal simply on the ground of misdirection or improper reception or rejection of evidence unless, in the opinion of the court, substantial wrong or miscarriage of justice has been thereby occasioned (RSC, Order 90, r 16(6)). It has been said that appeals which concern the welfare of children are not subject to special rules (*G v G (Minors: Custody Appeal)* [1985] 2 FLR 894, HL). Thus even if the appellate court would have preferred a different conclusion it must leave the decision of the lower court undisturbed unless it amounts to a wrongful exercise of discretion. A court which takes irrelevant matters into account or disregards relevant matters is not exercising its discretion in a proper manner. It has been suggested that an appeal should ordinarily be allowed against the decision of a magistrates' court which disregards the recommendation of a guardian ad litem without justification (Sir John Arnold in *Devon CC v C* [1985] 2 FLR 1159 at p 1163).

An appeal may be dismissed by the registrar for want of prosecution or with the consent of the parties.

Stay pending appeal

An appeal does not stay proceedings in the lower court (RSC, Order 55, r 3(3)). If, therefore, a juvenile court refuses to confirm a s 3 resolution or makes an order discharging it the local authority will have no right to detain the child in care if a parent demands his return (unless he has been in care for the preceding six months, when twenty-eight days' notice of removal is required).

The local authority can in such circumstances apply to a Divisional Court of the High Court (a single judge in chambers or a registrar) for an interlocutory order staying any action on the juvenile court's decision until the appeal is heard, but it may not have sufficient time to do this if a parent is not required to give any notice of his intention to remove the child.

A juvenile court, itself, has no express power to grant a stay pending appeal. In guardianship cases, however, it is approved practice for a magistrates' court to postpone the operation of any order transferring the custody of a child, either pending the outcome of an appeal or at least for a sufficient period to enable the appellant to apply for an interlocutory order maintaining the status quo. To achieve this the court simply expresses its desire 'that the order should not take effect immediately', and at the same time adjourns any proceedings for non-compliance with the order. In *Hereford and Worcester CC* v *EH* (cited above) the power of the juvenile court to grant 'a stay of execution' in cases involving a transfer of care and control from a local authority to a parent was implicitly recognised and it was further stated that any stay so granted should seldom exceed fourteen days. If a further stay is required application should then be made to the appellate court.

2 Court of Appeal and House of Lords

Appeal lies from the High Court, Family Division with leave, to the Court of Appeal, Civil Division and thereafter to the House of Lords. For procedure and circumstances in which leave is granted see pp 91–92.

3 Application for judicial review

Any person aggrieved by proceedings in the juvenile court may apply with leave to the High Court for judicial review and relief may be granted in the form of one of the prerogative orders of certiorari, prohibition and mandamus. (See p 93 for procedure and circumstances in which leave will be granted.)

Chapter 15

Legal aid and costs

1 Legal aid

This section deals only generally with the availability of legal aid in s 3 proceedings. For detailed guidance on procedure readers are referred to the current edition of *The Legal Aid Handbook*.

Legal advice and assistance

Any person divested of his or her parental rights may seek advice and assistance from a solicitor under the legal advice and assistance scheme (commonly known as the 'green form scheme'), provided that he or she satisfies the financial criteria for eligibility. A solicitor acting under the scheme may not take any step on a client's behalf in the institution and conduct of proceedings. He may, however, advise on whether a parent should object to a s 3 resolution or apply for its discharge. He may also conduct negotiations with the local authority on behalf of a parent and draft a letter of objection under the CCA, s 3(4). These are all steps preliminary to proceedings.

There is an exception to the general rule that the green form scheme cannot be used to provide legal representation in court. Under the Legal Aid Act 1974, s 2(4) a magistrates' court may, at the time of the hearing, appoint or authorise any solicitor who is present before the court to represent any party to proceedings who is not legally aided but is eligible for assistance under the green form scheme. This power is rarely used in proceedings under the CCA, ss 3 or 5 since the usual practice of the court is to adjourn the proceedings so that an unrepresented parent may apply for assistance by way of representation.

For further details of the green form scheme the reader should refer to p 96.

Assistance by way of representation

A parent who is a party to proceedings under ss 3 or 5 of the CCA may apply for assistance by way of representation to cover the cost of legal representation. This will only be granted if the applicant's disposable income and capital fall within the limits prescribed under the legal advice and assistance scheme *and* he has reasonable grounds for taking or being a party to the proceedings. The applicant may be required to pay a contribution towards the costs of representation. This will be assessed in accordance with the criteria laid down under the legal advice and assistance scheme.

Application should be made to the Secretary of the appropriate Legal Aid General Committee. The Secretary has power to grant the application or may refer it to the Committee. Any decision of the Committee is final. Prior approval must be obtained from the Committee to instruct counsel or to obtain an expert opinion or to tender expert evidence. If authority is not obtained the disbursement may be disallowed.

There is an alternative procedure whereby a person who is not eligible for assistance by way of representation on financial grounds may still qualify for legal aid under the civil legal aid scheme. This is because the methods for calculating financial eligibility under the two schemes differ slightly. Application should be made to the appropriate Legal Aid General Committee on Form A4.

Legal aid for the child

A child who is made a party to proceedings under ss 3 or 5 of the CCA may apply for assistance by way of representation so that he may be legally represented. In most cases when making a child a party to the proceedings the court will appoint a guardian ad litem and any application for assistance by way of representation will then be made by the guardian ad litem on the child's behalf. If the child is made a party to an appeal to the High Court under the CCA, s 6 he will be eligible for legal aid under the civil legal aid scheme. Application should then be made to the appropriate Legal Aid Area Committee on Form 1. A guardian ad litem appointed by the court will be able to apply on the child's behalf.

Legal aid on appeal

A parent or a child who has been made a party to proceedings may apply for legal aid under the civil legal aid scheme to appeal to the High Court or to be represented in an appeal made by another party to the proceedings. Application should be made to the appropriate Legal Aid Area Committee on Form A1. A guardian ad litem appointed by the court below may apply on the child's behalf.

2 Costs

Juvenile court costs

The juvenile court may order an unsuccessful party to proceedings under the CCA, ss 3 or 5 to pay all or such part of his opponent's costs as the court considers just and reasonable (MCA, s 64). The amount ordered, which may include solicitor's fees and witness expenses, should be stated in any order made by the court including an order dismissing the complaint.

Local authorities will often decline to make an application for costs against a parent since this may damage any future relationship between the family and the authority. The same considerations do not apply to a successful parent and if he is legally aided he has a duty to claim costs if in the same circumstances a paying client would do so in his own interests. Any costs recovered by a legally aided party will be paid directly into the legal aid fund.

Costs on appeal

The High Court has a discretionary power to award costs, and, if exercised, costs will usually follow the event. This also applies on appeal to the Court of Appeal and House of Lords.

For costs in the High Court generally see RSC, Order 62.

Costs against a legally aided party

In certain circumstances a successful party to proceedings may be awarded costs from the legal aid fund if his opponent is legally aided and does not have sufficient means to pay any costs ordered. However, a successful local authority is unlikely to be able to take advantage of this provision since the court can only order costs from the legal aid fund if it is just and equitable to do so in the circumstances; a transfer of public funds from one body to another will not often be justified.

Chapter 16

Unauthorised removal from care

1 Assisting, harbouring or concealing a runaway child

Any person who
   (a) knowingly assists or induces, or persistently attempts to induce a child who has been in care under the CCA, s 2 for the preceding six months or is the subject of a resolution under the CCA, s 3, to run away; or
   (b) removes such a child without lawful authority; or
   (c) knowingly harbours or conceals such a child who has run away or been taken away, or prevents him from returning,
commits a criminal offence punishable on summary conviction by a fine not exceeding £2000 or a term of imprisonment or both (CCA, s 13). Proceedings may be instituted in the magistrates' court by the local authority (CCA, s 84). A parent or guardian who has not been divested of his parental rights may remove a child who has been in care under s 2 for the preceding six months without committing an offence provided that he has given twenty-eight days' notice of his intention to remove the child. This applies even if the child is the subject of a s 3 resolution depriving the other parent of parental rights. The term 'parent' in this context does not include the natural father of an illegitimate child. When the FLRA 1987, s 8(3) is implemented the term parent or guardian will include any person who has been granted actual custody of the child by court order or a natural father who has been granted a parental rights order under the FLRA 1987, s 4 whereby actual custody is shared between the child's parents. Note also that no offence will be committed by any person who removes a child with the consent of the authority.

2 Refusal to return a child

If a local authority has allowed a child in respect of whom a s 3 resolution is in force to be in the charge of a parent, guardian, relative or friend under the CCA, s 21(2), and has served a written notice requiring that person to return the child at a specified time, any person who harbours or conceals the child after that time or prevents him from returning commits an offence punishable on summary conviction by a fine not exceeding £400 or a term of imprisonment not exceeding two months or both (CCA, s 14). Proceedings may be instituted in the magistrates' court by the local authority (CCA, s 84). A person conceals a child by refusing to divulge the child's whereabouts if known to him, whether or not he has actual custody at the time.

If a child is placed in a person's charge under s 21(2) for a fixed period, then the local authority cannot serve notice requesting his return before the expiry of that period. If it purports to serve such notice, non-compliance with the notice will not be an offence.

3 Recovery of a missing child

A justice, if satisfied by information on oath that there are reasonable grounds for believing that a specified person can produce a missing child in care, may issue a summons requiring that person to produce the child to a magistrates' court acting for the same petty sessional area as the justice (CCA, s 15(2)). He may also issue a search warrant authorising an officer of the local authority responsible for the child's care to search specified premises. A warrant will not be issued unless a justice is satisfied by information on oath that there are reasonable grounds for believing that the child is on the premises named (CCA, s 15(3)). Failure to comply with a summons under s 15(2) without reasonable excuse is an offence punishable on summary conviction by a fine not exceeding £2000.

Section 15 applies to any child in care under CCA, s 2 in respect of whom a s 3 resolution is in force who has
  (*a*) run away from accommodation provided by the local authority under the CCA, Part III; or
  (*b*) has been taken away from such accommodation contrary to the CCA, s 13(1); or
  (*c*) has not been returned to the local authority as required by a notice under the CCA, s 14.

4 Abduction abroad

Under the Child Abduction Act 1984 a person connected with a child in care under the age of sixteen years who takes or sends that child abroad without the consent of the local authority commits an offence punishable on summary conviction by a term of imprisonment not exceeding three months or a fine of £1000 or both, and on indictment by a term of imprisonment not exceeding three years or a fine or both (Child Abduction Act 1984, s 1(1) and Sched, para 2).

A person connected with a child for the purposes of the Act includes a parent or guardian, a person granted custody whether solely or jointly, by order of a court in England or Wales, and the natural father of an illegitimate child.

Part III

Children in the care of voluntary organisations

Chapter 17

Statutory controls

Children may be placed in the care of voluntary organisations without being received into care by a local authority under the CCA, s 2. A child is considered to be in the care of a voluntary organisation when that organisation has actual custody of him, or it has placed him in the charge of a person who does not have legal custody of him, eg a foster parent (CA, s 88). A voluntary organisation is any body, not being a public or local authority, which is not run for profit (CCA, s 87(1)).

Although there are no specified grounds for admission into the care of a voluntary organisation certain provisions of the Child Care Act 1980, which restrict the removal of a child from local authority care, also apply to children in care of voluntary organisations. Such children may be offered in addition the after-care facilities of the local authority if they cease to be in care after reaching school-leaving age (CCA, s 69 and see p 184).

1 The welfare principle

In reaching any decision relating to a child in its care a voluntary organisation must give first consideration to the need to safeguard and promote the welfare of the child throughout its childhood. It must, as far as practicable, ascertain the wishes and feelings of the child and give due consideration to them having regard to the child's age and understanding.

In providing for a child in its care the organisation must also make reasonable use of facilities and services available for the use of children in the care of their own parents (CCA, s 64A inserted by the HSSA, Sched 2, para 55).

2 Parental rights and duties

Section 64 of the CCA empowers a local authority to pass a resolution vesting parental rights and duties in a voluntary organisation in respect of any child in the care of the organisation, provided that:
    (*a*) the child is not in the care of any local authority; and
    (*b*) one of the grounds specified in the CCA, s 3(1) is satisfied (see Chapter 12); and
    (*c*) it is necessary in the interests of the child's welfare for parental rights and duties to be vested in the organisation; and
    (*d*) the child lives within the area of the authority, either in a voluntary home or with foster parents with whom he has been boarded out by the organisation; and
    (*e*) the organisation is an incorporated body.

A local authority will only pass a resolution at the request of a voluntary organisation. The resolution will vest in the organisation 'all the rights and duties which by law the mother and father have in relation to a legitimate child and his property' (CA 1975, s 85(1)). This does not include the right to consent to an adoption order or an order under the Adoption Act 1976, ss 18 or 55 providing for the child's eventual adoption. Neither can the organisation arrange for the child's emigration without the consent of the Secretary of State (CCA, s 62(1) and Emigration of Children (Arrangements by Voluntary Organisations) Regulations 1982 (SI No 13)). Once a s 64 resolution has been passed the voluntary organisation must serve a notice on the child's parent or guardian if parental access is to be terminated or denied and the parent may then apply to the juvenile court for an access order. See p 170 for procedure, generally.

A s 64 resolution will only assume the parental rights and duties of the parent it names. If immediately before the resolution was passed that person shared parental rights and duties with another person, eg the child's other parent or a testamentary guardian, then the voluntary organisation will also share parental rights and duties with that person (CCA, s 64(3)). (See p 116 for an examination of the joint exercise of parental rights.) A parent or guardian retaining parental rights in these circumstances must give twenty-eight days' notice of his intention to remove the child if the child has been in the care of the voluntary organisation for the preceding six months.

Note that in this context the term 'parent' includes a guardian appointed by will or court order, or any other person who has been granted custody of the child by court order. It does not include the natural father of an illegitimate child unless he has been granted custody of the child by court order or there is in force a parental rights order made under the FLRA 1987, s 4 (not yet implemented) whereby both parents share actual custody of the child (CCA, s 64 as amended by the FLRA 1987, s 8(5) (not yet implemented)).

A resolution will terminate automatically on a child's eighteenth birthday or prior to that if
 (*a*) he is adopted; or
 (*b*) an order is made under the Adoption Act 1976, s 18 or s 55 providing for his eventual adoption; or
 (*c*) a guardian is appointed under the Guardianship of Minors Act 1971, s 5 (CCA, s 64(7)).

A resolution may also be terminated by a subsequent resolution of the local authority, transferring parental rights and duties from the voluntary organisation to itself if the interests of the child require it (CCA, s 65(1)). The child will then be in the same position as if a resolution had been passed under s 3. The voluntary organisation and each parent, guardian or custodian whose whereabouts are known must be given notice of a resolution transferring parental rights and duties to a local authority within seven days although there is no right of objection as such, only a right of appeal to the juvenile court (CCA, s 65(2)).

Section 3(2)–(7) of the CCA applies to resolutions passed under the CCA, s 64 as to resolutions made under the CCA, s 3. Thus a parent must be given written notice of the resolution and may lodge a notice of objection within one month thereafter, in which case the resolution will lapse unless the local authority applies to a juvenile court for its confirmation. A person divested of parental rights may also apply to a juvenile court for the discharge of a resolution made under the CCA, ss 64 or 65 on the ground that:
 (*a*) there was no ground for passing the resolution; or
 (*b*) the resolution should in the interests of the child be determined (CCA, s 67(2)).

Proceedings will be the same as in an application under the CCA, s 5(4), the parties being the local authority and the parent. The voluntary organisation in which parental rights are or were vested will not be a party to the proceedings. Either party has a right of appeal to the High Court against a juvenile court's decision to confirm or discharge a resolution.

For procedure after parental objection and on application to discharge readers are referred to Chapters 12 and 13.

142 CHILDREN IN CARE OF VOLUNTARY ORGANISATIONS

3 Removal from care

Any person who:
  (a) knowingly assists or induces or persistently attempts to induce a child who has been in the care of a voluntary organisation for the preceding six months or is the subject of a resolution under s 64 to run away; or
  (b) without lawful authority takes away such a child; or
  (c) knowingly harbours or conceals such a child who has run away or been removed, or prevents him from returning,
commits an offence punishable on summary conviction by a fine not exceeding £2000 or a term of imprisonment not exceeding three months or both (CCA, ss 13(1), 63(1)). A parent or guardian who has not been divested of his parental rights may remove a child who has been in the care of a voluntary organisation for the preceding six months without committing an offence provided that he has given twenty-eight days' notice of his intention to remove the child. This applies even if the child is the subject of a resolution under s 64 depriving the other parent of parental rights. Note also that no offence will be committed by any person who removes a child with the consent of the organisation.

4 Supervision of accommodation

All voluntary homes, ie homes maintained wholly or partly by voluntary contributions (other than homes for the mentally disordered) must be registered with the Secretary of State for Social Services (CCA, s 57). Registration may be refused or a home removed from the register if it is not run in accordance with the Administration of Children's Homes Regulations 1951 (SI No 1217) or is otherwise unsatisfactory.

The 1951 Regulations govern such matters as medical care, religious instruction and discipline within homes. (These regulations are currently under review and new regulations are expected shortly.) Regulation 12(1) authorises the Secretary of State to give directions limiting the number of children who may be accommodated at any one time in a voluntary home. Failure to comply with a ministerial direction is an offence punishable on summary conviction by a fine not exceeding £1000 (CCA, s 60(2)).

Local authorities have a duty to inspect all voluntary homes within their areas from time to time and any person who obstructs the authority in exercise of this duty commits an offence punishable on summary conviction by a fine not exceeding £100 (CCA, s 68).

Children who are boarded-out by voluntary organisations are protected by the Boarding-Out of Children Regulations 1955 (SI No 1377), which regulate all boarding-out arrangements whether the child is placed by a local authority or by a voluntary organisation. If the voluntary organisation is unable to discharge its supervisory duties as required by the regulations, the local authority in whose area the child is placed may take over this function (reg 14(2)).

Part IV

What care means

Chapter 18

Powers, rights and duties of the local authority

This part of the book will discuss the respective rights, duties and powers of local authority, parent and child when a child is in care, and will concentrate on those aspects of care and upbringing most likely to give rise to dispute.

A local authority has certain powers and duties in respect of a child in its care under the CCA, s 2 whether or not a resolution has been passed under s 3. Part III of the CCA governs the treatment of a child while he is in the care of a local authority; it also applies, subject to certain variations, to a child who is the subject of a care order (including an interim order) under the CYPA 1969 and to a child committed to care in matrimonial, guardianship or wardship proceedings although in the case of children committed to care by the High Court or by the county court in matrimonial proceedings the local authority must exercise its statutory powers subject to any directions the court may give.

1 To safeguard and promote the child's welfare

In reaching any decision relating to a child in its care a local authority must give first consideration to the need to safeguard and promote the welfare of the child throughout his childhood. This must be balanced, however, against other statutory obligations which the local authority may have (*R* v *Avon CC, ex parte K and Others* [1986] 1 FLR 443). The authority must, as far as practicable, ascertain the wishes and feelings of the child and give due consideration to them, having regard to his age and understanding (CCA, s 18(1)). However, the local authority may act in a manner inconsistent with this duty if it is necessary to protect members of the public (CCA, s 18(3)), or to comply with a direction given by the Secretary of State in relation to a particular child (CCA, s 19). The term welfare has been variously described as referring to the education, general surroundings, stability and happiness of a child and not merely to his material well-being.

If a local authority decision will affect a number of children in care, the authority must give first consideration to the welfare of each individual child and not consider them as a group. Thus in *R* v *Avon CC* (above) a local authority decision to close a children's home was quashed on judicial review because the authority had failed to give first consideration to the welfare of each child accommodated in the home.

2 To review cases

A local authority must as soon as practicable review the case of any child who has been in its care throughout the preceding six months and, if a care order is in force, it must consider during the course of any review whether to make an application for the order to be discharged (CCA, s 20 as modified by s 90(3)). At present there is no specified procedure for reviewing cases and practice varies from authority to authority. Regulations specifying the manner in which cases are to be reviewed, relevant considerations on review, and the timing of the first and any subsequent review are now in preparation and are likely to be implemented in the near future.

3 To use available facilities

A local authority in providing for a child in care should make reasonable use of facilities and services available for the use of children in the care of their own parents (CCA, s 18(2)). This provision is designed to ensure that children in care are, as far as possible, given all the advantages of their more fortunate contemporaries. It can apply to such diverse facilities as schools, hospitals, youth clubs, play groups and community health services.

4 Accommodation

A local authority has a duty to provide accommodation for a child in its care. This can be with foster parents, in a community home, a voluntary home, a private home or in some sort of specialist unit if the child needs special facilities (CCA, s 21). A local authority also has a general power to make any other arrangements which seem appropriate. It can, for example, place a child in the charge of a parent, guardian, relative or friend for a fixed or indeterminate period (CCA, s 21(2)) unless the child is the subject of a care order made in criminal proceedings or after the offence condition has been found proved and an order has been made under the CYPA 1969, s 20A (see p 180). Whatever accommodation is provided the local authority has a duty to ensure, so far as practicable, that it is near to the child's home unless this is inconsistent with its overriding duty to safeguard and promote the child's welfare under the CCA, s 18 (CCA, s 21 as amended by the HSSA, Sched 2, para 49).

Community homes

The term community home covers all types of residential accommodation provided by local authorities for children in care. It also covers certain accommodation provided by voluntary organisations known as 'controlled' and 'assisted' community homes. A community home is controlled when the local authority is entitled to nominate two-thirds of the members of the management committee and is responsible for the management, equipment and maintenance of the home. An assisted community home is equipped, maintained and managed by the voluntary organisation providing it although the local authority is entitled to nominate one third of the membership of the management committee. Any dispute between the local authority and the management committee of an assisted or controlled community home can be referred to the Secretary of State for Social Services for resolution.

Local authorities are responsible for providing a range of accommodation in community homes suitable for the varying needs of children in care (CCA, s 31 as amended by the HSSA, s 4). Provision is no longer planned on a regional basis and community homes may now be used to accommodate a wider category of children than was previously the case including, for example, those on intermediate treatment programmes under a supervision order.

Part IV of the CCA (as amended by the HSSA, s 4) contains detailed provisions relating to the provision and management of community homes and the Community Homes Regulations 1972 (SI No 319) govern day-to-day management. These regulations are currently under review and it is envisaged that new regulations will be forthcoming in the near future. The aim of the regulations will be to provide a common framework for all children's homes within which they will be able to operate flexibly.

Voluntary homes

A voluntary home is one that is supported wholly or in part by voluntary contributions. All voluntary homes must be registered and they are subject to regulations made by the Secretary of State governing the numbers accommodated, standard of accommodation and equipment, and general management. If a home fails to register or to comply with the regulations the local authority can require its closure although there is a right of appeal against this.

Any person authorised by a local authority may enter a voluntary home outside the area of that authority to visit any child in the authority's care who has been placed in the home (CCA, s 68(2)). A local authority has a duty to visit all voluntary homes within its own area from time to time, whether or not any child in its own care is accommodated there (CCA, s 68(1)). Any person who obstructs a local authority official exercising his right of entry is guilty of an offence, punishable on summary conviction by a fine not exceeding £100 (CCA, s 68(5)).

Detailed provisions relating to the registration and control of voluntary homes are contained in Part VI of the CCA 1980 (as amended by HSSA, Sched 4 and Sched 10) and in the Voluntary Homes (Registration) Regulations 1948 (SI No 2408), the Voluntary Homes (Return of Particulars) Regulations 1949 (SI No 2092) and the Administration of Children's Homes Regulations 1951 (SI No 1217). These regulations are currently under review and new regulations are expected shortly.

Private homes

These are children's homes run by individual proprietors or non-voluntary organisations. There are believed to be about 170 such homes accommodating some 2,500 children in care. Most of these homes are run on a commercial basis and they are not subject to any regulation. When the Children's Homes Act 1982 is fully implemented such homes will have to be registered with the local authority and conducted in accordance with regulations made under the Act. It is anticipated that the Children's Homes Act 1982 will be fully implemented in the near future.

Secure accommodation

A local authority may not place a child in care (whether by reason of a care order or otherwise) in secure accommodation unless it appears that:

(*a*) he has a history of absconding and is likely to abscond from any other description of accommodation; and
(*b*) if he absconds, it is likely that his physical, mental or moral welfare will be at risk; or
(*c*) if he is kept in any other description of accommodation he is likely to injure himself or other persons (CCA, s 21A as substituted by the HSSA, Sched 2, para 50).

These criteria are modified slightly in the case of children remanded to care in criminal proceedings who are charged with offences of a serious or violent nature (see the Secure Accommodation (No 2) Regulations 1983 (SI No 1808), reg 7).

Secure accommodation is described in the Secure Accommodation (No 2) Regulations 1983 as accommodation provided for the purpose of restricting the liberty of children. It may be within a community home, a youth treatment centre, a regional assessment secure unit within the National Health Service or within a private home or hospital. Thus a behaviour modification unit within a hospital has been held to be secure accommodation because the treatment regime involved restricting the liberty of patients (*R* v *Northampton Juvenile Court, ex parte London Borough of Hammersmith and Fulham* [1985] FLR 193). Youth treatment centres were established by the Department of Health and Social Security under the CCA, s 80 to provide specialised treatment facilities for severely disturbed and anti-social children between the ages of twelve and nineteen years. All secure accommodation within the community homes system must be approved by the Secretary of State for Social Services and no child under the age of ten years may be placed there without his prior approval. The use of single secure rooms within community homes is no longer approved and approval will only be granted for the use of single rooms within approved secure units subject to strict conditions governing their use.

A local authority is not permitted to restrict the liberty of a child in care otherwise than in approved secure accommodation. It may not, therefore, lock a child in a single room or confine a child to a certain section of a home even when accompanied by a responsible adult. Neither may it erect a continuous fence or wall more than six feet in height around a home without the approval of the Secretary of State. It may, however, secure windows and lock external gates and doors at any time to prevent intruders gaining access to the home, provided that the children are not prevented from going out during the daytime (DHSS Circular LAC (83) 18, Annex B).

The Secure Accommodation (No 2) Regulations 1983 (SI No 1808) provide that a child may not be kept in secure accommodation for more than seventy-two hours consecutively or in aggregate in any consecutive period of twenty-eight days without the authority of the juvenile court. The twenty-eight day period will restart on the expiry of any authority given by the court. If the seventy-two hour period expires late on a Saturday, Sunday or public holiday, it will be automatically extended to midday on the first working day thereafter. Application to the juvenile court should be made by the local authority responsible for the child's care and it must inform the child's parent or guardian, if practicable, and his independent visitor (if one has been appointed—see p 174) of its intention to make an application as soon as possible. If the child is detained in accommodation maintained by another local authority, that authority may apply to a juvenile court in the name of the authority responsible for the child's care. Procedure is governed by Part III of the CYPR as amended by the Magistrates' Courts (Children and Young Persons) Amendment (No 2) Rules 1983 (SI No 1793) and the child's parent or guardian must be sent notice of the date, time and place of hearing.

If the juvenile court determines that the criteria for restricting the child's liberty are satisfied it may make an order permitting the local authority to keep the child in secure accommodation for a maximum period of three months. Thereafter, it may extend authority for further periods not exceeding six months on application by the local authority. A child remanded to care in criminal proceedings may only be detained in secure accommodation for the period of remand. If the hearing is adjourned at any time the court may make an interim order authorising the child's placement in secure accommodation for the period of adjournment. Any order made by the juvenile court is permissive and does not oblige or empower the local authority to continue the placement in secure accommodation once the criteria under which the order was made cease to apply.

The juvenile court cannot exercise its power to restrict a child's liberty in this manner if the child is not legally represented unless he has been refused legal aid on financial grounds or having been informed of his right to apply for legal aid has refused or failed to apply. As a matter of practice it is for the local authority to ensure that the child's right to legal representation is explained to him and that, where appropriate, arrangements are made to ensure that he is represented. Legal aid is available under the criminal legal aid system as with care proceedings generally (see Chapter 9).

Both the local authority and the child have a right of appeal to the Crown Court against a juvenile court's decision under the CCA, s 21A. An appeal must be lodged within twenty-one days of the juvenile court's decision and this period is calculated from the day after the day of the hearing. If a local authority is appealing against a juvenile court's decision not to approve a placement in secure accommodation the child must not be retained or placed in secure accommodation during consideration of the appeal. If the child is appealing against an order authorising his placement in secure accommodation, the placement may continue pending the hearing of the appeal.

A ward of court committed to the care of a local authority may only be placed or kept in secure accommodation by order of a judge exercising wardship jurisdiction. It will not then be necessary to obtain additional authority from a juvenile court. This applies whether a care order has been made under the FLRA 1969, s 7(2) or by a judge exercising his inherent jurisdiction in wardship (the Secure Accommodation (No 2) (Amendment) Regulations 1986 (SI No 1591)).

Each local authority has a duty to appoint at least two people to review the case of each child in its care and detained in secure accommodation in a community home at intervals not exceeding three months. The purpose of the review is to determine that the criteria for keeping the child in secure accommodation continue to apply and that the placement continues to be appropriate for the child. Due regard must be had to the welfare of the child and those carrying out the review must ascertain and take into account the views of the child, his parent or guardian (if practicable), any other person who has had care of the child (if practicable), the child's independent visitor (if one has been appointed) and the authority responsible for the child's care. If possible, all these parties should be advised of the outcome of the review. If the child is a ward, the court should be notified and further directions sought if those reviewing the case decide that continued detention in secure accommodation is not justified or appropriate (the Secure Accommodation (No 2) (Amendment) Regulations 1986 (SI No 1591), reg 4).

There are strict requirements for records to be kept relating to children in secure accommodation in community homes. There are also guidelines covering the administration of tranquillising medication to children in secure accommodation (see DHSS Circular LAC (83) 18). Such drugs may only be administered on clinical and therapeutic grounds where all other appropriate responses have failed and the child is at imminent risk of harming himself or others. Even in such cases medication must only be used if the care and medical staff jointly decide that the likelihood of such a situation arising is sufficient to justify the use of a drug to avert it. If the child is only in care under the CCA, s 2 the consent of his parent or guardian should be obtained before a tranquillising drug is administered, except in an emergency.

Note that the provisions of s 21A apply to children detained under place of safety orders and accommodated in community homes even though they are not in care. The provisions do not apply to children who may have their liberty restricted under other statutory provisions, eg CYPA 1933, s 53 (children detained after committing grave or serious offences) and the CYPA 1969, s 28(4) and s 29(3) (children detained in a place of safety for up to eight days by the police or detained for up to seventy-two hours after arrest pending a court appearance). Neither do they apply to certain categories of children who may not have their liberty restricted under any circumstances, eg children in the care of voluntary organisations, children not in care but accommodated in community homes for purposes connected with their welfare within the meaning of the CCA, s 31 and young people over school age accommodated in convenient community homes under the provisions of the CCA, s 72 (see p 184).

Boarding-out with foster parents

The Boarding-out of Children Regulations 1955 (SI No 1377) currently apply to all children in care who are boarded-out with foster parents. This does not include children detained under a place of safety order. The regulations lay down procedures for selecting and supervising foster parents and stipulate who may or may not be appointed.

A child in care may only be boarded-out with:
(*a*) a husband and wife jointly; or
(*b*) a woman; or
(*c*) a man who is the grandfather, uncle or elder brother of the child.

If these requirements are no longer complied with because of the death or departure of a foster parent, the child may still be allowed to remain in the foster home in the care of the remaining spouse or another suitable member of the household.

Strict records must be kept of all fostering placements and the local authority must visit the child at specified intervals, which vary depending on whether the placement is short-term (less than eight weeks) or long-term (over eight weeks). A local authority must remove a child from a foster home if it appears that boarding-out is no longer in his best interests or that the conditions in the home are a danger to his health, safety or morals.

The existing regulations are currently being revised and it is anticipated that new regulations will be introduced shortly. The revised regulations will abolish the distinction between short-term and long-term placements and will stipulate that all children should be visited within one week of placement in a foster home and thereafter at intervals not exceeding six weeks during the first year and three months during the second and subsequent years.

It will only be possible to place children with approved foster parents, except for short placements in emergency situations. Foster parents may, however, be specially approved for a particular child.

The new regulations will specify the matters to be taken into account by local authorities when approving foster parents. All foster parents will be expected to enter into an agreement with the local authority in relation to each placement. The agreement will contain particular arrangements for the care of each foster child and will cover his health, education, arrangements for parental access and provision for his financial support. Foster parents will be required to give an undertaking to care for the child as if he were a member of their own family and to promote his welfare.

The regulations governing the boarding-out of children in care should not be confused with the provisions of the Foster Child Act 1980 which provide a protective code for children fostered by private arrangement.

Charge and control placements

There are at present no regulations governing the position of children in care who are placed under the charge and control of a parent, guardian, relative or friend. Under the CYPAA 1986, s 1 (not yet implemented) the Secretary of State has power to make regulations and these have now been prepared in draft. It is anticipated that these regulations will be brought into force before the end of 1988.

The draft Charge and Control Placement Regulations specify the persons to be consulted before a decision is made to place a child and who must be notified of that decision. Time limits are laid down for supervisory visits by the local authority. These correspond with time limits for visiting laid down in the revised boarding-out regulations (see above). The local authority will have a duty to make appropriate arrangements for the child's health care and will be obliged to remove a child if at any time it becomes contrary to the child's welfare to leave him in a placement. The authority will have to take certain specified matters into account in considering a person's suitability to have a child placed in his charge. Those approved will have to enter into a formal agreement with the authority before the child can be placed with them. The agreement will set out the obligations of the person with whom the child is placed as well as the practical arrangements for the child's health care, supervision and access to his natural family. It will be necessary to obtain the prior approval of the local authority if the child is to move to a different household, even temporarily.

Note that the charge and control regulations will apply to arrangements commonly known as placement at 'home on trial'—when a child is placed with his own family as part of a rehabilitation process.

5 Maintenance

Contribution order

While a child is in care the local authority has a duty to maintain him, although it can demand a contribution from the parents of any child under the age of sixteen (but not the putative father of an illegitimate child, see p 158) and from the child himself if he is over the age of sixteen even if he is not in employment and is in receipt of income support (CCA, s 45(1) as amended by the HSSA, s 19(1)). A parent who is in receipt of income support or family credit cannot be required to contribute (CCA, s 45(1A) as inserted by the HSSA, s 19(2) and amended by the Social Security Act 1986). There is no liability to contribute if a child is only in care under an interim care order. A local authority's duty to maintain extends to feeding, clothing and generally satisfying the material needs of the child. This includes the provision of such things as pocket money, books, sports equipment, holidays and anything else a child might need in the normal course of growing up.

The maximum contribution a local authority can demand towards a child's maintenance is the amount it would be prepared to pay to foster parents if the child was boarded-out. This limit will apply whether the child is in fact boarded-out or accommodated in a community or voluntary home. Subject to this upper limit a local authority may fix a standard contribution applicable to all children in its care or it may demand such amount as it considers reasonable in the circumstances (CCA, s 46 as amended by the HSSA, s 19(3)).

The authority has a discretion not to request any contribution in circumstances where it would be unreasonable to do so (CCA, s 46(4)). Obvious examples would be where parents are unemployed, retired or of very limited means. A parent who has had no contact with a child for some years before the child's admission into care may still be required to pay a contribution. In these circumstances a local authority may require a parent to supply details of his or her financial position before deciding whether other circumstances warrant the exercise of its discretion under the CCA, s 46(4) (*R* v *Essex CC, ex parte W* [1987] 1 FLR 148).

A local authority before it demands a contribution must serve on the proposed contributor written notice of the amount proposed. This is termed a contribution notice. If within one month the parties do not then reach an agreement on the amount of any contribution, or an agreement is reached but the contributor defaults on one or more payments, the authority may apply to a magistrates' court for a contribution order (CCA, s 47 as amended by the HSSA, s 19(4)). The court may order the contributor to pay such weekly amount as it thinks fit having regard to his means and subject to the upper limit specified in the contribution notice. No contribution can be demanded for any period when a local authority allows a child to be under the charge and control of a parent, guardian, relative or friend even though he remains in care (CCA, s 45(3)).

A contribution order will remain in force as long as the child is in the care of the local authority (CCA, s 47(3)) and a resolution under the CCA, s 3 divesting a parent of his parental rights and duties will not affect his liability to contribute.

A contribution order is enforceable in the same way as an affiliation order (or when the FLRA 1987, Sched 2, para 75 is implemented, a magistrates' court maintenance order), ie by distress, by an attachment of earnings order, or by imprisonment if other methods of enforcement are inappropriate and the contributor's failure to pay results from wilful default or culpable neglect (CCA, s 47(4) and MCA, s 93 as amended by the FLRA 1987, s 33 and Sched 2, paras 75 and 84 (not yet implemented)). The court has power to revoke, revive or vary an order (MCA, s 60 and CCA, s 48(1)) and it can, after considering the representations of the local authority, remit any arrears due (MCA, s 95).

Arrears order
If there is no contribution order in force and a contributor falls into arrears with agreed contributions, the local authority may apply to a magistrates' court within three months of the period of default for an arrears order (CCA, s 51). Under an arrears order the court may order a contributor to pay such weekly amount as it considers reasonable having regard to his means. There is a complicated formula governing the amount the court can order him to pay in total. Basically, this cannot exceed the amount the court would have ordered him to pay under a contribution order for the period of default less any sums actually paid. If, however, the period of default exceeded three months, arrears can only be recovered for the last three months of that period, plus any period of default after the application for an arrears order was made. A person liable to make payments under an arrears order must keep the local authority informed of his address and failure to do so is an offence punishable on summary conviction by a fine not exceeding £50 (CCA, s 51(4)).

Order against a putative father
The above provisions do not at present apply to the recovery of contributions from the putative father of an illegitimate child. If an affiliation order is already in force the magistrates' court which made the order or a court having jurisdiction over the area in which the father lives may order him to make any payments under the order direct to the local authority (CCA, s 49).

If no affiliation order has been made the local authority for the area in which the mother resides may apply, within three years of the date on which the child last came into care or was made the subject of a care order, for an order against the putative father under the Affiliation Proceedings Act 1957 (CCA, s 50). The application will be dealt with in the same way as an ordinary application for an affiliation order by the mother of the child although the court will also have to hear any evidence produced by the local authority. Any order made will provide for payment direct to the local authority.

In either case an order against a putative father will not remain in force after a child ceases to be in care or is placed in the charge and control of a parent, guardian, relative or friend, and it will terminate automatically on the child's sixteenth birthday. A local authority can apply for a lapsed affiliation order to be revived if a child under the age of sixteen is re-admitted to care or ceases to be in the charge of a parent, guardian, relative or friend. The child's mother has a similar right to apply for the revival of an affiliation order obtained by her but transferred to the local authority if the child ceases to be in care or is placed at home with her although still in care.

Effect of Family Law Reform Act 1987

When the FLRA 1987 is fully implemented affiliation proceedings will be abolished. It is intended that a local authority will be able to seek a contribution from the natural father of an illegitimate child in the usual way and the court will have power to make a contribution order. Unfortunately, due to a drafting error the relevant provisions of the FLRA 1987 do not effect this reform but it is anticipated that amending legislation will be enacted before the due implementation date. Subject thereto the natural father of an illegitimate child will be obliged to keep the local authority informed of his address if a contribution order is made against him and failure to do so will be a criminal offence punishable on summary conviction by a fine not exceeding £50 (CCA, s 47(5) as amended by the FLRA 1987, Sched 2, para 75 (not yet implemented)).

Collection of contributions

In all cases contributions are payable to the local authority for the area in which the parent/contributor lives and it is that authority which must bring proceedings in the magistrates' court. Contributions are then paid over to the local authority responsible for maintaining the child if other than the collecting authority (CCA, s 53).

Right of appeal

Any person required to make a contribution whether by contribution order or arrears order has a right of appeal to the Crown Court (CCA, s 52(1)(*a*)). A person entitled to receive payments under an affiliation order has a similar right of appeal against an order transferring those payments to a local authority (CCA, s 52(1)(*b*)).

6 Access to information

In the case of *Gaskin* v *Liverpool City Council* [1980] 1 WLR 1549 the Court of Appeal refused to order the disclosure of a local authority's case records on the basis that confidentiality was necessary for the proper functioning of the child care service. Since then the position has altered considerably and many local authorities now operate an 'open files' policy under which a child in care is permitted access to his own case records subject to certain safeguards. This follows guidance given to local authorities by the Secretary of State in DHSS Circular 83(4). In the circular all local authorities were advised to review their policies on the availability of information and to formulate a standing procedure for dealing with requests for access to case records. The following information may be protected from disclosure:

(a) information which is subject to a statutory requirement of confidentiality;
(b) information about a third party unless that party consents to disclosure;
(c) information obtained in confidence from a third party unless that party consents to disclosure;
(d) information likely to cause physical, mental or emotional harm to the recipient;
(e) confidential judgments and opinions recorded by social workers in the case records in accordance with good professional practice.

Requests for information from children of sufficient age and understanding should be treated in the same way as requests from adults. Some local authorities have stipulated a minimum age for this purpose which may be as low as seven years. Schemes currently in operation vary considerably. Where children are given access to case records this is often in the presence of a social worker who can explain the nature of the information and assist the child in assimilating it.

Parents have no absolute right of access to the case records of their children as in many cases a conflict of interest may exist. The DHSS Circular advises that sensitive information about a child should not be disclosed to a parent without the child's consent unless the child is unable to give an informed consent by reason of age or mental disorder.

Many of the principles advocated in the circular have now been given statutory force. Thus under the Data Protection Act 1984, s 21 a person is entitled to be supplied with a copy of any personal information about himself which is held on computerised records. Note, however, that local authorities are exempt from providing certain information from their records if this would prejudice the carrying out of social work for reasons (*b*) (*c*) and (*e*) above (the Data Protection (Subject Access Modification) (Social Work) Order 1987 (SI No 1904)).

At present most case records held by Departments of Social Services are not computerised. The Access to Personal Files Act 1987 creates a statutory obligation for local authorities to give access to case records. Regulations have yet to be laid before Parliament to implement the Act. These regulations will in due course replace the guidelines laid down in the DHSS Circular. It is likely that they will incorporate similar safeguards to prevent the disclosure of sensitive information.

Chapter 19

General matters of care and upbringing

1 Religion

A local authority cannot change the religion of a child in care or cause him to be brought up in any religious creed other than his own (CCA, ss 4(3), 10(3)). As a consequence of this the local authority, when boarding out a child with foster parents or placing him in the charge of a relative or friend, must, wherever possible, place him with a person of the same religious persuasion or willing to bring him up in that faith. Regulation 19 of the Boarding-Out of Children Regulations 1955 (SI No 1377) requires a foster parent to sign an undertaking to bring the child up in his own religion. Regulation 8 of the Community Homes Regulations 1972 imposes a similar duty on the managers of all community homes or, if there are no managers, the local authority, to ensure that as far as practicable every child resident in the home has the opportunity to attend such religious services and receive such religious instruction as are appropriate to his religion. A similar provision applies to children living in voluntary homes (the Administration of Children's Homes Regulations 1951 (SI No 1217), reg 4).

Although a local authority clearly has a duty to bring up a child in his own religion it may not be easy in some cases to determine which religion that should be. As a general rule a child will have the same religion as his parents. Formerly, where the parents were of different religions, this meant the religion of his father unless the father had by his own misconduct, acquiescence or neglect forfeited this right. Now that the Guardianship Act 1973, s 1 gives both parents equal rights in relation to a child's upbringing, he could equally well take the religion of his mother. Parents who are in dispute over a child's religious upbringing may refer the matter to a court for resolution under the Guardianship Act 1973, s 1(3). A local authority does not have a similar right and is best advised in the case of a child of mixed religious parentage to continue to bring the child up in the religion he has so far adopted, be it the religion of his father or mother. This would clearly be in accord with the local authority's duty to give first consideration to the child's welfare (CCA, s 18(1)) since any change would be bound to cause distress.

Further problems may arise if a child professes to hold religious beliefs different to those of either parent, especially as a local authority has a general duty to ascertain a child's wishes and feelings and give them due consideration, having regard to his age and understanding. There is no definite age at which a child may be considered mature enough to choose his own religion. The now defunct Poor Law Act 1930, s 73 recognised that children might have definite religious views by the age of twelve. Others have suggested that sixteen is the appropriate age since a child over that age is considered to be self-supporting unless he is undergoing full-time education or training. Obviously each case must be considered on its merits, having regard to such factors as the child's level of understanding and his strength of feeling. In the event of a dispute between the local authority and the child or his parents it might be advisable for the local authority to seek the intervention of the High Court in wardship proceedings (see p 187).

2 Education

Every parent is under a duty to ensure that his or her child receives efficient full-time education suitable to his age, ability and aptitude and to any special educational needs he may have either by regular attendance at school or otherwise. A parent who fails to ensure that his child regularly attends the school at which he is a registered pupil commits an offence (Education Act 1944, ss 36, 39). A parent in this context includes any person with actual custody, ie possession of a child. In the case of a child in care it will therefore apply to a foster parent if the child is boarded-out, to the managers or the persons in charge if the child is placed in a voluntary home or a controlled or assisted community home, and to the local authority itself if the child is accommodated in a community home run by the authority.

Neither the Community Homes Regulations 1972 (SI No 319) nor the Boarding-Out of Children Regulations 1955 (SI No 1377) expressly stipulate that a child must be sent to school or otherwise educated in a satisfactory manner, but presumably a local authority mindful of its duty 'to safeguard and promote the welfare of the child throughout its childhood' (CCA, s 18(1)) will ensure that this is done.

Disputes may occasionally arise with a parent as to what school a child in care should attend especially if he has been assessed as in need of special schooling or is shortly to transfer from primary to secondary school. Section 76 of the Education Act 1944 provides that as a general principle, and so far as this does not incur unreasonable public expense, children should be educated in accordance with the wishes of their parents. In the case of a child in care his parent for the purposes of s 76 is the local authority if a s 3 resolution is in force or the child is the subject of a care order. If a child is only in care under the CCA, s 2 it is obviously good practice for his parents to be consulted and their wishes taken into account on any changeover of schools, so as to avoid any further unnecessary change of schools if and when he leaves care.

3 Medical treatment

It is generally accepted that a parent is under a duty to ensure that his child receives medical attention and treatment when necessary.

Any failure to carry out this duty, resulting in serious consequences, may amount to ill-treatment or neglect sufficient to support a criminal charge under the CYPA 1933, s 1 (*R v Hayles* [1969] 1 QB 364). A local authority has a similar duty in respect of a child in care and this is reflected in the regulations governing boarding-out arrangements and the administration of residential homes.

Thus the Administration of Children's Homes Regulations 1951 (SI No 1217), regs 5 and 6 and the Community Homes Regulations 1972 (SI No 319), reg 5 impose a duty on those running residential homes to arrange medical and dental care for all resident children and to ensure that satisfactory standards of hygiene are maintained in the premises. (These regulations are currently under review and it is likely that new regulations expected shortly will deal in some detail with the health provisions for children in residential care.) The Boarding-out of Children Regulations 1955 (SI No 1377), regs 6 and 7 require similar arrangements to be made for children accommodated in foster homes; they must be medically examined before they are boarded-out and at least once every six months thereafter if they are under the age of two, and once a year in other cases. In addition all foster parents must give an undertaking to

GENERAL MATTERS OF CARE AND UPBRINGING 165

consult a doctor whenever a child is ill and to allow him to be medically examined whenever the authority requires it.

If a s 3 resolution is in force or a child is the subject of a care order then the local authority may clearly consent on his behalf to any medical treatment requiring parental consent, for example, surgery or a blood transfusion. If parental rights are shared by the local authority and a parent (see p 116) the consent of the parent retaining parental rights is not required. If a child has been committed to care in wardship proceedings the consent of the High Court is necessary. If the child is in care under the CCA, s 2 a parent's consent should be obtained to any major medical procedure unless he or she has authorised the local authority to consent on his or her behalf, for example, as a term of any document signed on admission into care. In practice most local authorities will consult a parent on the question of medical treatment even if they have full power to give any consent required. A local authority which is reluctant to override the wishes of a parent regarding medical treatment may seek the guidance of the High Court in wardship proceedings. Thus in *Re P (A Minor)* (1982) 80 LGR 301 a local authority was able to obtain approval for a termination of pregnancy in a fifteen year old girl who was the subject of a care order even though this was against the wishes of her father. A parent is entitled to be informed if his child is seriously ill or has suffered a serious injury and a person in charge of a residential home has a duty to notify him.

A child over the age of sixteen may consent to medical treatment on his own behalf (FLRA 1969, s 8). A child under that age may also give valid consent provided that he is capable of understanding what is proposed and he is able to express his wishes (*Gillick* v *West Norfolk and Wisbech Area Health Authority and Another* [1986] 1 FLR 224). A parent or local authority having parental rights cannot consent to medical treatment on behalf of a child over the age of sixteen years who does not have the capacity to consent. Thus, in *Re B (A Minor)* [1987] 2 WLR 1213 it was necessary to seek the consent of the High Court in wardship proceedings before a sterilisation operation could be performed on a seventeen year old, mentally-handicapped girl.

It was established in the *Gillick* case (above) that a child under the age of sixteen may receive contraceptive advice and treatment without parental consent in exceptional circumstances. Local Authority Circular 86(3) on *Family Planning Services for Young*

People accordingly stipulates that a doctor may provide contraceptive advice and treatment without parental consent if satisfied that:
  (*a*) the child can understand the advice and is mature enough to appreciate the moral, social and emotional implications;
  (*b*) the child is unwilling to tell her parents or let the doctor tell them;
  (*c*) the child is likely to have sexual intercourse with or without contraception;
  (*d*) without contraception the child's physical or mental health is likely to suffer; and
  (*e*) the child's best interests require advice and/or treatment without parental consent.

If a s 3 resolution or a care order is in force parental consent in this context means the consent of the local authority and references to disclosure to a parent should be construed accordingly. If a child has been committed to care in wardship proceedings, parental consent will mean the consent of the High Court.

If a child requires emergency treatment and there is insufficient time to obtain parental consent a doctor has implied consent to do whatever is necessary without running the risk of a trespass action. If a parent refuses to give consent to a life-saving operation or blood transfusion, then a doctor may go ahead and treat the child without consent provided that he obtains the written opinion of a colleague confirming that the child's life will be in danger unless the procedure is carried out (Ministry of Health Circular F/P9/IB, 14 April 1967).

Any person with a legitimate interest in a child who objects to any form of elective medical treatment which he is required to undergo may make the child a ward of court and seek an order prohibiting or terminating the treatment. In *Re D (A Minor) (Wardship: Sterilisation)* [1976] 1 All ER 326, an educational psychologist by this method successfully obtained an injunction prohibiting the sterilisation of an eleven-year old mentally-defective girl, even though her mother had consented to the proposed operation. In this case the child was not in care. The High Court may well have been unwilling to intervene had the child been in care and the relevant consent given by the local authority, although local authorities may be well advised to invoke the wardship jurisdiction themselves when faced with difficult decisions of this nature.

4 Discipline

Corporal punishment

A parent or person acting in loco parentis has a right to exercise discipline over a child in his care and this includes inflicting reasonable physical punishment where circumstances warrant it. The use of punitive measures against children in care who are accommodated in residential homes, however, is strictly controlled.

Regulation 11 of the Administration of Children's Homes Regulations 1951 (SI No 1217) provides that no corporal punishment is to be administered to any girl over the age of ten or any boy over the age of sixteen resident in a voluntary home. A child under the age of ten may be smacked on the hand and a boy over that age may be given six strokes of the cane on his buttocks over his ordinary clothing. No other forms of physical punishment may be administered.

The Community Homes Regulations 1972 (SI No 319) do not specifically mention corporal punishment but reg 10 states that the control of a community home should be maintained by good personal relationships between the staff and children. Where personal contact alone is inadequate to maintain order a local authority is given power to authorise such additional measures as may be necessary to maintain control having regard to the character of the home and the type of children placed there. A scale of additional punitive measures and the circumstances in which they may be used must be approved in advance by the local authority and rigidly adhered to by the person in charge of a community home. A full and permanent record must be kept of all punishment administered.

Each local authority is therefore free to decide whether and to what extent corporal punishment should be used within its own residential homes. Practice obviously varies but a departmental circular published in 1972 (DHSS Circular 18/1972) noted (with approval) a marked decline in the use of corporal punishment in children's homes.

Any unauthorised use of corporal punishment within a community home is a disciplinary matter between the local authority and the staff of the home and, if it is excessive, may also provide grounds for criminal proceedings against the person responsible under the CYPA 1933, s 1.

There is no code governing the disciplinary methods that may be employed by foster parents and they are presumably in much the same position as parents, unless the local authority expressly limits their powers. If there is any evidence that a foster parent is administering excessively harsh punishment then the person supervising the fostering arrangements (usually a local authority social worker) can remove the child immediately.

Restriction of liberty

See p 150 for the manner and extent to which placement in secure accommodation may be used as a disciplinary measure.

5 Access

The right of access has been described as being a right of a child rather than a parent (*M* v *M* [1973] 2 All ER 81). Nevertheless, it is a common area of dispute between local authorities and the parents of children in care.

The Code of Practice, *Access to Children in Care*, published by the Department of Health and Social Security in 1983, lays down certain basic principles to be adopted by local authorities with regard to access generally. The Code is a guide to good practice and has no statutory force. It assumes that the aim of the local authority from the outset will be to return a child in care to a parent, guardian, relative or friend provided that this is consistent with his welfare. From this it follows that local authorities have 'a positive responsibility to promote and sustain access'. It is, however, accepted in the Code that there may be circumstances in which access to a parent or guardian would not be in the child's best interests.

In such cases the Code of Practice recommends that parents should be informed in writing that termination or refusal of access is being considered. At the same time they should be told how to make their views known, what their position is in law and the procedure once a decision has been made. In all cases the Director of Social Services should be involved in making the decision but each local authority is left to formulate its own procedures and to decide the extent to which elected members of the council should be consulted.

Denial or termination of access

Once a decision has been taken to terminate access arrangements or deny access from the outset the local authority must comply with the procedure laid down in Part 1A of the CCA (added by the HSSA, s 6 and Sched 1) unless:

(a) the child is in care under the CCA, s 2 and there is no resolution in force under the CCA, s 3 assuming parental rights and duties, or
(b) the child was committed to care by the High Court, or
(c) the child was committed to care by the county court in matrimonial proceedings.

Part 1A does not apply to children in care under the CCA, s 2 as they may be removed by a parent dissatisfied with access arrangements at any time subject to the requirement for twenty-eight days' notice if the child has been in care for the preceding six months. Both the High Court and the county court (in matrimonial proceedings) may give directions on access when committing a child to care and any problems with regard to access may be referred back to the original court at any subsequent time. Note that Part 1A does apply to children committed to care by a magistrates' court or by a county court in guardianship proceedings (*Re L (Child in Care: Access)* [1986] FLR 95). It also applies to children in the care of voluntary organisations if a resolution has been passed under the CCA, s 64 vesting parental rights in the organisation. Although the CCA, Part 1A does not expressly mention children who are the subject of a parental rights resolution made under s 2 of the Children Act 1948 (now repealed and replaced by the CCA, s 3), the access provisions do apply to these children (*R v Corby Juvenile Court, ex parte M* [1987] FLR 490).

In all cases in which Part 1A does apply the local authority must serve a notice on the child's parent, guardian or custodian (whichever is appropriate) in the prescribed form (see Appendix 1) informing him of his right to apply to a juvenile court for an access order (CCA, s 12B). The notice may be served in person or by post although the Code of Practice recommends that it should be delivered personally by the social worker involved in the case. Postal service is deemed to be effective at the time at which the notice would be delivered in the ordinary course of the post. The decision to terminate access takes effect from the date of service of the notice.

Note that a proposal to substitute new arrangements for existing ones does not amount to a termination of access even if access is to be reduced as a result. Similarly, a decision to postpone access for a reasonable period in order to consider what arrangements, if any, should be made will not amount to a refusal to make access arrangements. There is no statutory definition of what constitutes a reasonable period. In *R v Bolton Metropolitan BC, ex parte B* [1985]

1 FLR 343 it was held that a local authority should make a decision on terminating access within fourteen days, or in exceptional circumstances within twenty-one days. A slightly longer period may be allowed to decide whether access should be denied from the outset if, for example, the local authority needs to seek an expert opinion. The court said, however, that once a decision was reached the local authority must inform the parents and serve the requisite notice without delay. A local authority which fails to serve a notice under s 12B within a reasonable period may be compelled to do so by an order for mandamus made on application for judicial review (see p 188).

A local authority may sometimes make access arrangements which are so limited as to amount to a denial or termination of access. It may be possible to challenge such decisions by judicial review. In *Re M (A Minor) (Wardship: Jurisdiction)* [1985] 1 All ER 745, Cumming-Bruce LJ remarked, obiter, that an order for mandamus might lie against a local authority which granted access at long intervals as a tactic in order to frustrate any possible rehabilitation but prevent a parent from applying for more frequent access.

Application for access order

A parent, guardian or custodian served with a notice terminating or refusing access may apply to the juvenile court for an access order (CCA, s 12C). Parent in this context does not at present include the natural father of an illegitimate child. It is intended that it will do so when the FLRA 1987, Sched 2, para 74 is implemented although a drafting error in that Act at present precludes this. It is anticipated that amending legislation will be enacted before the date of implementation and a natural father will then be able to apply for an access order.

It has already been established that the natural father of an illegitimate child in care will not be granted an access order under s 9 of the Guardianship of Minors Act 1971 (*Re M and H (Minors) (Local Authority: Parental Rights)* [1987] 3 WLR 759 and *Re P (Minors: Access) P v P (Gateshead Metropolitan BC intervening)* (1988) *The Times*, 19 February). Until the implementation of the relevant parts of the FLRA 1987, therefore, he is left without a remedy.

Application is by way of complaint which should be made within six months of the date of service of the notice (*Y v Kirklees BC* [1985] FLR 927). A parent who has not made a complaint to the juvenile court within this time limit can make a fresh request for access to the local authority which will then have to issue a fresh notice of refusal.

The appropriate forum is the juvenile court having jurisdiction in the area of the local authority which served the notice. The proceedings are civil and the procedure at the hearing follows that of proceedings under the CCA, ss 3(6) and 5(4) (see Chapter 12). The parties are the parent, guardian or custodian and the local authority, although the child may also be made a party to the proceedings if this is necessary to safeguard his interests. If the child is made a party, a guardian ad litem should be appointed to represent his interests unless this is deemed to be unnecessary. (The role and duties of the guardian ad litem are discussed more fully at p 40.)

Difficulties may arise when there are concurrent proceedings for adoption in another court. In these circumstances it is for the juvenile court and not the local authority to decide whether the access application should proceed or be adjourned. In *Southwark London BC* v *H* [1985] 2 All ER 657, a juvenile court's decision not to adjourn was upheld on appeal on the basis that the juvenile court provided the only machinery to consider parental access in the circumstances. In *C* v *Berkshire CC* [1987] 2 FLR 210, however, Heilbron J held that there was no general proposition that access proceedings should take precedence. The magistrates had a discretion which they had to exercise judicially and on the basis of sufficient and relevant material. Each case had to turn on its own facts but the welfare of the child was always the paramount consideration.

The court may make an order requiring the local authority to permit access subject to such conditions as the order may specify as to the commencement, frequency, duration and place of access and any other matter which seems appropriate. An order should not specify that access take place at the discretion of the local authority (*Devon CC* v *C* [1985] FLR 1159). The court can continue to control access by making an initial order for a specified period and seeking further reports at the end of that period (*Hereford and Worcester CC* v *EH* [1985] FLR 976).

The welfare of the child must always be the first and paramount consideration in access proceedings. A parent is not automatically entitled to an access order in the absence of evidence that he is not a fit and proper person to have contact with the child (*Hereford and Worcester CC* v *JAH* [1986] FLR 29). Once the jurisdiction of the court is invoked to protect a child, parental privileges do not terminate but become immediately subservient to the paramount consideration which is the welfare of the child (*Re KD (A Minor)* (1988) *The Times*, 19 February).

Variation or suspension of an access order

Once an access order has been made the local authority cannot vary access arrangements without the consent of the juvenile court. Both the local authority and a parent, guardian or custodian may apply for variation or discharge of an order at any time. The local authority may, in addition, apply (ex parte, if necessary) to a single justice who is also a member of the juvenile court panel, for an order suspending the operation of an access order for up to seven days. If the order is suspended the local authority will then be able to apply during the period of suspension for the access order to be varied or discharged and the order will remain suspended until the application has been determined. Before making a suspension order a justice must be satisfied that continued access in accordance with the terms of the order will place the child seriously at risk. The Code of Practice and DHSS Circular (LAC (83)19) on access to children in care both make it clear that this is an emergency procedure to be used when an unexpected crisis occurs.

Appeals

Any party to the proceedings has a right of appeal to the High Court (Family Division) against any decision made by a juvenile court in connection with access. This includes a decision to adjourn an access application pending the outcome of other proceedings (*R v Slough Justices, ex parte B* [1985] 1 FLR 384), and a decision not to adjourn in similar circumstances (*Southwark London BC v H*, cited above).

Procedure is governed by the RSC, Order 55. Appeal is by originating motion and must be entered within twenty-eight days of the date of the decision appealed against. Speed is of the essence in hearing appeals in matters relating to children and the maximum period which should elapse between entry of the appeal and hearing is twenty-eight days (*Hereford and Worcester CC v EH*, cited above). Application should be made for an expedited hearing when the appeal is entered *R v Slough Justices, ex parte B*, cited above). Although the juvenile court has no express statutory power to grant a stay of execution pending appeal it was said in *Hereford and Worcester CC v EH*) that it could do so, although any stay so granted should not usually exceed fourteen days. Thereafter application for a further stay should be made to the High Court.

The appellate court has a discretion to admit new evidence. It may do so, for example, if the evidence is helpful to all concerned and admitted by agreement (*Devon CC* v *C* [1985] FLR 1159). For procedure on appeal generally, see Chapter 14.

An access order will be overruled on appeal if it is plainly wrong on the facts (*Coventry CC* v *J* [1986] 2 FLR 301). Magistrates who reject the recommendation of a guardian ad litem without any reason or justification may also be overruled (*Devon CC* v *C*, cited above). An appellate court can remit a case for rehearing by the juvenile court but it must then specify that the matter be heard by a different bench (*Hereford and Worcester CC* v *JAH*, cited above). A local authority may choose to invoke the wardship jurisdiction of the High Court rather than exercise its right to appeal against an access order. This course was adopted in *Re LH (A Minor) (Wardship: Jurisdiction)* [1986] 2 FLR 306 after magistrates had made an ambiguous and uncertain access order which effectively thwarted the local authority's plans for the child's adoption. Wardship is not available to a parent in these circumstances (see p 187).

Legal aid and costs

Legal aid is available for parents, guardians and custodians (and any child who is made a party to the proceedings) under the civil legal aid scheme. For proceedings in the juvenile court, application should be made to the appropriate Legal Aid General Committee for assistance by way of representation. On appeal application should be made on Form A1 to the Legal Aid Area Secretary. Note that a person who is not eligible for assistance by way of representation on financial grounds may still apply for civil legal aid to cover representation in the juvenile court as the method of determining financial eligibility under the two schemes differs. Application is made on Form A4 to the appropriate Legal Aid General Committee.

Since proceedings are by way of complaint, the juvenile court has the power to order an unsuccessful party to pay all or such part of his opponent's costs as the court considers to be just and reasonable (MCA, s 64).

Complaints procedure

Relatives, however close, have no right to apply for an access order. The Code of Practice does, however, advise that 'consideration of access should take into account the child's wider family'. Siblings, grandparents and putative fathers are specifically mentioned in this context. The Code requires local authorities to set up a complaints procedure for parents who are dissatisfied with access facilities and it is suggested that these also be available to deal with complaints from relatives. Certain guidelines are laid down for all complaints procedures although each authority is left to devise its own system. Thus, all procedures should provide an opportunity for parents (or relatives) to discuss their grievances with a senior officer. If no agreement can be reached arrangements should be made for the situation to be reviewed by the Director of Social Services, and if necessary, elected members of the council.

6 Maintaining contact

A parent of a child in care has no duty to maintain contact with his child but he must keep the local authority informed of his current address unless the child is only committed to care by an interim care order (CCA, ss 9 and 12). Any parent who fails to comply with this requirement is guilty of an offence, punishable on summary conviction by a fine not exceeding £50, unless he can show (in the case of a child in care under the CCA, s 2) that at the material time he was residing with the child's other parent and had reasonable cause to believe that the other parent had kept the authority informed of their address. A parent has no duty to keep a local authority informed of his whereabouts if a child is kept in care beyond the age of eighteen and he will not be guilty of an offence if he is unaware that a care order has been made.

Although a parent has no duty to visit a child in care a local authority may offer financial assistance to any parent who would not otherwise be able to visit the child without suffering undue hardship (CCA, s 26). Parents are generally encouraged to visit their children and all community homes are required to provide suitable visiting facilities for parents, relatives and friends. A local authority has a duty to appoint an independent visitor to visit, advise and befriend any child over the age of five who is the subject of a care order and accommodated in a community home if:

(a) communication with his parent or guardian is so infrequent as to justify the appointment of a visitor; or
(b) he has not lived with or visited or been visited by his parent or guardian during the preceding twelve months; and
(c) in either case he has not been allowed to leave the home within the preceding three months either to attend school or work (CCA, s 11).

A visitor appointed under s 11 must be a person who is entirely independent of the local authority and the community home although he may recover his legitimate expenses from the authority. The Children and Young Persons (Definition of Independent Persons) Regulations 1971 (SI No 486) list persons who may not be appointed visitors. In addition to his general duty to advise, assist and befriend, an independent visitor may apply on the child's behalf for discharge of a care order.

7 Adoption

A local authority has no right to consent to the adoption of a child in care or to an application under the Adoption Act 1976, s 18 freeing a child for adoption.

A court can, however, dispense with the need for parental consent to adoption if a parent:
  (*a*) cannot be found or is incapable of giving consent; or
  (*b*) is withholding consent unreasonably; or
  (*c*) has persistently failed without reasonable cause to discharge the duties of a parent in relation to the child; or
  (*d*) has abandoned or neglected the child; or
  (*e*) has persistently ill-treated the child; or
  (*f*) has seriously ill-treated the child and it is unlikely that the child will ever be rehabilitated in the home again (Adoption Act 1976, s 16(2)).

In many cases the reasons why a child came into care and/or the grounds on which a s 3 resolution was passed may also provide evidence for a subsequent application to dispense with parental consent to adoption.

A local authority which intends to place a child in care for adoption will usually terminate existing access arrangements by notice before seeking an order freeing the child for adoption. If there is an access order in force application should be made to the juvenile court for discharge although there is nothing to preclude a court from making a freeing for adoption order while there is an access order in force. See the Adoption Agencies Regulations 1983 (SI No 1964), reg 7(1)(*a*) and Local Authority Circular (84)(3), para 35 for the procedure to be followed by a local authority acting as an adoption agency in these circumstances.

8 Custodianship

A local authority may consent to an application for a custodianship order in respect of a child who is subject to a care order or a parental rights resolution under the CCA, s 3. The following can apply for a custodianship order in these circumstances:

(*a*) a relative or step-parent (but not a natural parent) applying with the consent of the local authority and with whom the child has had his home for the three months preceding the application;

(*b*) any person who applies with the consent of the local authority and with whom the child has had his home for a period or periods of at least twelve months before the application, including the three months immediately preceding it;

(*c*) any person with whom the child has had his home for a period or periods of at least three years before the application including the three months immediately preceding it, whether or not the local authority consents (CA 1975, s 33(3)).

If a child is in voluntary care under the CCA, s 2 parental consent and not the consent of the local authority is required in appropriate cases.

A custodianship order vests in the applicant(s) the right to legal custody of the child. Unlike adoption the order is revocable and does not sever the child's legal relationship with his natural family. Foster parents may apply for a custodianship order if the child has lived with them for the requisite period.

A custodianship order made with the consent of the local authority can be a means of achieving for a child long-term security and stability in a substitute family in situations in which adoption would be inappropriate. If a foster parent makes an application without the consent of the local authority the child cannot be removed from the foster home during the proceedings without the leave of the court even if there is a care order or parental rights resolution in force. The local authority will, however, have an opportunity to express its opposition to a custodianship order as a party to the proceedings and in the report which it is required to make to the court.

A custodianship order will expire when a child reaches eighteen years of age unless revoked earlier. A local authority may apply for revocation. When an order is revoked the rights of the person entitled to legal custody before the order was made are revived unless the court orders otherwise. If, therefore, the child was originally subject to a care order or a parental rights resolution he will revert to local authority care.

9 Emigration

A local authority cannot procure or assist in procuring the emigration of a child in care without the consent of the Secretary of State for Social Services (CCA, s 24(1)). Consent will not be forthcoming unless the Minister is satisfied that:
  (a) emigration would benefit the child;
  (b) suitable arrangements have been or will be made for the child's reception in his new country;
  (c) his parents or guardian have been consulted or that this is not practicable; and
  (d) the child consents.

If a child is too young to express a proper opinion on the matter the Secretary of State may consent on his behalf if he is either emigrating in the company of or in order to join a parent, guardian relative or friend (CCA, s 24(3) as amended by the HSSA, Sched 2, para 51).

A parent or guardian who has been deprived of his parental rights should still be consulted about a child's proposed emigration. Under the FLRA 1987, s 8(4) (not yet implemented) the natural father of an illegitimate child will also have to be consulted if there is in force an order granting him actual custody of the child or a parental rights order under the FLRA 1987, s 4 whereby actual custody is shared by both parents. A guardian means a person appointed by deed or will or court order (CCA, s 87(1)). A relative means a grandparent, sibling, uncle or aunt of the full or half-blood or by affinity (CCA, s 87(1)). At present it can also include the natural father of an illegitimate child and his relatives within the specified categories but this will no longer be the case once the FLRA 1987, Sched 2, para 79 is implemented. The term 'friend' is not defined in the Act and has its usual meaning; it could include a foster parent.

A local authority should always consider the effect on parental access when it proposes to seek consent to the emigration of a child in care. If emigration would effectively terminate parental access it may be necessary to comply with the procedures laid down in Part

1A of the CCA (see p 168). Applications for ministerial consent should be submitted before any travel arrangements are made.

If the parent of a child in care under the CCA, s 2 wishes to arrange the child's emigration he is free to remove the child from care in order to do so, provided he gives twenty-eight days' notice, if necessary. It may, however, be advantageous, if the local authority approves of the emigration plans, for him to leave the child in care and to apply through the local authority for ministerial consent to emigration. The local authority may then agree to provide some financial assistance towards the cost of emigration, in accordance with its general duty under the CCA, s 1 to provide 'such . . . assistance as may promote the welfare of children by diminishing the need . . . to keep them in care'.

The Secretary of State will require a great deal of information before he consents to the emigration of a child in care. Local Authority Circular No 16/1975 (12 November 1975) stipulates that all applications should, wherever possible, be accompanied by:

(1) a report on the home conditions in the place where the child is going to live including, in the case of a child going to join a parent, guardian, relative or friend, some background detail on that person's circumstances and suitability;
(2) a brief history of the child and his family including details of the child's period in care, his placements, and any special problems he presents;
(3) information on the parents' views of the proposed emigration and whether or not they consent, or, if it has been impracticable to consult them, an explanation to this effect;
(4) information on the child's view of the proposed emigration and confirmation that he consents; and
(5) information about the sources of social-work help in the country to which the child is going in the event of difficulties developing.

Information on conditions abroad is often obtained with the assistance of the International Social Service of Great Britain (Cranmer House, 39 Brixton Road, London SW9 6DD).

10 Travel abroad

Difficulties may arise if a child in care requires a passport to take part, for example, in a school holiday abroad. A child under the age of sixteen may be issued with a separate passport or his particulars may be included on the passport of a parent or relative. A passport will not be issued to a child under the age of eighteen without parental consent. In the case of a child in care the consent of the local authority will be sufficient if a s 3 resolution is in force or the child is the subject of a care order. This is so even if parental rights are vested jointly in the local authority and another person.

If a child is only in care under the CCA, s 2 the consent of the local authority *and* a parent will be required, although the Passport Office may be prepared to accept the consent of the local authority alone if a parent cannot be found or is incapable of giving consent. Any special circumstances should be explained by the local authority in a letter accompanying the application. Each individual case will be considered on its merits but in no case will a passport be issued to a child in care under s 2 if a parent refuses consent.

In some cases a local authority may wish to prevent a child in care from obtaining a passport; it may fear that the child will be snatched from care and taken abroad by a parent or relative. No enquiries are made to ascertain whether a child is in care when an application for a passport is made. An application supported by parental consent may therefore seem perfectly proper on the face of it and a passport may be issued. To prevent this a local authority can, if a child is committed to care by a court order, lodge an objection with the Passport Office which may then refuse to grant the child passport facilities. If a valid passport has already been issued to the child or his particulars have already been included in the valid passport of an adult the Passport Office cannot require the surrender of that passport although it may confiscate it if it comes into its possession for any reason. The Passport Office will only accept an objection based on a court order.

The objection procedure does not apply to the issue of British Visitors' Passports, which may be obtained on personal application from main post offices and are valid for one year for holiday travel to certain Western European countries, Bermuda and Canada.

11 Legal proceedings

Criminal

A juvenile court when dealing with a child in care who has committed a criminal offence has the usual sentencing powers applicable to any child. Magistrates should not, however, make a care order in criminal proceedings if there is already in force a matrimonial care order; the appropriate procedure is to adjourn any criminal proceedings so that the existing care order can be discharged (*W v Heywood* [1985] FLR 1064). It is not clear whether this also applies if the existing care order was made under CYPA 1969, s 1 (but not on the offence ground) as s 20(2A) of the same Act seems to envisage the making of a further care order when there is already one in existence.

It may be particularly important to the court to impose a care order in criminal proceedings as it will then have additional powers to deal with the child if he commits a further offence. Thus if a child is already the subject of a care order made in criminal proceedings or after the offence condition has been found proved and he commits a further offence punishable by imprisonment in an adult, the court may make an order under s 20A of the CYPA 1969 as an alternative to a custodial sentence. The effect of such an order is to preclude the local authority from releasing the child into the charge of a parent, guardian, relative or friend for a period of up to six months. As an alternative the court can direct that the child may only be released into the charge of a specified parent, guardian, relative or friend. An order under s 20A can only be made if the child is legally represented, unless he has refused to apply for legal aid or his application has been rejected on financial grounds. If the child commits a further offence punishable by imprisonment in an adult while an order under s 20A is in force the court may extend the restriction for a further period not exceeding six months. The court may only exercise its powers under this section if the seriousness of the offence warrants it and if no other method of dealing with the child is appropriate.

Both the child and the local authority have a right of appeal to the Crown Court against an order made under s 20A (CYPA 1969, s 20A(7) and MCA 1980, s 108). In addition, the local authority and the child (or his parent or guardian on his behalf) may apply to the juvenile court for the order to be varied or revoked.

A local authority cannot be ordered to pay compensation under the CYPA 1933, s 55 if a child in its care is found guilty of a criminal offence (*Leeds City Council v West Yorkshire Metropolitan Police and Others* [1982] 1 All ER 274). The victim of the crime must instead rely on his remedy in civil law or make claim for compensation under the Criminal Injuries Compensation Scheme.

If the authority has actually transferred the charge and control of a child in care to a parent, guardian, relative or friend in accordance with the CCA, s 21(2), that person may be ordered to pay compensation under s 55. An arrangement whereby a child merely returns

GENERAL MATTERS OF CARE AND UPBRINGING 181

home for a short visit will not amount to a transfer of control so as to render a parent liable to pay compensation if the child commits an offence during the visit.

Civil

A person under the age of eighteen cannot bring or defend civil proceedings. He must act through an adult known as his 'next friend' if he is the plaintiff in the proceedings, and his 'guardian ad litem' if he is the defendant. In normal circumstances a child's next friend or guardian ad litem is a parent or guardian, or possibly a relative or family friend. A child in care who wants to institute civil proceedings because, for example, he has been injured in a motor accident, may not be able to call upon any of the usual people to act as his next friend.

In such cases a local authority, being a legal person capable of bringing or defending proceedings, may step in and act as next friend or guardian ad litem since it has a statutory power 'to do anything which is . . . incidental to the discharge of any of its functions' (Local Government Act 1972, s 111). If a s 3 resolution is in force or a child is committed to care by a care order it is clearly incidental to the local authority's functions as a 'parent' to bring or defend proceedings on the child's behalf if necessary.

If an authority is reluctant to act, the Official Solicitor may always be asked to act on the child's behalf and he may also be asked to replace a parent already acting as next friend who has failed to conduct the proceedings properly or with due expedition.

Apart from acting on behalf of a child in its care a local authority may also be involved directly in civil proceedings arising out of the child's actions. If, for example, the authority has failed to exercise proper supervision over the child with the result that he causes damage to others, an action may lie against the authority for negligence (*Home Office* v *Dorset Yacht Co Ltd* [1970] 2 All ER 294; *Vicar of Writtle and Another* v *Essex CC* (1979) 77 LGR 656).

A child in care may claim damages against foster parents if he is injured as a result of their negligence. No action will lie against the local authority which is not vicariously liable for the negligence of foster parents (*S* v *Walsall Metropolitan BC* [1985] 3 All ER 294). A local authority may be liable if a child is injured in local authority accommodation but this will depend on the circumstances giving rise to the injury.

12 Consent to marriage

Parental consent is required to the marriage of any child between the ages of sixteen and eighteen. If a child in care under the CCA, s 2 wishes to get married the consent of the local authority is not required and parental consent should be obtained in the usual way. If a s 3 resolution is in force, only the consent of the local authority is required. If the child is committed to care by a care order, the usual practice is to require the consent of the local authority and the parent(s). (See the Marriage Act 1949, Sched 2 as amended by the FLRA 1987, s 9 (not yet implemented), for the usual consents required to the marriage of a minor.)

When notice of marriage involving a minor is given, a superintendent-registrar has a duty to establish whose consent is required by questioning the parties to the proposed marriage or by other means. He may refuse to issue a licence or certificate for the marriage until satisfied that all necessary consents have been obtained (Family Law Reform Act 1969, s 2(3)).

If a child in care under the CCA, s 2, or committed to care by a care order, wishes to marry but cannot obtain parental consent because the whereabouts of his parents are unknown or they are incapable of giving consent, the Registrar-General may dispense with this requirement or a court may on application give the necessary consent (Marriage Act 1949, s 3(1)(*a*)).

If a parent or a local authority refuses to give consent a child may apply to a magistrates' court, a county court or to the High Court for consent to marry (Marriage Act 1949, s 3(1)(*b*)).

Although care proceedings cannot be commenced in respect of a child who is or has been married, the subsequent marriage of a child in care will not determine an existing care order or parental rights resolution.

13 Welfare benefits

Parent's entitlement to benefit

A parent's entitlement to certain welfare benefits is affected if a child dependant is admitted to care.

> *Child benefit*—A parent is not entitled to child benefit in respect of a child for any week in which the child is in the care of a local authority under CCA, s 2 or by reason of a care order made under the CYPA 1969 (Child Benefit Act 1975, Sched 1, para 1, and

Child Benefit (General) Regulations 1976 (SI No 965), reg 16(5)). Where a parent is entitled to child benefit in a particular week and the child then goes into care, benefit will continue to be payable for the first eight weeks of his absence after which it will be discontinued even if the parent is contributing voluntarily or by court order to his maintenance (reg 16(6)(*a*)). For the purposes of this rule a week means from midnight on Sunday to midnight on the following Sunday.

After a child has been in care for eight weeks child benefit may be payable to any person with whom he stays on a visit which lasts a complete week, or with whom he normally lives for at least one complete day (midnight to midnight) in each week, provided that these weekly visits are arranged on a long-term basis (reg 16(6)(*b*)). In no circumstances can a foster parent with whom a child is boarded out by a local authority claim child benefit (reg 16(8)).

Social security benefits—A parent who is entitled to a social security (national insurance) benefit eg unemployment or sickness benefit, can only claim an increase for a child dependant if he is also entitled to claim child benefit for that child. The position regarding dependency increases for children in care is therefore governed by the Child Benefit Act 1975 and Child Benefit (General) Regulations 1976 (see above).

Income support—A child's requirements can only be aggregated with those of his parent for supplementary benefit purposes if he is actually living in the parent's household.

If a child under the age of sixteen is allowed to return to his parents' home for a holiday or for a trial period while still in care, his requirements can be aggregated with those of his parents for income support purposes, since there is no statutory provision for the local authority to contribute towards his maintenance in such circumstances. The same applies to a young person in care aged sixteen or over who is continuing in full-time education.

Child's entitlement to benefit

A young person aged sixteen or over who has completed his secondary education may normally claim income support in his own right if he is unemployed or is prevented from working by illness. This also applies to a young person in the care of a local authority.

It is likely that the age at which a young person can claim benefit will be raised from sixteen to eighteen years in the near future. Young people between these ages will be expected to accept a place on the government's Youth Training Scheme. There will be a discretionary power to allow payment of benefit to those under eighteen in cases of severe hardship. Young people who have been in care for more than two years are likely to be included in this category.

14 After-care

A local authority's duty to a child in care does not automatically terminate when the child leaves care. It can, and in certain circumstances must, continue to provide support, both material and moral, to children formerly in care, in some cases until they reach the age of twenty-one.

Duty to advise and befriend

A local authority has a duty to advise and befriend all children within its area who are over minimum school-leaving age (at present sixteen) but under the age of eighteen, and were either in local authority care under the CCA, s 2, or in the care of a voluntary organisation at the time they reached school-leaving age, or at any subsequent time, but who are no longer in care (CCA, ss 28 and 69). The duty to advise and befriend does not arise if the local authority is satisfied that the child's welfare does not require it. A voluntary organisation with the necessary facilities can make its own arrangements for after-care and the local authority will then be relieved of this duty. The Child Care Act 1980 contains provisions to ensure that the duty to advise and befriend is transferred from one local authority to another if a child moves, provided that he notifies the local authority of his change of address.

Accommodation and maintenance

A local authority may contribute towards the cost of accommodating and maintaining any person between the ages of seventeen and twenty-one in any place where he is working, seeking a job or receiving full-time education or training if he was in care when he reached school-leaving age and is no longer in care (CCA, s 27). Accommodation can be provided in a community home (CCA, s 72), and contributions towards maintenance may take the form of a grant which may continue beyond the recipient's twenty-first birthday if he is in the middle of a course at the time, or has had to interrupt his education or training for any reason. A young person formerly or still in care can, of course, apply for a grant for higher education in the usual way. For the purposes of assessment he will be treated as a child of parents without resources to pay for his education (Local Authorities and Local Education Authorities (Allocation of Functions) Regulations 1951 (SI No 472)). He may also participate in the various government training schemes.

A local authority can guarantee any deed of apprenticeship or articles of clerkship entered into by a child in care under the CCA, s 2, a care order under the CYPA 1969 and a care order made by a magistrates' court in matrimonial proceedings (CCA, s 23 and Sched 4, para 3).

Help on request

A local authority may visit, advise, befriend and, in exceptional circumstances, provide financial assistance to any person between the ages of seventeen and twenty-one who left care after his seventeenth birthday and who requests such assistance (CCA, s 29).

15 Death of a child in care

If a child in care dies in a voluntary or community home the person in charge of the home has a duty to notify any parent or guardian whose whereabouts are known. If the child dies in a foster home or in hospital then the duty falls upon the local authority in most cases, although this is not expressly stated.

The local authority can arrange for the child to be buried or cremated unless cremation is contrary to the tenets of his religion. If the child was under the age of sixteen the cost of burial may be recovered from either parent (CCA, s 25).

A local authority can pay the travelling, subsistence and other expenses of a parent, relative or any other person who wishes to attend the child's funeral but cannot afford to do so (CCA, s 26).

Chapter 20

Resolution of disputes

While a child is in care disputes may arise between the local authority and a parent or relative or between the local authority and the child himself. Some disputes may be resolved by informal contact between the aggrieved parties and officers of the local authority. Some authorities have a formal complaints procedure involving senior officers and/or elected members. The Code of Practice: Access to Children in Care (see p 168) requires local authorities to set up a complaints procedure for parents who are dissatisfied with access facilities and suggests that this also be available to deal with complaints from relatives.

If a dispute cannot be resolved by formal or informal procedures within the local authority there are several options, some less effective than others.

1 Local Government Ombudsman

The Local Government Ombudsman (properly known as the Commissioner for Local Administration) investigates complaints of maladministration within local authorities. Complaints no longer have to be submitted first to a local councillor but may now be referred to the Ombudsman direct.

The procedure is of limited use in child care cases for several reasons. First, the Ombudsman cannot consider the merits of any decision made by a local authority; he can only review the procedure by which that decision was reached. He does not usually have any special expertise in child care law and the welfare of the child will not be his paramount consideration. The adjudication process itself may be lengthy and even if a complaint is proved the Ombudsman cannot overturn a local authority's decision although he may make recommendations.

2 Wardship

Recent cases have now firmly established the principle that a parent or relative cannot use wardship proceedings to challenge the decision of a local authority relating to a child in its care (*Re M (An Infant)* [1961] 1 All ER 788; *A v Liverpool City Council* [1982] AC 363, HL; *Re W (A Minor) Wardship: Jurisdiction)* [1985] AC 791, HL).

The High Court will not exercise its wardship jurisdiction to interfere with the exercise of those powers and duties which Parliament has entrusted to local authorities by statute. This principle does not just apply where there is a care order in force or the local authority has passed a resolution assuming parental rights. It has been held to apply when there is only an interim care order in force (*Re W (A Minor) (Wardship: Jurisdiction)*, cited above); when care proceedings have been commenced in the juvenile court but no order yet made (*Re E (A Minor) (Wardship: Court's Duty)* [1984] FLR 457); and when care proceedings have not yet been commenced but would undoubtedly succeed (*W v Shropshire CC* [1986] 2 FLR 359).

At one time it was thought that wardship jurisdiction would be exercised where existing statutory provision appeared to leave a lacuna in the law. Following the decision of the House of Lords in *Re W* above this may no longer be the case. The courts have now decided that the proper remedy where a local authority has abused its powers or has acted in breach or disregard of its statutory obligations is to apply for judicial review (*Re DM (A Minor) (Wardship: Jurisdiction)* [1986] 2 FLR 122; *Re RM and LM (Minors) (Wardship Jurisdiction)* [1986] 2 FLR 205; *Re S (A Minor) (Care Proceedings: Wardship Summons)* [1987] 1 FLR 479). It is, however, recognised that judicial review may not be the best remedy in the circumstances and in *R v Newham London BC, ex parte McL* (1987) *The Times*, 25 July it was suggested that judges, when granting leave to apply for judicial review, should add a recommendation, in appropriate cases, that wardship proceedings be commenced by agreement. This would have no binding effect but could persuade a local authority to invite or agree to the exercise of wardship jurisdiction in appropriate cases.

It is always open to a local authority to consent to the use of wardship to resolve disputes even in cases where the jurisdiction would not otherwise be exercisable (*A v B and Hereford and Worcester CC* [1986] 1 FLR 289). An authority can also invoke the jurisdiction itself to supplement its powers when these cannot adequately protect a child or to assist when it is faced with decisions of a particularly difficult or sensitive nature (*Re B (A Minor) (Wardship: Child in Care)* [1975] 2 WLR 302). Thus in *Re P (A Minor)* (1982) LGR 301 a local authority used wardship to obtain judicial approval for a termination of pregnancy in a fifteen year old girl subject to a care order, contrary to the wishes of her father.

If a child was originally committed to care in wardship proceedings the local authority must exercise its statutory powers subject to any directions which the High Court may give (FLRA 1969, s 7(3)). It must also consult the court on all major decisions which affect the child's welfare (*Re CB (A Minor) (Wardship: Local Authority)* [1981] 1 All ER 16). A parent will usually be a party to these proceedings and will therefore have an opportunity to be heard. The main advantage of wardship in tandem with care for a local authority is that it gives immediate recourse to the High Court, if necessary.

Note that wardship jurisdiction may also be invoked by a local authority:

(*a*) to secure a child's compulsory admission into care where no grounds exist to proceed under the CYPA 1969, s 1;
(*b*) as an indirect means of 'appealing' against a juvenile court's decision to discharge a care order or a finding that the case for such an order has not been made out, there being no statutory right of appeal;
(*c*) to prevent a parent from removing a child who has been in voluntary care under the CCA, s 2 for less than six months in circumstances where the child's return has been requested and there are no grounds for passing a resolution under the CCA, s 3;
(*d*) to retain in care a child who has been in the care of the local authority for less than three years when there are no grounds for passing a resolution under the CCA, s 3.

3 Judicial review

A local authority decision relating to a child in care may be challenged by application for judicial review. Application can only be made by a person with sufficient interest in the matter to which it relates (RSC Order 53, r 3(7)). A parent, relative, foster parent and the child himself could fall into this category. For procedure generally, see p 94.

On judicial review the court will only be concerned with the decision making process and not the merits of the decision itself. It will only intervene if the local authority has:
  (a) reached a decision based upon an error of law, or
  (b) acted improperly by failing to follow proper and fair procedures; or
  (c) acted unreasonably by reaching a decision which defies logic or accepted moral standards (per Lord Roskill in *Council of Civil Service Unions and Others* v *Minister for Civil Service* [1985] AC 374).

A local authority will act improperly if it fails to consider all the relevant matters (*Associated Provincial Picture Houses Ltd* v *Wednesbury Corporation* [1948] 1 KB 223).

Thus in *R* v *Bedfordshire CC, ex parte C* [1987] 1 FLR 239 a local authority decision not to place children with their father was quashed because it was found to be based on unsubstantiated allegations against the father which he was not given an opportunity to rebut. In another case heard at the same time (*R* v *Bedfordshire CC, ex parte B* [1987] 1 FLR 239) a local authority decision to remove a child from a placement 'at home on trial' was not quashed because it was found to be based on evidence from various agencies and not just on one incident of drunkenness on the part of the mother. The court's concern in each case was not whether the decision was right or fair but whether it was made in a fair manner.

The welfare of the child is of no concern to a court hearing an application for judicial review and this is the principal disadvantage of the procedure. The court cannot substitute its own decision for that of the local authority. The two orders which it is most likely to grant are certiorari (quashing the decision of a local authority) and mandamus (directing the authority to comply with its statutory duties). The effect in each case will be to remit the matter to the local authority for fresh consideration. This may result in further delay in making decisions which vitally affect a child's future.

The unsatisfactory nature of judicial review proceedings as a means of resolving disputes in child care cases has been recognised judicially (see *R* v *Newham London BC, ex parte McL*, cited above). Parents and relatives have little option, however, now that wardship proceedings are all but barred to them.

4 Action for breach of duty

A claim for damages may lie against a local authority which has acted in breach of its statutory duties. An authority will also owe a common law duty of care when exercising its social services functions although this may be limited in scope by lack of resources or the need to act urgently. In most cases it is the child in care rather than a parent to whom a statutory duty is owed and it is therefore for the child to bring any proceedings for breach of that duty. For this reason, proceedings are usually brought after a child has grown-up and left care and problems may arise in obtaining disclosure of the relevant case records. This was the position in *Gaskin* v *Liverpool City Council* (see p 160) although many local authorities now operate a voluntary 'open files' policy which should help considerably (see Access to information—p 160).

In *Guevera* v *London Borough of Hounslow* (1987) JSWL 374 whilst it was confirmed that a local authority could be liable to pay damages for breach of statutory duty it was held that the proper procedure was to apply for judicial review. Damages may be awarded on a successful application for judicial review together with one of the prerogative orders.

5 European Court of Human Rights

The European Convention of Human Rights, to which the United Kingdom is a party, establishes certain basic human rights. Article 8 of the Convention protects a person's right to a private and family life and Article 6 provides the right to a fair hearing in the determination of a person's civil rights and obligations.

The European Commission on Human Rights and the European Court of Human Rights exist to investigate alleged violations of these fundamental rights and to ensure that the Convention is observed by member states. Any individual who claims that his rights under the Convention have been violated may complain to the Commission provided that he has exhausted all domestic remedies available to him.

The Commission will investigate the facts and decide whether these disclose a breach of the Convention by the state concerned. The Commission may then make proposals at this stage to ensure compliance with the Convention. The individual case may then be referred to the European Court of Human Rights for a decision on its merits. Whilst the Commission can direct a member state to alter its domestic law to comply with its treaty obligations, it cannot overrule any decision which has already been made. The powers of the European Court are similarly restricted although it may award compensation against a member state.

The machinery of the Convention has been used to challenge local authority actions relating to children in care, particularly with regard to access (see *O, H, W, B and R v UK* (1987) *The Times*, 9 July). The procedure is nevertheless unsatisfactory as a means of resolving individual disputes. It may take many years for a case to reach final adjudication and even then a decision which violates an individual's rights under the Convention cannot be reversed. Monetary compensation in these circumstances may be of little value.

Applications under the Convention have, however, led to important changes in child care legislation in England and Wales in recent years. The provisions of Part 1A of the CCA 1980 governing access to children in care (see p 168) and the Secure Accommodation Regulations (see p 150) are examples of this.

Part V

Future Developments

Chapter 21

Proposed reform of child care law

In January 1987 the Government published a White Paper (Cm 62) setting out its proposals for the reform of child care law in England and Wales. Legislation has yet to be introduced to implement these proposals but it is anticipated in the near future. The proposals take into account the recommendations of the Inter-departmental Working Party on Child Care Law published in September 1985 (Review of Child Care Law, DHSS, September 1985). The present Lord Chancellor has expressed his support for the proposals in the White Paper and indicated that the attention of the Government will turn to the establishment of a Family Court once the substantive changes in child care law have been achieved. The following summary highlights the main changes proposed.

1 Investigation of child abuse

Local authorities are to have a more active duty to investigate in any case where it is suspected that a child is suffering harm or likely to do so. Statutory and voluntary agencies will have a legal duty to co-operate in the investigation of harm and the protection of children at risk.

2 Emergency protection orders

The emergency protection order will replace the present place of safety order. Any person will be able to apply to a magistrate for an order if there is reasonable cause to believe that damage to a child's health or wellbeing is likely unless he can be immediately removed to or detained in a place of protection.

The respective obligations and powers of the applicant, local authority and parent during the period of an emergency protection order will be more clearly defined than at present. The applicant will have the responsibilities of a parent with actual custody of the child. There will be a specific requirement to notify parents of the making of an order and a presumption of access unless specified otherwise by the magistrate. If the applicant is not a local authority, he or she will have to inform the relevant local authority of the order with details of the arrangements made for the child's care. The local authority will then be able to apply for a transfer of the order if this would be in the child's interests.

The maximum duration of an order will be eight days. In exceptional cases a local authority may apply on notice for a further extension of up to seven days but this may be challenged by the parents or child.

The present power of the police to detain in a place of safety without recourse to a magistrate will be retained but limited to 72 hours instead of eight days. The police will have power to apply on notice to a single magistrate or a juvenile court for an extension of up to eight days from the date on which the initial detention began.

3 Care proceedings

The present power of the police and local education authorities to initiate care proceedings will be removed. Only local social services authorities and the NSPCC will have this power. There will be a positive duty to consult the local education authority if a child who is the subject of care proceedings has a history of poor school attendance. In other cases of non-school attendance, where care proceedings are not appropriate, local education authorities will be able to apply for a special supervision order relating to educational need.

The present specific grounds for making an order in care proceedings will be replaced by new general grounds. A court will be able to make an order if satisfied:
    (*a*) that there is evidence of harm or likely harm to the child, and
    (*b*) that this is attributable to the absence of a reasonable standard of parental care or the child is beyond parental control, and
    (*c*) that the order proposed is the most effective means available to the court of safeguarding the child's welfare.

The inclusion of likely harm in the new grounds is intended to eliminate the present need for recourse to wardship proceedings in certain cases and will cover children in care on a voluntary basis where a return home is likely to cause harm. The test of a reasonable standard of parental care will be an objective one.

Anyone whose legal position could be affected by the proceedings will be entitled to party status. This will include any person who is able to seek legal responsibility for the child and wishes to do so. The court will have power to call as witnesses others who may have important evidence, opinions or views to contribute.

A local authority (or the NSPCC) will have a duty to disclose its case in advance of the hearing. A party contesting an application will have to disclose an outline of its reasons. Each party will have to disclose in advance all documents it proposes to rely on at the hearing.

There will be a partial relaxation of the doctrine of privilege. For example, where a party already has a copy of a privileged document it will be possible to rely on this in evidence at the hearing. A guardian ad litem will have a statutory right of access to all records, privileged or otherwise. The use of hearsay evidence as permitted under the Civil Evidence Acts 1968 and 1972 will be allowed.

The present duty to appoint a guardian ad litem wherever there is a conflict of interest between a parent and child will be replaced by a positive duty to appoint in all cases except where this appears unnecessary in order to safeguard a child's interests.

4 Interim care orders

The court will only have power to make an interim care order after care proceedings have been commenced and if:
 (a) there is reasonable cause to believe that the first two limbs of the grounds for a full order may exist, and
 (b) the power to remove or detain the child is necessary in order to safeguard his welfare during the interim period.

The maximum duration of an interim order will be eight weeks with power to apply for extensions of up to fourteen days in exceptional circumstances.

5 Supervision orders

The court will have the power to impose conditions on a parent rather than just the child when making a supervision order. Thus a parent may be ordered to permit a supervisor to have access to the child, to allow the child to be medically examined or treated, to comply with a supervisor's direction with regard to the child's education and so on.

6 Custody orders

The court will have power to make a custody order between parents or spouses or in favour of a third party, eg a grandparent, if either the third party is qualified to apply for a custodianship order or the first two elements of the new ground for an order are made out and a custody order would be the most effective way of protecting the child. In the latter case a custody order will usually be coupled with a supervision order in favour of the local authority.

7 Discharge of care orders

Before discharging a care order the court will have to be satisfied that this would be in the child's best interests and that if control is needed (to protect the public as well as the child) it will be provided.

8 Appeals

All parties to the original proceedings will have a right of appeal. This will be to the High Court, Family Division and not to the Crown Court as at present.

If a court of first instance makes a decision which would result in a child leaving care pending appeal, it will have power to grant a stay of its decision for a specified period. In other cases, where a court refuses to make a care order, an application may be made for an emergency protection order if there is immediate risk to the child. In addition, the appellate court will have power to make an interim care order.

9 Duties of local authority

Local authorities will have a statutory obligation to safeguard and promote the health, development, education and welfare of children in care and, in particular, to afford them opportunities for the proper development of their characters and abilities. They will be required to set up procedures with an independent element to resolve disputes and complaints from either the child or parents. Whilst a care order will pass all parental powers and responsibilities to the local authority it will still be required to inform and consult parents on all major decisions affecting the child unless this would not be in the child's best interests.

There will be a legal presumption of reasonable access. Local authorities will be encouraged to agree access arrangements at an early stage so that any disputes can be dealt with by the court when making a care order. The court will have power to determine what is reasonable access. A local authority wishing to vary an order will have to refer the matter back to court if a parent or child objects to its proposals.

Local authorities will have a duty to advise and assist children in care so as to promote their welfare when that care ends. The existing power to advise and befriend those who leave care on leaving school will be extended to apply to young people up to the age of twenty-one years instead of eighteen years as at present.

10 Unauthorised removal from care

In relation to children subject to a care order or an emergency protection order, there will be a single offence consisting of knowingly or without reasonable excuse or lawful authority:

(*a*) taking the child, or
(*b*) detaining or harbouring him, or
(*c*) assisting, inducing or inciting him to run away.

The present power to arrest an absconding child without a warrant will be abolished in respect of children committed to care in civil proceedings. In its place a local authority will be able to seek an order authorising a police officer, a court officer or a specified person to take charge of an absconding child. The court will have power to compel disclosure by any person who may have relevant information about a missing child. If it has reasonable cause to believe that any person intends to remove or detain a child without permission, it may order him not to do so.

11 Voluntary care

Local authorities will no longer be able to assume parental rights and powers over children in voluntary care by administrative resolution. If compulsory powers are required a care order will have to be sought in appropriate cases. In urgent cases, it will be possible to apply for an emergency protection order. If a child has been abandoned the local authority will be able to apply for guardianship under the Guardianship of Minors Act 1971.

There will be a substantial change of emphasis in the provision of care on a voluntary basis. Whilst local authorities will continue to have specific statutory responsibilities to children in voluntary care these will have to be carried out as far as possible in partnership with parents. To this end parents will no longer be required to give twenty-eight days' notice of their intention to remove a child who has been in voluntary care for more than six months.

Appendix 1
Forms

(Prescribed forms are reproduced as in Schedule 2 to the Magistrates' Courts (Children and Young Persons) Rules 1970 although forms in use in most juvenile courts vary slightly from the prescribed form and may differ from court to court)

APPENDIX 1

Notice of care proceedings (Form 7 CYPR):

To the Clerk of the Juvenile Court sitting at

Take notice that A.B. of   (hereinafter called the relevant infant), who is believed to be a child/young person, is to be brought before the Court under section 1 of the Children and Young Persons Act 1969 on the grounds hereinafter mentioned.

It is alleged that the following condition is satisfied with respect to the relevant infant, that is to say, (*specify in the terms of section* 1(2)(*a*) *to* (*f*) *identifying, in the case of paragraph* (*f*), *the offence*).

It is further alleged that the relevant infant is in need of care or control which he is unlikely to receive unless an order is made under the said section 1.

In pursuance of Rule 14 of the Magistrates' Courts (Children and Young Persons) Rules 1970 a copy of this notice is being sent to each of the following persons, that is to say, to:—

Dated the   day of   , 19 .
                                  C.D.,
    [On behalf of the council of the
      county/county borough of   ].
    [A constable].
    [An authorised person].

Notice of care proceedings under CYPA 1969, s 1(2)(b) when court is required to make a finding in respect of a child not before the court:

To the Clerk of the Juvenile Court sitting at

Take notice that A.B. of   (hereinafter called the relevant infant) who is believed to be a child/young person, is to be brought before the Court under section 1 of the Children and Young Persons Act 1969 on the grounds hereinafter mentioned.

It is alleged that the following condition is satisfied with respect to the relevant infant, that is to say, it is probable that the condition set out in section 1(2)(*a*) of the Children and Young Persons Act 1969 will be satisfied in his case having regard to the fact (which the court will be asked to find) that the condition was satisfied in the case of another child who was a member of the household to which he belongs.

It is further alleged that the relevant infant is in need of care or control which he is unlikely to receive unless an order is made under the said section 1.

In pursuance of Rule 14 of the Magistrates' Courts (Children and Young Persons) Rules 1970 a copy of this notice is being sent to each of the following persons, that is to say, to:—

Dated the   day of   , 19   .
                                  C.D.,
          [On behalf of the council of the
            county/county borough of   ].
          [A constable].
          [An authorised person].

APPENDIX 1

Notice of application to vary/discharge a care/supervision order:

To the Clerk of the Juvenile Court sitting at

Take notice that A.B. of   (hereinafter called the relevant infant) who is believed to be a child/young person, is to be brought before the Juvenile Court at   on the   day of   , 19 , at   a.m./p.m. under s 15[21] of the Children and Young Persons Act 1969.

The grounds of the application are that it is appropriate to vary/discharge the supervision/care order made on the   day of   , 19 , in respect of the relevant infant.

[It is further alleged that the relevant infant is in need of care or control which he is unlikely to receive unless the court makes an order under s 15].

In pursuance of Rule 14 of the Magistrates' Courts (Children and Young Persons) Rules 1970 a copy of this notice is being sent to each of the following persons, that is to say, to:

Dated the   day of   , 19 .
                    C.D.
       [on behalf of the council of the
         county/county borough of   ].
       [the relevant infant]
       [the parent/guardian of the relevant infant]
       [supervisor]

Summons: care proceedings and proceedings in respect of supervision order (Form 4 CYPR):

In the [county of   . Petty Sessional Division of   ].

To A.B. (hereinafter called the relevant infant) [and E.F. his/her parent/guardian] of

[The council of the county/county borough of   ] [C.D. a constable/an authorised person] [C.D. the relevant infant's supervisor] having given notice that the relevant infant is to be brought before the court under section [1][15] of the Children and Young Persons Act 1969 on grounds specified in the notice:

And application having been duly made in that behalf to [me the undersigned] [*or state name*] [Justice of the Peace] [Clerk to the Justices]:

You are hereby summoned [each of you] to appear on   day, the   day of   , 19 , at the hour of   in the noon before the Juvenile Court sitting at   to attend proceedings brought in pursuance of the said notice.

Date the   day of   , 19 .

J.P.,

Justice of the Peace for the [county] first above mentioned.

[*or* This summons was issued by the above-named justice of the peace.

J.C.,
Clerk of the Magistrates' Court sitting at   .]
[*or* J.C.,
Clerk to the Justices for the Petty Sessional Division aforesaid.]

APPENDIX 1

Summons for the attendance of parent or guardian of child or young person: care proceedings and proceedings in respect of supervision order (Form 5 CYPR):

In the [county of . Petty Sessional Division of].

To E.F. being a parent/guardian of A.B. (hereinafter called the relevant infant), who is believed to be a child/young person, of

[The council of the county/county borough of] [C.D. a constable/an authorised person] [C.D. the relevant infant's supervisor] having given notice that the relevant infant is to be brought before the court under section [1][15] of the Children and Young Persons Act 1969 on the grounds specified in the notice:

And application having been duly made in that behalf to [me the undersigned] [*or state name*] [Justice of the Peace] [Clerk to the Justices]:

You are hereby summoned to appear on day, the day of , 19 , at the hour of in the noon before the Juvenile Court sitting at to attend proceedings brought in pursuance of the said notice.

Date the day of , 19 .
J.P.,

Justice of the Peace for the [county] first above mentioned. [*or* This summons was issued by the above-named justice of the peace.

J.C.,
Clerk of the Magistrates' Court sitting at .]
[*or* J.C.,
Clerk to the Justices for the Petty
Sessional Division aforesaid.]

Notice of appeal to the Crown Court against finding and/or order made under CYPA 1969, s 1:

TO: The Clerk of the   Juvenile Court (*address*)

AND TO: The County/County Borough
of   (*address*)

    We,   of   , solicitors for A.B. of   , do hereby give you and each of you notice that it is his intention to appeal to the Crown Court sitting at   against [*either*] the finding of the Juvenile Court sitting at   on the   day of   19   , that he is (*here specify the finding in the terms of CYPA 1969, s 1(2)(a) to (f) identifying in the case of paragraph (f), the offence*) and that he is in need of care or control which he is unlikely to receive unless the court makes an order under section 1 of the Children and Young Persons Act 1969 and against the care/supervision/hospital/guardianship order made therein [*or*] the care/supervision/hospital/guardianship order made by the Juvenile Court sitting at   on the   day of   19   , under section 1 of the Children and Young Persons Act 1969.

    And that the general grounds of appeal are:

Dated the   day of   19 .

      (Signed)

      Solicitor for the above named Appellant

APPENDIX 1

Summons to discharge an interim care order under CYPA 1969, s 22 (Form 107, Supreme Court Practice Vol 2 Appendix A):

In the High Court of Justice,
  Queen's Bench Division.

Let all parties concerned attend the judge in chambers on the   day of   19 , at   o'clock, on the hearing of an   application on behalf of A.B. for the discharge of an interim order made on the   day of   by a juvenile court sitting at   [or by C.D. a justice of the peace for the petty sessions area of   ].

Dated the   day of   19 .

This summons was taken out by   , of   [agent for   of   ] solicitor for the said A.B.

Notice to parent under rule 22 (Form 8 CYPR):

To C.B. of

Take notice that I have complained to the Juvenile Court sitting at   for an order against the council of the county/county borough of   , directing them to bring A.B. before the court on the ground that I am unable to control him/her.

The complaint will be heard by the Court on   day, the   day of   , 19   , at the hour of   in the   noon.

You may if you wish speak to the Court about him/her before the Court reaches a decision upon the complaint.

(Signed) B.B.

APPENDIX 1

Authority to remove to a place of safety (Form 9 CYPR):

In the [county of   . Petty Sessional Division of   ].

C.D. of   (hereinafter called the applicant) has this day applied under section 28(1) of the Children and Young Persons Act 1969 for authority to detain and take to a place of safety A.B. of   a child or young person (hereinafter called the relevant infant):

And I, the undersigned Justice of the Peace, am satisfied that the applicant has reasonable cause to believe (*specify belief in terms of section* 28(1)(*a*), (*b*) or (*c*)) and hereby grant the said application:

And the relevant infant may be detained in a place of safety by virtue of this authorisation for a period of   days beginning with the date hereof.

Dated the   day of   , 19   .
                             J.P.,
Justice of the Peace for the [county] aforesaid.

Warrant to search for or remove a child or young person (Form 10 CYPR):

In the [county of   . Petty Sessional Division of   ].

To each and all the constables of   .

Information on oath [*or* affirmation] has this day been laid before me, the undersigned Justice of the Peace, by C.D. of   , a person acting in the interests of a child or young person, namely (*insert name and address or other identifying particulars*) (hereinafter called the relevant infant) that there is reasonable cause to suspect (*specify in the terms of section* 40(1)(*a*) *or* (*b*) *of the Children and Young Persons Act 1933*):

[You are hereby authorised to search for the relevant infant and, if it is found that (*specify in the terms of section* 40(1)), to take him to a place of safety:]

[You are hereby authorised to remove the relevant infant with or without search to a place of safety:]

[And for the purposes hereof you are hereby authorised to enter (*specify house etc.*):]

[It is hereby directed that when executing this warrant you shall not be accompanied by the said C.D./shall be accompanied by a duly qualified medical practitioner:]

And the relevant infant may be detained in a place of safety by virtue of this warrant until he can be brought before a juvenile court, except that the relevant infant shall not be so detained for a period exceeding   days.

Dated the   day of   , 19 .
                                J.P.,
Justice of the Peace for the [county] aforesaid.

APPENDIX 1

Order for removal of foster child or protected child to a place of safety (Form 11 CYPR):

In the [county of   . Petty Sessional Division of   ].

[Before the Juvenile Court sitting at   ].

To each and all the constables of   [and to C.D. of   , a person authorised to visit foster/protected children].

[Complaint having this day been made by the council of the county/county borough of   ] [Application having this day been duly made to me, the undersigned Justice of the Peace, by C.D. of   , a person authorised to visit foster/protected children], on the ground that A.B. of   , a foster/protected child (hereinafter called the child) is (*state briefly grounds of complaint or application*):

[Proof having been given that there is imminent danger to the health or well-being of the child:]

It is hereby ordered that the child [and all other foster children kept at (*specify premises*)] be removed to a place of safety:

And the child [and any other foster child so removed] may be detained in a place of safety by virtue of this order until restored to a parent, relative or guardian or until other arrangements can be made, except that the child [and any other foster child so removed] shall not be so detained for a period exceeding   days.

Dated the   day of   , 19   .
J.P.,
Justice of the Peace for the [county] first above mentioned.
[*or* By order of the Court,
J.C.,
Clerk of the Court.]

Summons: proceedings under Child Care Act 1980, s 3:

In the [county of . Petty Sessional Division of].

To A.B. of

Complaint has this day been made to me, the undersigned Justice of the Peace by C.D. duly authorised in that regard by the council of the county/county borough of   that on the   day of   , 19 , the council of the said county/county borough of   did resolve that with respect to E.F. of   (a child in their care under s 2 of the Child Care Act 1980) all your rights and duties should vest in the said council, you being the parent [*or* guardian] of E.F. and (*here insert ground upon which resolution passed in terms of s 3 Child Care Act 1980*)

And notice in writing of the said resolution having been served on you on the   day of   , 19 .

And you having served upon the said council on the   day of   , 19 , notice in writing objecting to the said resolution

Wherefore the said C.D. complains that the said resolution shall not lapse.

You are hereby summoned to appear on   day, the   day of   , 19 , at the hour of   in the   noon before the Juvenile Court sitting at   to answer the said complaint.

Dated the   day of   , 19 .
J.P.,
Justice of the Peace for the [county] first above mentioned.
[*or* This summons was issued by the above-named justice of the peace.

J.C.,
Clerk of the Magistrates' Court sitting at   .]
[*or* J.C.,
Clerk to the Justices for the Petty Sessional Division aforesaid.]

APPENDIX 1

Summons: proceedings under Child Care Act 1980, s 5:

In the [county of   . Petty Sessional Division of   ].

To the county/county borough of

Complaint has this day been made to me the undersigned Justice of the Peace by A.B. of   that on the   day of   , 19 , the council of the county/county borough of   passed a resolution under s 3 of the Child Care Act 1980 thereby assuming all parental rights and duties with respect to E.F. (a child then in the care of the said council under s 2 of the Child Care Act 1980 as it appeared to the council that (*here insert the ground upon which the resolution was passed in terms of s 3 Child Care Act 1980*))

The complainant having applied for an order that the resolution should in the interests of the child be determined you are hereby summoned to appear on   day, the   day of   , 19 , at the hour of   in the   noon before the Juvenile Court sitting at   to show cause why the said resolution should not be determined.

Dated the   day of   , 19 .
J.P.,

Justice of the Peace for the [county] first above mentioned.
[*or* This summons was issued by the above-named justice of the peace.

J.C.,
Clerk of the Magistrates' Court sitting at   .]
[*or* J.C.,
Clerk to the Justices for the Petty Sessional Division aforesaid.]

Notice of motion for appeal to High Court under Child Care Act 1980, s 6:

IN THE HIGH COURT OF JUSTICE No.   of 19
FAMILY DIVISION (DIVISIONAL COURT)

In the Matter of an appeal under The Child Care Act 1980

Between

        A.B.   Appellant

and

        C.D.   Respondent

TAKE NOTICE that the High Court of Justice, Family Division, Royal Courts of Justice, Strand London WC2A 2LL will, on a date to be fixed and notified to the parties, consider an appeal by A.B. (the father/mother of the child) against the order of the juvenile court dated the   day of   19 .

1. The said order (*here set out the details of the magistrates' order*) and (*if appropriate*) the full name, surname and date of birth of the child referred to in the order is ....

2. The appellant appeals against the whole of the said order or (*here set out the part or parts of the order appealed against*)

3. The appellant seeks an order that (*here set out the order that is sought from the Divisional Court*)

4. (*If appropriate*) Leave to appeal out of time is required because (*here set out briefly the reason giving any dates that are relevant*).
[N.B. Where the delay is more than six weeks (i.e. this notice is being filed within 12 weeks of the hearing) and has been occasioned by the obtaining of documents or legal aid and the respondent has been notified of the likelihood of an appeal, it will normally suffice to say so without giving details]

5. The grounds of appeal are (*all the grounds should be set out; it is not sufficient to state merely that the finding was against the weight of the evidence*)

APPENDIX 1

Dated the   day of   19

This notice was filed by

                        (Signed)

whose address for service is:–

                        (Solicitor for the above named Appellant)

To   of

Notice of appointment of guardian ad litem (Form 7A CYPR):

Date:

Name of child or
young person
(hereinafter called
the infant):

Address:

    Take notice that ....
of ....
has been appointed guardian ad litem of the above named infant in proceedings which are in the list for hearing at this Juvenile Court on .... at .... am/pm

    In pursuance of rule 14A(5) of the Magistrates' Courts (Children and Young Persons) Rules 1970 (notice of appointment) is being sent to each of the following persons:

                              J.C.
                              Clerk of the Court

Address of Court
Telephone number

APPENDIX 1

Notice of order depriving parent or guardian of right to represent child or young person (Form 7B CYPR):

Date:

Name:

Address:

    Take notice that it appears to the Court that in the proceedings concerning the child/young person named .... (hereinafter called the infant) of whom you are a parent/guardian which are in the list for hearing at this Juvenile Court on .... at .... am/pm there is or may be a conflict on relevant matters between your interests and those of the said infant. Accordingly the Court has ordered that in relation to the proceedings you are not to be treated as representing the infant or as otherwise authorised to act on his behalf.

                            J.C.
                       Clerk of the Court

Address of Court
Telephone number

Notice of refusal of arrangements for access prescribed by the Access (Notice of Termination and of Refusal) Order 1983:

Notice of Refusal of Arrangements for Access

Child Care Act 1980: section 12B

From: (Local authority/Voluntary organisation)

To: (Name of Parent/Guardian/Custodian)

Name of child:

.... (name of child) of whom you are the .... (parent/guardian/custodian) is in the care of this .... (authority/organisation). The purpose of this notice is to advise you that the .... (authority/organisation) have decided that your request for arrangements for access to .... (name of child) should be refused. You have a right under section 12C of the Child Care Act 1980 to apply to the Juvenile Court at .... (name of Court) for an order granting you access to .... (name of child).

The application must be made within six months of the date this notice is served on you. If you wish to apply to the Court for an order granting you access or if you need any help in connection with this notice, you are advised to seek legal advice as soon as possible. Depending on your financial circumstances, you may be entitled to free or low-cost help under the Legal Aid or Legal Advice and Assistance schemes. Your local Citizens Advice Bureau will be able to give you the names of solicitors in the area who operate these schemes.

Dated

....
(signed)
An officer authorised to
sign on behalf of the
local authority/voluntary
organisation

APPENDIX 1

Notice of termination of arrangements for access prescribed by the Access (Notice of Termination and of Refusal) Order 1983:

Notice of Termination of Arrangements for Access

Child Care Act 1980: section 12B

From: (Local authority/Voluntary organisation)

To: (Name of Parent/Guardian/Custodian)

Name of child:

.... (name of child) of whom you are the .... (parent/guardian/custodian) is in the care of this .... (authority/organisation). The purpose of this notice is to advise you that the .... (authority/organisation) have decided that the arrangements for you to have access to .... (name of child) should be terminated. Your access will be terminated from the date this notice is served on you. You have a right under section 12C of the Child Care Act 1980 to apply to the Juvenile Court at .... (name of Court) for an order granting you access to .... (name of child).

The application must be made within six months of the date this notice is served on you. If you wish to apply to the Court for an order granting you access or if you need any help in connection with this notice, you are advised to seek legal advice as soon as possible. Depending on your financial circumstances, you may be entitled to free or low-cost help under the Legal Aid or Legal Advice and Assistance schemes. Your local Citizens Advice Bureau will be able to give you the names of solicitors in the area who operate these schemes.

Dated

....
(signed)
An officer authorised to
sign on behalf of the
local authority/voluntary
organisation

Appendix 2

Draft letters

Example 1:
Parental request under the Children and Young Persons Act 1963, s 3

                                                    87 Municipal Towers,
                                                       Corporation Street,
                                                          Bruford BX16 5QZ.

The Chief Executive,
Bruford County Council,
Town Hall,
Bruford BZ11 3SW.   25th March 1978

Dear Sir,

                                Herbert Alan Jones

I, Arthur Frederick Jones of 87 Municipal Towers, Corporation Street, Bruford hereby inform you that I am unable to control my son. Herbert Alan Jones (date of birth 14th March 1963) and request your council to bring him before a juvenile court under s 1 of the Children and Young Persons Act 1969.

If your council refuses to do so or fails to act within twenty-eight days of the date this notice was given I intend to apply to Bruford Juvenile Court for an order directing it to do so.

Would you kindly acknowledge receipt of this notice served in accordance with the provisions of s 3 of the Children and Young Persons Act 1963.

                                    Yours faithfully,

                         (*signed*) Arthur Frederick Jones

APPENDIX 2

Example 2:
Counter notice under the Child Care Act 1980, s 3(4)

62 Nirvana Street,
Bruford BR33 7TS.

The Chief Executive,
Bruford County Council,
Town Hall,
Bruford BZ11 3SW.   14th April 1977

Dear Sir,

Tracy Wallis

I, Sylvia Mary Wallis of 62 Nirvana Streeet, Bruford acknowledge receipt of your notice dated 8th April 1977 and hereby object to the resolution dated 6th April 1977 vesting parental rights and duties in respect of my daughter, Tracy Wallis, in your council.

Would you kindly acknowledge receipt of this notice served in accordance with the provisions of s 3(4) of the Child Care Act 1980.

Yours faithfully,

(*signed*) Sylvia Mary Wallis

Appendix 3

Children and Young Persons Act 1933—First Schedule

Offences against children and young persons with respect to which the special provisions of this Act apply:

—the murder or manslaughter of a child or young person
—infanticide
—any offence under ss 27 or 56 of the Offences against the Person Act 1861 and any offence against a child or young person under ss 5, 42 or 43 of that Act.
—any offence under ss 1, 3, 4, 11 or 23 of this Act
—any offence against a child or young person under any of the following sections of the Sexual Offences Act 1956 that is to say ss 2 to 7, 10 to 16, 19, 20, 22 to 26 and 28 and any attempt to commit against a child or young person an offence under ss 2, 5, 6, 7, 10, 11, 12, 22 or 23 of that Act
—any other offence involving bodily injury to a child or young person

NB Under the Indecency with Children Act 1960, s 1(3) references in the CYPA 1933 to offences mentioned in the above schedule (except in s 15) shall include offences under s 1 of the Indecency with Children Act 1960.

Appendix 4

Useful addresses

Family Rights Group
6–9 Manor Gardens
Holloway Road
London N7

Tel: 01–272 7308

Information Officer
Register of Expert Witnesses
Contentious Business Department
The Law Society
113 Chancery Lane
London WC2 1PL

Tel: 01–242 1222

Parents against Injustice (PAIN)
'Conifers'
2 Pledgden Green
Near Henham
Bishop's Stortford
Hertfordshire

Tel: 0279–850545

Children's Legal Centre
20 Compton Terrace
London N1 2UN

Tel: 01–359 9392

Panel Administrator
Child Care Panel
Contentious Business Department
The Law Society
113 Chancery Lane
London WC2 1PL

Tel: 01–242 1222

National Association of Young
   People in Care (NAYPIC)
6–9 Manor Gardens
Holloway Road
London N7

Tel: 01–272 7308
and 0912–612 178

NSPCC
67 Saffron Hill
London EC19 8RS

Tel: 01–242 1626

Advisory Centre for Education
18 Victoria Park Square
Hackney
London E2

Tel: 01–980 4596

National Council for One
   Parent Families
255 Kentish Town Road
London NW5

Tel: 01–267 1361

Legal Action Group
242 Pentonville Road
London N1

Tel: 01–833 3931

Appendix 5

Sexual abuse: some recent medical publications

Clayden G, *Anal appearance and child sexual abuse*, Lancet 1987; i:620–21.
Hey F, Buchan PC, Littlewood JM and Hall RI *Differential diagnosis in child sexual abuse*, Lancet 1987; i:283.
Hobbs CJ and Wynne JM *Buggery in childhood: a common syndrome of child abuse*, Lancet 1986; ii:792–96.
Hobbs CJ and Wynne JM *Differential diagnosis in child sexual abuse*, Lancet 1987; i:510.
Roberts REI *Examination of the anus in suspected child abuse*, Lancet 1986; i:1100.
Letters to the Editor. Lancet 1987; ii:1017–19.
Letters to the Editor. Lancet 1987; ii:1396–98.

Note The above list is by no means exhaustive but will provide a useful starting point for the lawyer who needs to know more about this subject. The medical papers contain references to further reading material. The correspondence with the Editor of The Lancet will be of additional interest to the lawyer seeking potential expert witnesses in the field.

The National Society for the Prevention of Cruelty to Children publishes bibliographies of introductory material and staff publications on sexual abuse. These are available from The Headley Library, NSPCC (see Appendix 4 for address).

Index

Abroad—
  abduction, 103–4, 136
  consent to child's removal, 103–4
  emigration—
    generally, 177–8
    Secretary of State's consent, 177, 178
    voluntary organisation with parental rights, 140
  entertainers (juvenile), sending of, 12
  travel, 178–9
Access, right—
  appeals, 172–3
  Code of Practice, 168, 173–4
  complaints procedure, 174
  denial, 168–70
  generally, 168
  limited, 170
  new arrangements, 169
  order—
    application, 170–1
    concurrent adoption proceedings, 171
    conditional, 171
    discharge, 172
    procedure, 171
    suspension, 172
    variation, 172
  relatives, 173–4
  representation, 173
  termination, 168–70
  welfare of child, 171–2
Adoption—
  access proceedings concurrent, 171
  care order made, 5–6
  freeing for, 175
  local authority's position, 175

Adoption—*contd*
  unsatisfactory prospective adopters, 107
Appeals—
  bail pending, 92–3
  by local authority, 94–5
  generally, 86
  judicial review, *see* Judicial review
  stating case, 89
  refusal, 90
  to—
    Court of Appeal, 91
    Crown Court—
      abandonment, 88
      appellant, 87
      hearing, 88
      powers of court, 88
      procedure, 87–8
      right of appeal—
        child, 86–7
        parent, 87
    Divisional Court—
      amicus curiae, 90
      hearing, 90
      powers of court, 90–1
      procedure—
        Crown Court, 90
        juvenile court, 89–90
      right of appeal, 89
    House of Lords, 91–2

Care—
  unauthorised removal from—
    absence without leave, 102
    third party's intervention, 102
  voluntary, *see* Voluntary reception into care

INDEX

Care orders—
  appeal by local authority, 62
  cessation, 63
  discharge, 74
    procedure, *see* Procedure, order variation/ discharge
  effect, 62–3
  extension, 74
    procedure, *see* Procedure, order variation/discharge
  following supervision order, 74
  hospital order simultaneously, 72
  interim, *see* Interim care orders
  making in—
    adoption order refusal, 5–6
    criminal proceedings, 6–7
    custodianship, 5
    guardianship proceedings, 4–5
    matrimonial proceedings, 3–4
    wardship, 5
  variation, 74
    procedure, *see* Procedure, order variation/discharge
Care proceedings—
  age of child, 20
  bringing, 19
  care or control test, 32–3
  court's jurisdiction, 20
  grounds—
    beyond control, 28–9
    development of child, 21–3
    education, 29–30
    generally, 20–1
    health, 21–2, 23
    ill-treatment, 21–2, 23–4
    moral danger, exposure to, 27–8
    need to satisfy, 44
    neglect, 21–6
    offence, commission, 30–2, 36
      proof, 48–9
    potential risk to child, 26–7
    sexual abuse, 24–5, 27
  meaning, 1–3
  procedure, *see* Procedure, care proceedings
  simultaneous, several children, 26
  welfare principle, 43–4
Certificates of unruliness, 67–8
Child—
  access, *see* Access, right
  after-care, 184–5
  apprenticeship, 185

Child—*contd*
  attendance at court, care proceedings, 36, 45, 47
    inability, 37
  contact with, maintaining, 174–5
  death in care, 185
  discipline—
    corporal punishment, 167–8
    liberty, restrictions, *see* Secure accommodation
  education—
    care proceedings on ground of, 29–30
    duty, 163
    higher, 185
    parent—
      prosecution, 30
      wishes, 164
    special needs, 29, 163
  evidence by, 56
  foster, *see* Foster child
  maintenance—
    after-care, 184–5
    contribution order, 156–9
  marriage, consent, 182
  medical treatment—
    consent to, 165
    contraceptive advice, 165–6
    emergency, 166
    generally, 164
  passport, 178–9
    objection to grant, 179
  recognisance, 72–3
  religion—
    change, 162
    choice, child's, 163
    generally, 162
    parental—
      dispute, 162–3
      rights, assumption, 116
  reports at court hearing, 49–51
  representation—
    care proceedings, 37–40
    separate, 80–1, 88
  residence, meaning, 35–6
  visiting of, 174
  visitor, 174–5
  welfare benefits, 183–4
Civil proceedings, 181
Community homes—
  death of child, 185
  discipline, 167

INDEX

Community homes—*contd*
  generally, 149
  religion, 162
  secure accommodation, 154
  visiting facilities, 174
Costs—
  against child, 100–1
  approval, legal aid, 98–9
  award, 100–1
  ss 3 or 5 proceedings—
    appeal, 133
    juvenile court, 133
    legally aided party, against, 133
    local authorities, 133
County court—
  power to make guardianship order, 4
Criminal proceedings—
  bail pending appeal, 92
  care orders made in, 6–7, 32
  certificates of unruliness, 68
  compensation order, 31–2, 73, 180–1
  concurrent with care proceedings, 25–6
  generally, 179–81
  member of child's household, 26–7
  offence as ground, care proceedings, 30–2, 36
  prevention of child's return to authority, 135
  removal of child from voluntary care, 110
  runaway child, assisting, 134
  secure accommodation, 152–3
  supervision order, 70
    variation, 75
  third party's intervention, 102, 103
  voluntary organisation, removal from care of, 142
Custodianship, 5, 176–7

Disputes, 186

European Commission on Human Rights, 190–1
European Convention of Human Rights, 190–1
European Court of Human Rights, 190–1
Evidence—
  admissions of fact, 52–3
  character, person's, 53
  confidentiality, 55–6
  conviction, previous, 57

Evidence—*contd*
  disclosure, advance, 61
  documentary, 57–8
  expert, 53–4
  hearsay, 54–5
  insufficient for decision, appeal, 93
  interim care order application, 64–6
  meaning, 52
  nature, 52–3
  offence condition cases, 49
  oral, 56–7
  order at hearing, 44–7
  privilege, 55–6
  proof—
    burden, 52
    standard, 52
  real, 58–9
  refusal to give, 57
  relevance, 53
  reports, 58
  rules, 53
  statement of facts, 58
  tape recordings, 59–60
  video recordings, 24, 59–60

Foster child—
  child benefit, 183
  custodianship, 176
  death, 185
  discipline, 167–8
  education, 163
  medical treatment, 164–5
  negligence of foster parents, 181
  place of safety, removal to, 16–17
  regulations, 154–5
  religion, 162
  representations at hearing, foster parent's, 46, 82
  unsuitable private foster home, 107

Green form scheme, *see* Legal advice and assistance scheme
Guardian ad litem—
  access order application, 171
  appeal—
    appointment for, 88
    lodging by, 87
  appointment, 38, 40
    failure to make, 38
  assumption of parental rights, 122–4
    appeal, 128
  civil proceedings, 181

INDEX

Guardian ad litem—*contd*
  discharge of orders, 77, 79–80, 81, 82
  duties, 41
  evidence—
    advance disclosure to, 61
    hearing, at, 46
  interlocutory order, 129–30
  panel, 39, 40
  reports, 49, 50–1, 84–5, 122–3
  role, 40–2, 81
  solicitor also appointed, 39–40
Guardianship—
  care order under, 4–5
  generally, 71–2

Habeas corpus, 112

Interim care orders—
  appeal, 67
  discharge, 67
  further interim orders, 64, 65
  interests of child, 66
  local authority's—
    duties, 66
    powers, 66
  making, 37, 47–8, 63–4
  meaning, 63
  place of safety proceedings preceding, 13, 14, 18, 63–4
  procedure, 64–5

Judicial review—
  application, 94, 188–9
  assumption of parental rights, 118, 130
  certiorari, 93
  damages, 190
  dispute—
    challenging authority's decision, 188–9
    joint exercise of parental rights, 117
    use to resolve, 187
  generally, 93
  mandamus, 94
  procedure, 94
  prohibition, 93
  s 3 resolution procedure, 118, 130
  welfare of child, 189
Juvenile court—
  constitution, 42
  power to make care order, 2
  presence at sitting, 42–3

Legal advice and assistance scheme—
  generally, 96
  Mental Health Review Tribunal cases, 72
  parental rights, divesting, 131–2
  representation—
    child, 132
    parent, 132
  ss 3 or 5 proceedings, 131–2
Legal aid—
  access proceedings, 173
  appeal—
    advice on, 99
    application, 99
  application, 97
  care proceedings, 29, 97
  contributions payable, 98, 99, 100
  costs, prior approval, 98–9
  counsel's fees, 98
  detention by police, 15
  grant, 98
  High Court, 99–100
  interim care orders, discharge application, 67
  juvenile court, 97–9
  parents, 100
  secure accommodation cases, 97
  ss 3 or 5 proceedings—
    appeal, 132–3
    child, 132
  statement of means, 97–8, 100
  variation of orders, 79, 97
Local authority—
  charge and control placements by, 155–6
  Commissioner for Local Administration, 186–7
  community homes, 149, 154
  confidentiality, 160–1
  duties—
    access, right of, 168–74
    accommodation, 148–56, 184
    advice and befriending, 184
    after-care, 184–5
    breach, action for, 190
    care, common law duty of, 190
    committal to care, following, 4, 7
    discipline, 167–8
    education, 163–4
    facilities, use of available, 148
    group of children, 148
    information, disclosure by, 160–1
    maintenance, 156–9, 184–5
    medical treatment, 164–6

Local authority—*contd*
  duties—*contd*
    protection of public, 147
    receiving into care, 2
    religion, 162–3
    review of cases, 148
    voluntary reception into care, 108–10
    welfare of child, 147–8
    generally, 147
  home on trial placements by, 156
  powers—
    assumption of parental rights, 2
    committal to care, following, 4, 7
    restriction of child's liberty, 151
    secure accommodation, *see* Secure accommodation
Local Government Ombudsman, 186–7

Magistrates' court—
  power to make care order, 3–4
Matrimonial proceedings, 3–4, 179–80
Medical examination—
  place of safety, child in, 17–18

National Society for Prevention of Cruelty to Children, 19, 31, 37
Next friend, 181

Orders—
  access, 170–2
  affiliation, 158–9
  care, *see* Care orders *and* Interim care orders
  compensation, 31–2, 73
  generally, 62
  guardianship, 4, 71–2
  hospital, 71–2
    interim, 71
  maintenance—
    appeal, 159
    arrears, 158
    collection of contributions, 159
    contribution, 156–8
      interim care order, 156
    enforcement, 157
    maximum amount, 156–7
    putative father, 158–9
  prerogative, *see* Judicial review
  recognisance, 72–3
  separate representation, parent and child, 80–1
  supervision, *see* Supervision orders

Parent—
  address, notification of authority of, 174
  contact with child, maintaining, 174
  hearing—
    attendance, 37
    cross-examination by, 46
    exclusion, 47
    reports at, 49–51
  recognisance, 72
  representation—
    of child by, 37–8
    separate, 80–1, 88
  visiting child, 174
  welfare benefits, 182–3
Parental rights, assumption—
  access, 169
  appeals to—
    Court of Appeal, 130
    High Court—
      decision, 129
      dismissal, 129
      hearing—
        expedited, 128–9
        time, 128–9
      procedure, 127–9
      right, 124, 127
      stay pending, 129–30
    House of Lords, 130
  guardian ad litem, 122–4
  hearing—
    absence of—
      child, 123
      complainant, 120
      defendant, 119–20
    adjournment, 120–1
    attendance, 119–20
    child as party, 122
    evidence, 120, 121–2
    exclusion from, partial, 121–2
    generally, 119
    order, 124
    procedure, 120
    proof, burden, 121
    report stage, 123–4
    representation, 119
      separate, 123
    speeches, 120
  joint exercise with another, 116–17
  disputes, 117
  notification, 118
  procedure, 118

INDEX

Parental rights, assumption—*contd*
  resolution—
    child's—
      abandonment, 114
      wishes, 114
    complaint to court by authority, 118–19
    discharge—
      applicant, 125
      discretion of court, 125–6
      grounds, 125
      hearing, 126
      procedure, 126
      time to apply, 125–6
    grounds for, 113, 114–15
    lapse, 118
    one parent only affected, 115–16
    order confirming, 124
    parents' representations before, 114
    passing, 113–14
    termination, 117–18
  return of child to authority, prevention, 135
  runaway child, assisting, 134
  voluntary organisation, by, 140–1, 169
    termination of resolution, 141
Place of safety—
  abroad, child taken without court consent, 103
  absence from, 103
  detention in—
    arrest, after, 17
    generally, 11
    medical examination, 17–18
  foster children, 16–17
  hospital order cases, 71
  notification of local authority, 14–15
  order—
    appeal, 13
    application, 11–12
    emergency, 12–13
    period for detention, 12, 13
  protected children, 17
  secure accommodation requirements, 154
  warrant—
    application, 13–14
    period for detention, 14
Police officer—
  arrest without warrant, 102, 103
  care proceedings, bringing, 19

Police officer—*contd*
  detention by, 15
    release, 15–16
  offence ground, care proceedings, 31
  search by, 15
Press—
  presence at juvenile court sittings, 42–3
Private homes, 150
Procedure, care proceedings—
  adjournment, 47–8
  attendance, 36–7
  commencement, 34–5
  conflict of interest, 38
  court's jurisdiction, 35–6
  defect in process, 44
  exclusion of persons, 47
  guardian ad litem, *see* Guardian ad litem
  hearing, 43, 47–8
  notification, 34–5
  offence condition, proof, 48–9
  parties, 37, 46–7
  regulation, 44–7
  report stage, 49–51
  speeches, order, at hearing, 44–7
  summons for child, 35
Procedure, order variation/discharge—
  adjournment, 83–4
  applications—
    unopposed, 80–1
    withdrawal, 81–2
  attendance—
    child, 77–8
    local authority, 79
    parent, 78–9
    supervisor, 79
  commencement, 76–7
  conflict of jurisdiction, 83–4
  court's jurisdiction, 76, 83–4
  generally, 76
  hearing, 82–4
  notification, 76–7
  report stage, 84–5
  representation, 79–80
Protected children, 17

Reform of law, proposed—
  abuse of children, investigation, 195
  access, 199
  appeals, 198
  care proceedings, 196–7
  custody orders, 198

INDEX

Reform of law, proposed—*contd*
  discharge of care orders, 198
  emergency protection orders, 195–6
  generally, 195
  guardian ad litem, 197
  interim care orders, 197
  local authority's duties, 198–9
  place of safety, 195, 196
  removal from care, unauthorised, 199
  supervision orders, 197–8
  voluntary care, 199–200
Reports—
  assumption of parental rights cases, 123–4
  hearing—
    consideration at, 49–51
    reading before evidence given, 58
  variation of orders, proceedings, 84–5

Secure accommodation—
  approval, Secretary of State's, 151
  criminal proceedings, 152–3
  legal aid, 97
  meaning, 151
  medication, tranquillising, 153–4
  period for keeping in, 152
  placing child in, 150–1
  records, 153
  review of cases, 153
  ward of court, 153
Sexual abuse, 24–5, 27, 59–60
Solicitor—
  appeal, advice about, 87
  appointment by—
    court, 38, 39
      notification, 38
    guardian ad litem, 41
  assumption of parental rights cases, 123
  Child Care Panel, 39
  choice of, 39
  guardian ad litem, acting with, 39–40, 41, 123
  legal advice and assistance scheme, 96
  need for, 7
  privilege, 55
  representation—
    child, 38–9
    parent, 39, 40
    separate, 39, 40
  variation of orders, 79

Summons—
  attendance of—
    child, care proceedings, 35
    parent, 35
  issue, 35
  missing child, recovery, 135
  witness, 60–1
Supervision orders—
  discharge, 74–5
    procedure, *see* Procedure, order variation/discharge
  duties of supervisor and child, 68–9
  following care order, 74
  generally, 68
  intermediate treatment, 69–70
  mental treatment requirement, 69, 75–6
  inclusion, 75
  notification by copy, 70
  powers of supervisor, 70
  variation, 74–5
    procedure, *see* Procedure, order variation/discharge

Voluntary organisations—
  boarding-out of children by, 143
  homes—
    community, 149, 154
    death of child, 185
    education, 163
    generally, 150
    inspection, 142, 150
    registration, 142, 150
    religion, 162
  meaning, 139
  placing children in care of—
    accommodation, supervision, 142–3
    generally, 139
    grounds for admission, 139
    removal from care, 142
    welfare principle, 139
Voluntary reception into care—
  abandoned child, 107
  assumption of parental rights, *see* Parental rights, assumption
  grounds for admission, 107–8
  homelessness, 108
  improper, 109
  leaving care, 110–12
  local authority's—
    cessation of authority, 110, 111
    discretion, 109
    duties, 108–10

Voluntary reception into care—*contd*
  local authority's—*contd*
    refusal to return child, 112
    termination of care, 110–12
  runaway child, assisting, 134

Wardship—
  care order made, 5
  medical treatment, 165, 166
  use—
    difficult cases, 188
    generally, 188
    resolving disputes, 187–8
  voluntary care, relationship with, 111–12
Warrant—
  arrest, 17, 35
  place of safety, 13–15
  search, missing child, 135
  witness, 60–1

Witnesses—
  child's, 45
  competent, 56
  cross-examination, 45–6
  exclusion from hearing, 47
  expert—
    evidence, 53–4
    presence at hearing, 47
    Register, 54
    social workers, independent, as, 54
  incompetent, 56
  summons, 60–1
  warrant for arrest, 60–1
  see also Evidence

Youth treatment centres, 151